Only a Few Blocks to Cuba

POLITICS AND CULTURE IN MODERN AMERICA

Series Editors: Keisha N. Blain, Margot Canaday,
Matthew Lassiter, Stephen Pitti, Thomas J. Sugrue

Volumes in the series narrate and analyze political and
social change in the broadest dimensions from 1865 to
the present, including ideas about the ways people have
sought and wielded power in the public sphere and the
language and institutions of politics at all levels—local,
national, and transnational. The series is motivated by
a desire to reverse the fragmentation of modern U.S.
history and to encourage synthetic perspectives on
social movements and the state, on gender, race, and
labor, and on intellectual history and popular culture.

ONLY A FEW BLOCKS TO CUBA

Cold War Refugee Policy, the Cuban Diaspora,
and the Transformations of Miami

Mauricio Castro

PENN

UNIVERSITY OF PENNSYLVANIA PRESS

PHILADELPHIA

Published by
University of Pennsylvania Press
Philadelphia, Pennsylvania 19104-4112
www.pennpress.org

Printed in the United States of America on acid-free paper
10 9 8 7 6 5 4 3 2 1

Hardcover ISBN: 978-1-5128-2572-5
eBook ISBN: 978-1-5128-2573-2

A Cataloging-in-Publication record is
available from the Library of Congress

For Adrian

CONTENTS

A NOTE ON TERMS

Given the slew of caveats and geopositioning that often follows the phrases "I'm going to Miami" or "I'm from Miami," I offer a note on my use of the term. I often use the name *Miami* to refer to the Greater Miami metropolitan area, a section of South Florida so poorly defined in the popular imagination that it has very little to do with the limits of the city of Miami. When discussing a specific jurisdiction or a governmental entity tied to a specific city or municipality, I use the official name of those jurisdictions. This applies to cities (Miami, Miami Beach, Hialeah, etc.) and to counties (Dade or Miami-Dade County, Broward County, etc.).

In terms of how I refer to my historical subjects, I will usually refer to individuals or to the broader community as "refugees." This is largely because it denotes a designation given to the arriving Cubans by the federal government and because it is tied to the policy decisions made in the aftermath of the Bay of Pigs Invasion. I will use the word "exile" to denote individuals who specifically embraced the term as a political identity and in relation to political organizations prevalent in the Cuban community in the United States for decades. These two identities are not mutually exclusive—there is often significant overlap—but I have often chosen to use one term or the other to denote particular political identifications. The term *exile*, or *exilio*, is sometimes used to refer to the tenure of Cubans who came to the United States after the revolution, as Cuban Americans often use it. As the book moves into the 1970s and beyond, I use the term *Cuban American* more often to reflect the growing number of Cubans who naturalized and became American citizens. I still use the term *refugee* for Cubans who arrived after 1980, but sometimes specific terms tied to particular migrations are also used, such as Marielito.

"The Seventh Province of Cuba"

aniel San Román was a realist. This, the readers of *America libre*, the Cuban exile newspaper where San Román served as editor and publisher, could count on. San Román and his publication were much like other newspapers that served the Cuban community in Miami. *America libre*'s nameplate declared it "In the Service of Democracy in the Continent," and the opinions of its editor and publisher and his staff were staunchly anticommunist. In the October 27, 1972, issue of *America libre*, for example, San Román responded to any potential negotiation with Fidel Castro's government in Cuba by titling his editorial "A River of Blood Separates Us from Coexistence."[1] At other points, the editor denounced clergy that opposed the Vietnam War as "pro-communist," worried that Richard Nixon might "sell out" the cause of a free Cuba as part of his détente with the Soviet Union, and speculated whether Democratic presidential candidate George McGovern was a demagogue or a fellow traveler.[2] But when it came to the actual mechanics of bringing about regime change in Cuba, San Román saw himself as part of a realist camp beset by bad faith critiques, a camp that understood that any real change would only come through the Cuban community reaching beyond Miami and exerting real influence on Washington, DC, and on American foreign policy. The "Battle of Washington" that San Román referenced several times in his editorials pointed to this as the only realistic avenue for achieving the goals of Miami's Cuban community.[3] Those who thought that Cubans living in the U.S. could overthrow the revolution on their own through force of arms were either foolish or ill-intentioned. After all, if the Bay of Pigs Invasion had failed to dislodge Castro a decade before, how could any new attempts at military action overthrow what had become "the second greatest military power in the Americas"? These opinions were not without controversy, and San Román noted the fierce opposition to the overtures toward Washington as a strategy for change in Cuba.[4]

San Román's self-perception as a realist probably drove him to challenge one of the great abiding truisms of Cuban life in the United States after the 1959: that Cubans would return home in droves the moment Fidel Castro was no longer in power. On August 6, 1971, San Román declared that Miami was, spiritually, "the seventh province of Cuba," given the large population of Cubans who had settled in the city. In fact, they now had such extensive roots in the city that should communism disappear from the Cuba overnight, Miami would not lose all, or even most, of its Cuban population. San Román estimated that after Castro's fall no more than 30% of Miami's Cubans would return to their homeland. More might deeply desire to do so, but the economic realities of life in Cuba and life in Miami would keep them rooted in South Florida. Those who had eked out a living in Cuba as workers, peasants, and fishermen now owned automobiles and homes in Miami. Doctors, dentists, and engineers would remain in the United States, making far more money than they ever could in Cuba and working in far more advanced facilities. And if the liberation were to take place in ten years, rather than a day, the percentage of returnees would be smaller still. Most Cuban residents of the island's seventh province would stay where they were. "Their heart will fly toward Cuba," San Román wrote, "but their bodies will remain here."[5]

That many, if not most, Cubans would remain in South Florida, in the economically successful enclave they had constructed, was not an opinion unique to San Román, it was a belief held by many Cubans but not one to be expressed publicly without potential backlash. It was common for Cubans to refer to themselves as exiles, as many would for decades after San Román wrote his editorial, and to envision a future return home as an expression of common identity in the city they had made their home. To many, who were often the loudest voices in the community, the entire point of a sojourn in the United States was to chart a path to a different future for themselves and for Cuba, one necessarily entwined with their vision of the Cuba they had lost to the revolution. A decade on, however, that common expression of identity and a shared future was wearing thin as the basis for a plan of action, and the concept of "home" left many with the pained question of "which one?" Miami was not Cuba, but it was undergoing transformations that made the city a home and a site of continued struggle for waves of Cuban Cold War migrants.

The politics of the Cold War shaped life in Miami, tying it to a broader global struggle, through the dual forces of Cuban migration and of federal refugee and foreign policies. San Román's seventh province would not have been nearly as welcoming and the Cuban community's economic success not nearly as impressive had both forces not coincided. The Cuban Revolution sparked a migration that brought an estimated 392,458 Cubans to the United States between 1959 and 1974.[6] This period of migration, and subsequent waves, turned a city where officials estimated a population of 46,000 Cubans in the mid-1950s into San Román's seventh province of Cuba.[7] By 2019 it was estimated that Miami-Dade County had nearly 700,000 Cuban-born residents.[8] During various periods of migration, the majority of these refugees either settled in South Florida immediately or returned to the area after a period of resettlement elsewhere in the United States. The U.S. government granted these refugees special entry and tenure in the United States based on Cold War concerns regarding the spread of communism in Latin America. Early on, federal officials shared the idea of a return from exile. They expected that the Cuban refugees to whom they were giving asylum would only stay in the United States for a short time. In the early years after the revolution, policymakers believed that the Castro government would collapse within a few months or years. They could not imagine that the revolution would be anything but transitory, and neither did the refugees who came to the United States with phrases like "Next year in Cuba" and "We'll be back in Cuba in six months" on their lips. The exile was meant to be a brief interlude in the history of the Cuban people. San Román's assertion that no more than three in ten Cubans would return to the island not only challenged these truisms but also undermined the logic that had driven the creation of federal policy, which, in turn, drove the creation of wealth for the Cuban community in Miami.

In the first two years after the fall of Fulgencio Batista's government, the influx of Cuban refugees into the United States and their concentration in Miami were seen by many as a humanitarian crisis; a logistical problem in need of a solution. The problem also presented an opportunity: the well-dressed Cuban civilians arriving on American soil seeking refuge could serve as living proof of the failures of Marxism, and the welcome they received could serve as evidence of the U.S. government's commitment to its Latin American allies in the fight against the spread of communism. The Dwight D. Eisenhower administration also sought to invest in directly overthrowing Castro's government by training an exile paramilitary force. The John F. Kennedy administration ultimately carried out those plans, which resulted in the disastrous Bay of Pigs Invasion in April of 1961.[9] While paramilitary action by Cuban exile groups would continue for years after the invasion, its failure brought about a new focus on how refugee civilians could serve American Cold War interests. The Bay of Pigs had not changed the belief in Castro's inevitable fall, but it demanded an adjustment in the expected timeline. With no short-term solution to the problem, policymakers looked to a solution that might take years instead of months, and the need to foster the economic well-being of the refugees became part of this new approach.

After this setback, high-level policymakers came to see Cuban refugee civilians as the core of a post-Castro Cuba that they could mold on American soil. They envisioned a new role for the Cuban Refugee Program (CRP), an aid program under the Department of Health Education and Welfare that had only existed for a few months. The CRP would not only address the humanitarian crisis caused by the continuing Cuban arrivals, but it would also provide them with the tools for economic empowerment in the United States. This would require a different level of sustained aid than had been provided to other refugee groups, which involved disbursing an estimated $2 billion.[10] Simple economic survival was not enough if these civilians were to be of use in establishing a pro-U.S. Cuban government and civil society after Castro's fall. This new vision required sustaining the skills the refugees brought with them. Cuban professionals among the refugees would practice in their field in the United States and be ready to return to Cuba without having their skills dulled by disuse. Cuban entrepreneurs would start businesses in South Florida and elsewhere, ensuring a commitment to capitalism and business ties to the United States on their return to the island. By providing assistance in the form of professional certification, language and work-skills classes, and small business loans, the U.S. government sought to foster the core of a capitalist society in Cuba in the near future.[11] The early waves of Cuban refugees embraced the opportunities provided by the federal government and built on them through their educational, social, and entrepreneurial backgrounds, adapting to social and business environments at once foreign and familiar.

The "inevitable" fall of Fidel Castro did not happen as policymakers expected, but the Cubans' presence and their embrace of the opportunities their strategic role had provided transformed Miami economically and politically, and spatially. In November of 1960, during the early refugee arrivals, *Miami Herald* reporter Juanita Greene wrote a story about the dire economic situation in which many of the refugees found themselves.[12] In the piece, she detailed a trip to SW Eighth Street and explained, "From downtown Miami, it's only a few blocks to Cuba."[13] The majority of Greene's Anglophone audience would not yet have recognized names like "Little Havana" and "Calle Ocho." But in the years that followed, those names and the Cuban community became synonymous with the city through a contentious process that led some to believe that Miami had become a foreign place on U.S. soil. This perception, whether in the form of an inquiry, a cliché reinforced by popular culture, or a xenophobic accusation, obscures how Miami reflects the structures that have shaped other American cities. The Cold War–influenced policy choices made in the early years after the Cuban Revolution had far-reaching, long-term consequences for South Florida, but they were not unique. Rather, this history is a particularly potent example of the convergence of local and global forces on urban life in the United States.

Only a Few Blocks to Cuba recounts this history of South Florida from the late 1950s to the mid-1990s by focusing on the interactions of three main historical entities: the federal government, the city of Miami, and the Cuban community. None of these entities is monolithic, and the distinctions between them have blurred over time and in reaction to the politics of different historical moments. They were, for example, discrete through the early 1960s, when the federal government, city elites, and the refugees themselves hoped and planned for a prompt change in the political situation in Cuba, a swift return, and the creation of a new, pro-U.S. government on the island. By the late 1960s and into the 1970s, the Cuban community in South Florida retained a distinct identity, but it was becoming a significant and ever-growing segment of the city, blurring the lines between "Miami" and "the Cubans." Throughout the 1980s, as Cuban Americans successfully ran for local and federal offices, these distinctions became hazier still. The federal government, the city of Miami, and the Cuban community, however, never blurred into one another entirely. South Florida's Cuban community garnered power and gained influence over city and federal policymakers, but never full control. When Cuban migrants being held in indefinite detention took over two federal detention centers in 1987, for example, the distinctions between the Cuban community and the federal government were sharper than ever. When Cubans and Cuban American leaders felt frustrated by the limits of their sway, they often abandoned the rhetoric of having "built" Miami and being partners in a global struggle against communism and instead hardened the distinctions between themselves, the city, and the federal government. Likewise, city leaders and federal authorities used the Cuban community and one another as partners or foils depending on their needs, and the evolving interactions between these three groups shaped the history of South Florida for decades.

Only a Few Blocks to Cuba builds on the established literature on South Florida's Cuban community and seeks to put it into conversation with other scholarship. Miami and the Cuban community were the subject of María Cristina García's groundbreaking 1996 study *Havana USA: Cuban Exiles and Cuban Americans in South Florida, 1959–1994.* García's study was not concerned with Miami as an urban space, but with a broad view of community formation that separated this history into a recounting of the Cuban migration since the revolution and an analysis of the culture and politics of the community in those years.[14] In her study, García noted the importance of the CRP as a significant factor in the community's success in South Florida, as have many other scholars who have focused on the federal government's unprecedented largesse and the social and political changes the diaspora brought to the area.[15] This federal intervention is often treated as a natural outgrowth of the Cold War and the anticommunism of the Cuban refugees, without a deeper examination of the processes that brought about these policies. Other scholars, like historians Lillian Guerra and Michael J. Bustamante, have addressed other aspects of this community's formation, writing extensively on how the politics of memory shaped life both in revolutionary Cuba and in exile. These works have shown how neither of the absolutist narratives harbored on either side of the Straits of Florida are borne out by the historical record and how the nostalgia for a "lost Cuba" post-1959 was not sufficient to overcome the political baggage these new arrivals brought with them to the United States.[16]

This study utilizes a materialist interpretation of this South Florida in the decades after the Cuban Revolution, from the ouster of Batista through the institution of the "wet foot, dry foot" policy and its aftermath in 1995, based on the intersection between urban, policy, and foreign relations history. It centers the CRP and other Cold War–inflected policies as the driver of multiple transformations for the city that had wide-ranging consequences at the local, state, and national levels and for American foreign policy as well. The connections between foreign policy, local politics, and urban development are at the core of this study, showing not only how larger foreign policy decisions affected Miami, but also how Miami helped shape Cold War policy starting in 1960. In this context, actions taken within a decidedly local context had significant foreign policy implications. For refugees to open a new business, train for a new job, or become involved in local politics became imbued with new layers of meaning and were sometimes considered conducive to a different future for the home they had left. As Cuban influence spread throughout Miami, as the city's space, economy, politics, and race relations were reshaped, the idea that this came with corresponding political power meant that a new Cuban future, one meant to restore that which had been lost, was being built with every new business, home, and cultural institution. What this new Cuban future would look like, along with that of Miami overall, however, would be deeply and consistently contested throughout the decades.

Only a Few Blocks to Cuba makes explicit the interactions and decision-making processes at the local and national levels that set into motion three distinct, but deeply entwined, transformations: the changes to the area's economic order, the changes to who held political power in the city, and the changes to the city's racial structures. Though the stunning economic transformation of the Miami area from the late 1950s to the early decades of the twenty-first century had distinctive characteristics, its underlying structures mirrored broader trends in urban development during the postwar period, particularly in the South. This transformation empowered the Cuban community and helped drive the growth in political power of the Cuban American voting bloc and the creation of an influential political lobby. The chapters that follow document this process and, in doing so, illuminate the specific decisions that both led to an electoral shift in Dade County and drove a growing association of Cuban Americans with the Republican Party. This book also builds on the literature of how Cold War concerns created an opening to challenge the impulse to restrict immigration by casting it as a liability in the ongoing struggles of the Cold War. Policymakers knew that the Soviet Union would undermine U.S. influence by using racist American immigration policies in their propaganda.[17] In the case of Miami, this influx would be seen as a propaganda and material benefit to the Cold War struggle and would challenge the established racial order in Miami, but only to a degree. The chapters that follow recount how this challenge built on previous migrations to continue eroding the Jim Crow structures that remained in the city, the reaction to the challenge by Black and white Miamians, and the reasons why these racial structures were bent but not broken.

The influx of Cuban refugees and the subsequent federal response were significant drivers in transforming Miami's economy from one dependent on seasonal tourism to one that fulfilled the long-held aspirations of the city's boosters and elites by making it an economic gateway to the Americas and the world. In 1961, the mayor of Miami, Robert King High, testified before

Congress on the Cuban refugee influx and noted that 62% of the city's residents depended on the seasonal tourism industry for all or part of their income.[18] Some local industries, including garment manufacturing, had experienced growth, but Miami's economic prospects did not suggest a future as global city. By the early twenty-first century, however, as Alejandro Portes and Ariel C. Armony note, South Florida's economy and built environment were much changed. In 1982, Dade County's gross regional product was $40.4 billion. Ten years later, in 1992, it was $50.9 billion. By 2012, Miami-Dade County's gross regional product was $124 billion, with the accommodation and food service industry, an indicator of the city's tourist trade, accounting for only 6% of the metropolitan economy. Portes and Armony also noted that throughout the 1960s, the tallest building in the city was the twenty-eight-story courthouse. By 2010, however, there were fifty buildings exceeding that height, with the tallest exceeding seventy stories (see Figures 1 and 2). While Portes and Armony focus on the position of Miami in the twenty-first century, they also tie the history of the Cuban presence and contributions to what they call Miami's "economic surge."[19]

This economic growth and physical change were intimately connected to the framework of federal spending that drove growth in the American South and West during the Cold War. Miami is not often considered part of the processes by which federal spending fundamentally changed the agrarian economy of the South, turning the region into what historian Bruce Schulman called "Fortress Dixie."[20] Most of the historical literature has focused on the federal government's disbursements in the acquisition of tangible assets: weapons, military bases, and new technologies. As Schulman notes, however, it was not defense spending that directly reshaped the economy of the South, but "the peculiar operation of a series of programs, many only tangentially related to defense but all under the aegis of the defense establishment."[21] In the 1950s, Miami's economy was not dependent on these expenditures. Cuban refugees arrived soon thereafter and quickly overwhelmed a city that viewed them as a threat to the city's tourism industry and weak job market. The federal government's reaction to the influx and the potential that they saw in these refugees in the context of the Cold War would bring the city in line with much of this regional development.

While the presence of refugees makes the Miami case appear to be an outlier among Sunbelt cities, the underlying structures that fueled South Florida's economic growth mirrored those that fueled the growth of other cities precisely because of the Cuban presence. Rather than an investment

Figure 1. Downtown Miami at night in the 1960s. The Cuban Refugee Center, which was formerly the Miami News and Metropolis Building and then rebranded as the Freedom Tower by federal authorities, is prominently featured on the right. Courtesy of the Cuban Heritage Collection, University of Miami Libraries.

Figure 2. Downtown Miami in 2009. The Freedom Tower can be seen on the right of the image. Now surrounded by much larger structures, it illustrates the vast transformation of the downtown area around the former Cuban Refugee Center. Photograph by Marc Averette. Courtesy of Wikimedia Commons through Creative Commons Attribution 3.0 Unported license: https://creativecommons.org/licenses/by/3.0/deed.en.

in materiel or the development of new technologies, policymakers were investing in human assets. Ordinary actions like opening a new business or starting a medical practice after certification became analogous, if much less expensive, to the purchase of a Minuteman missile or a B-52 bomber: federal funds were being invested in assets meant to bring the United States closer to victory in a global conflict. While officials did not broadcast their intent for the community, these plans and the very public disbursement of public funds related to U.S.-Cuba policy imbued everyday activities with larger meanings in that conflict.

The Kennedy administration's creation of the Cuban Refugee Program in 1961 and the paths to economic empowerment that were established through multiple programs throughout the 1960s and into the 1970s set the stage for the economic and political empowerment of South Florida's Cuban American community. Policymakers quickly became disillusioned with the usefulness of the Cuban refugee community and of Cuban exile political organizations, but they remained committed to making Cubans economically self-sufficient. This involved efforts to ensure the ability of refugee professionals to practice in their chosen fields, efforts to teach refugees skills and trades, and efforts to teach English to those Cubans who did not already speak it. These endeavors were both highly successful and highly visible. In other areas of the federal bureaucracy, officials saw a potential model for welfare reform at a national level. Miami then became not just a battleground in the global Cold War, but a laboratory for the study of initiatives that might serve the broader welfare state. The CRP continued in operation until the 1970s, but after the end of the so-called Freedom Flights from Cuba in 1973, the flow of refugees slowed to a trickle and the urgency to fund programs for the community faded. By this point, the Cuban community in Miami had embraced the economic structures that the CRP and related programs had provided and had helped construct a far more robust economy, complete with thousands of Cuban-owned businesses, than had greeted them on their arrival.

The length of the investment in the Cuban community was briefer than the federal investments in other areas, but it also created an economy with a broader base that was less dependent on the changing politics of the Cold War than many of these areas and that attracted significant foreign investment. There would be no renewed influx as part of Ronald Reagan's military buildup of the 1980s, even as the 1980 Mariel boatlift created long-term issues by bringing nearly 125,000 new refugees to the United States. Conversely, South Florida's economy would not see the disastrous effects that other areas that hosted military bases or defense industries experienced with the draw-down of military forces at the end of the Cold War. The presence of the Cuban community in Miami had not only created new businesses, but it also helped attract investment and tourism from Latin America. While the flow of capital across borders was also affected by the evolution of the Cold War in Latin America, the effects of these changes were sometimes quite beneficial to Miami's business and financial sectors. For instance, when Marxist insurgencies in Latin American countries directly challenged U.S. hegemony in the region and the interests of local elites, they could create situations that were both dangerous or even disastrous to American policymakers and extremely profitable for Miami's bankers and builders as Latin American elites sought a safe place to invest and shelter their wealth. An increasingly Spanish speaking Miami was geographically close to their home countries, welcoming to self-described anticommunists, and a world away in terms of the dangers posed by revolutionaries. Miami's new business environment was shaped by the federal investment of the 1960s and 1970s, but it adopted a framework that did not depend on those funding levels being maintained and that attracted investment in times of both peace and of turmoil.

Miami's Cuban community was a significant driver of the city's economic transformation, and this had downstream effects for the community's place in South Florida. This monograph traces that economic transformation through the lens of the Cuban community's own evolution from impoverished refugees in the 1960s to a powerful economic block starting in the 1970s. This perspective brings into focus the processes that transformed Miami politically and culturally.

Only a Few Blocks to Cuba also illustrates how policy decisions meant to aid and ensure the economic independence of the refugees in the early 1960s led to the rise of the Cuban American voting bloc in South Florida along with a powerful political lobby that sought to influence American foreign policy. This path to power was built with specific institutional and individual decisions that allowed the Cuban community to grow in size and influence in South Florida. These choices were not preordained. Much of the literature on the Cuban community in South Florida has treated the privileged position afforded the Cuban refugees as a natural outgrowth of their anticommunism in the Cold War without properly investigating the contingent nature of this aid and the choices of historical actors, including government officials, that led to those policy decisions.[22] Starting with Eisenhower, multiple presidential administrations made the choice to allow Cuban refugees entry into the United States. Once in the United States, federal authorities could have forcibly resettled the Cuban refugees throughout the country, as they had done with the influx of Hungarian refugees just a few years earlier, rather than offering voluntary resettlement with elements of coercion tied to aid. Federal authorities could have simply neglected the community, leaving the refugees to employ the same energies they did in the transformation of Miami but without the structures in place to prevent them from becoming an underclass in South Florida. That officials at multiple levels of government chose otherwise does not mean that the choices they made were a foregone conclusion. Rather, these policy choices were part of a contentious negotiation rooted in the belief that the Cuban refugees would be useful to the position of the United States in the Cold War. These choices, in turn, had unintended consequences for the political landscape of South Florida and the United States overall.

This book utilizes sources at the local, state, and federal levels to illustrate the contingent process by which political power is built. The case of the Cuban population in Miami provides a particularly clear view of the interactions between local and national power and between local politics and foreign policy, building on literature that ties both migration and the development of specific urban and suburban spaces to American imperial ambition.[23] The lived effects of choices driven by policy aimed at countering the Cuban government are at the center of this book, but it also brings into focus how local actors had a hand in influencing these policies from the very start of the refugee influx. Local leaders and institutions shaped the response to the influx of Cuban refugees, which would ultimately shift the economic, political, and social landscape around them. This applies to the established local elites that sought to bring a robust federal response to their city by enticing the Eisenhower White House with rhetoric of Miami as a Cold War battleground in 1960, as it does to the Cuban American power brokers who sought to align themselves with Reagan's foreign policy objectives in the 1980s. As with the economic dynamics described previously, the connections between foreign policy and local politics are by no means unique to South Florida, as when local politicians in multiple states envisioned the development of their cities as tied to Cold War priorities of research and defense. In Miami, these connections shaped political structures and brought rhetoric tied to foreign policy to the forefront of local politics, requiring local politicians to go beyond a broad embrace of anticommunism and pushing them to have specific opinions on U.S. Cuba policy as a purity test to compete for offices having little or no influence over that policy's creation. The structures of economic empowerment that the federal government provided the Cuban refugees set the stage for much of the influence of the Cuban American community, but they were effective in providing a path to political power only in conjunction with decisions that allowed for concentration in one area, a path to citizenship, and for shared political concerns. While the CRP sought to resettle as many Cuban refugees as possible from Miami and used economic pressure in pursuit of this goal, it did not make resettlement mandatory, in part because such actions would be antithetical to the rhetoric of freedom it sought to contrast with repression in Cuba. As the 1960s wore on and policymakers grew disillusioned with the potential for rapid change in Cuba and with their dealings with exile political and paramilitary organizations, the U.S. government provided the refugees with a path to citizenship through the Cuban Adjustment Act of 1966. This action, which government officials explicitly framed as having nothing to do with the permanence of the Cuban Revolution, was meant in part to reinforce measures taken to improve the ability of Cuban professionals and entrepreneurs to pursue their careers in the United States. It also provided Cuban refugees with the potential to become Cuban American voters. This led to the development of a politically engaged Cuban American voting bloc that developed in South Florida as refugees made the sometimes-painful choice of becoming naturalized as American citizens. While the Cuban community was always politically diverse, particularly in their views on how to approach the government in Havana, significant numbers of them embraced local politics in the late 1960s and into the 1970s in order to secure the gains they had made in the region. This pursuit of influence at the local level would position the community to project their political power beyond South Florida.

Only a Few Blocks to Cuba also complicates our understanding of how the Cuban American political identity came to be associated with the Republican Party. While the diversity of Cuban American political thought and experience is often flattened in American political discourse, there is a significant bloc of Cuban American voters whose allegiance to the Republican Party significantly changed the politics of South Florida. This work explicitly rejects any discussion of a foreordained or natural affinity between the Cuban Americans and the Republican Party, an unbridgeable chasm between the Cuban refugees and the Democratic Party after the Bay of Pigs, or of a Cold War partnership with conservative Republicans being a foregone conclusion. Cuban refugees, exile political organizations, and Cuban Americans all worked with both Democratic and Republican administrations in the context of the Cold War, with all parties pursuing their own aims.[24] While some Cuban Americans have been more inclined to praise Republican stances on foreign policy toward Cuba, the consensus among anti-Castro hard-liners was that neither party ever did enough to bring about change on the island. While anti-Castro politics became a way to appeal to Cuban American voters, it was hardly an appeal for South Florida votes restricted to one party. In fact, as this work shows, local politics in Miami were infused with the rhetoric of the Cold War in Latin America and beyond, regardless of political party.

The advances made by the Republican Party in courting Cuban American voters is tied to positions related to foreign policy, but there was an organized effort in Miami by the Republican Party ("Grand Old Party," or GOP) to actively court Cubans at the moment when they were becoming Cuban Americans. Using the communications between Dade County Democratic politicians with concerned Democrats, both inside and outside the Cuban American community, this work shows how new voter registrations in the Republican Party among new citizens were driven by programs specifically targeting these new voters. The Democratic Party met Republican organization in Dade County with neglect and, in doing so, fulfilled the predictions of political scientists, who by the late 1960s and 1970s expected a significant change in the politics of South Florida. The party loyalty of Cuban Americans was neither uniform nor unchanging, but this organizational work established connections between the GOP and new voters.

This history puts *Only a Few Blocks to Cuba* in conversation with the literature on the history of Latino voting and political affiliations. Historians like Geraldo Cadava and Benjamin Francis-Fallon have drawn significant insights into the role of Cuban American Republicans in national politics. Some illustrate the ways in which this association fed into their identity. Francis-Fallon argues that GOP Cubans "found that their Republicanism and their *Cubanidad* accentuated one another" during the 1980s as they could both be expressed in terms of their anticommunism.[25] For that moment to arrive in the 1980s, significant work had to be done at the local level. As Geraldo Cadava has argued about the development of these identities, "Hispanics don't vote Republican because they're Catholic or Cuban; they vote for Republicans because they've developed considerable loyalty to the Republican Party."[26] The local focus of this book and its coverage of the late 1960s and the 1970s illustrate not only how this association was solidified, as the pattern of Republican outreach and

Democratic neglect in South Florida would lead to increasing frustration by Cuban American Democrats and to previously solid Democratic areas electing Republican Cuban Americans; moreover, this local perspective is, in fact, necessary to understanding how Miami-based Cuban politics came to be understood as Cuban American politics by the broader public. Cuban American politicians from other areas of the country understood national Cuban American political organizations as being dominated by Miami, whether they agreed with their viewpoints or not.[27] The consequences of Cuban American politics and the community's relationship to the Republican Party on U.S. foreign policy and on the viability of Democratic candidates in the state of Florida, and by extension, in national politics, can only be understood through the study of the downstream effects of Miami politics.

The association between Cuban Americans and the Republican Party became more pronounced with the creation of the Cuban American National Foundation (CANF) in 1981. While CANF did not represent the political views of all Cuban Americans, it became the most visible example of the community's political power by reaching out to Washington policymakers to influence Cuba policy, as Daniel San Román and others had suggested during the previous decade. The foundation claimed to be nonpartisan and worked with politicians from both major political parties, but it developed a strong association with the Reagan White House and with its foreign policy. CANF was an outgrowth of the challenges to the gains made by Cuban Americans, in image, economic power, and political influence that came out of the Mariel boatlift of 1980 and the backlash that followed. Under Reagan's Cold War posture, despite still believing the president's actions did not go far enough on Cuba, CANF amplified the economic power of its founders and contributors and the political sway it had over a segment of Cuban Americans. Beyond rhetorical stances and foreign policy initiatives, CANF also embraced the neoliberal turn fundamentally changing the welfare state that had sown the seeds for the Cuban American community's own success. During the administration of George H. W. Bush, CANF embraced the conservative approach to government when it came to Cuban refugees by pioneering a private sector initiative that sought to provide new Cuban migrants with an echo of the safety net that had once welcomed the early arrivals, now bankrolled by the foundation and its donors.

This work also explores the limits of the power accumulated by the Cuban American community in the decades between the end of Batista's regime and the creation of the wet foot, dry foot policy. The growth of Cuban American economic and political influence over Miami and beyond was a contested process. By the late 1960s and into the 1970s, even institutions that had sought to bring federal aid to the refugees in the early 1960s had adopted an antagonistic stance against the Cuban community because of its permanence and because it continued to challenge established hierarchies. After the arrival in the United States of nearly 125,000 new Cuban refugees during the Mariel boatlift in 1980, the reaction against the Cuban community only intensified. The intensity of the flow of refugees combined with negative portrayals of the new arrivals in the media threatened political gains made during the 1970s, such as a 1973 ordinance declaring Dade County bilingual and bicultural. This led to divisions within the community as many people sought to aid the new arrivals and others worried that their poor reputation might tarnish all Cuban Americans. Even after Cuban Americans sought to consolidate those gains by creating CANF and organizations that sought to address anti-Cuban sentiment in South Florida, their reach was often limited by disputes within the Cuban American community and by having to compete with the concerns of other constituencies. The fear of increased migration from Cuba at a time when immigration was once again being used as a political cudgel helped bring about a change to decades of policy and a fundamental test for the influence of CANF and of Cuban Americans at large.

The xenophobic and racist responses that drove the creation of several Cuban American political organizations, including CANF, after 1980 are part of the contested process that redefined the boundaries of race in South Florida, which is the third transformation that is central to this book. The backlash from the Mariel boatlift in the early 1980s and the reaction to the rafter crisis in the mid-1990s, which largely grew out of the memory of Mariel, were not unprecedented. Previous waves of refugees were subject to xenophobic and racialized treatment from white Miamians, but the Cold War likewise influenced their reactions and the institutions they created provided significant support for the refugees and managed their image with the public at large. The policy choices of the early 1960s actively shifted the racial structures that were prevalent not only in South Florida, but throughout the United States. The complex relations between the Cuban refugee and Cuban American community, white Miamians, and African American Miamians serve as a particularly salient example of the multifaceted structures of race in the United States, which are often obscured by narrowing them to a strict Black-white binary.

Cold War concerns thus created an opening for exceptions to be made in the long history of racialized immigration exclusion of immigrants in the United States. Scholars of American foreign policy have made connections between the flows of immigrants to the United States and American aims abroad.[28] While the case of the open-door policy afforded to the Cuban refugees is unusual, it is not unique in the history of the Cold War. Historian Meredith Oyen, for example, has shown how Cold War–era policymakers used the influx of migrants from the People's Republic of China as a way to portray to the world that the United States was a haven for oppressed people.[29] As with the case of Chinese immigrants, the dynamics of the Cold War generated a powerful rhetorical response to long-standing attitudes aimed at restricting immigrants. In the early days of the Cuban refugee arrivals, city officials and local institutions embraced the rhetoric of an exemplary migration brought low by communist oppression, which was taxing the resources of South Florida not because of their qualities or characteristics, but rather because of their numbers. This rhetoric was useful in attracting federal assistance, but also in quieting some of the anxieties about the influx into the city.

As time went on and the expected "temporary" presence of the refugees became a more permanent feature of Miami's landscape, these divisions only intensified. By the time of the Mariel boatlift in 1980, the rhetoric of their usefulness to the Cold War struggle had fallen away and the restriction instinct was unchecked in the face of a migration that was more intense, more working class, more queer, more disabled, and more Afro descended. These refugees were also saddled with a worse reputation than any previous wave because Castro had characterized them as the scum of Cuban society. The media in the United States, for its part, largely obliged Castro in its portrayal of the Marielitos. The xenophobic wave of reaction that came from 1980 was not met with any concerted government effort. A decade and a half later, when thousands of Cubans took to the sea in makeshift rafts in an effort to escape the island and the ravages of the post-Soviet economy, they were arriving in a country in the midst of another panic related to immigration. Federal decision-makers feared another Mariel and saw no political advantage in fighting this new wave of xenophobia.

To draw out the complex context of race in this transformation this work draws from the insights of the literature on Latino urban history. Scholars of the Latino urban experience, like historian Lilia Fernández, have made significant contributions by demonstrating the need to move past an understanding of race in the United States along a strict Black-white binary.[30] *Only a Few*

Blocks to Cuba contributes to this work, but also to a movement of historians, cultural geographers, and other scholars who have brought the transnational context in which Latino communities have developed to the forefront of their work.[31] Of particular importance here is the work of Andrew K. Sandoval-Strausz and his study of the impact of Latino immigrants on American cities. As Sandoval-Strausz shows, Latino immigrants were often perceived as "racially undefined" in mid-century cities where race was usually defined in binary terms and were even used by real estate agents and others to serve as a buffer between white and Black communities.[32] Accordingly, this meant that for Latinos, their "uncertain identities sometimes advantaged them as not-black while also sometimes disadvantaging them as not-really-white."[33] Sandoval-Strausz focuses on the important contributions to urban America made by these immigrant groups despite the significant restrictions they experienced due to modest incomes, social marginalization, political demonization, and the undocumented status of many among them.[34]

The impact of the Cuban migrations to Miami has significant similarities to Sandoval-Strausz's case studies, but the assistance provided by the federal government demonstrates that the Cold War is an understudied factor in Latino urban history. To illustrate this, this work builds on the insights of another scholar of Latino urban history, Llana Barber, and her study of Lawrence, Massachusetts. Barber provides an important framework based on Juan González's "harvest of empire" conception of Latino migration to the United States. The case of Lawrence provides an important connection between U.S. imperial machinations in Latin America and the impact on American cities as the United States created the push factors that drove migrants from their homelands to go along with the pull factors that drew them to urban areas.[35] Barber describes the upheavals of the Cold War and post–Cold War periods as creating a wide-ranging set of experiences within the "harvest of empire" model.[36]

The Cubans who came to Miami starting in 1959 and well after the accepted end of the conflict were Cold War migrants whose movement across the Straits of Florida served a purpose for a particular phase of American empire. In this way, their experience represents a variant of the harvest of empire that brought the struggles of the global ideological conflict to the streets of the United States.[37] Because of the purpose the U.S. government intended them to serve, the Cubans in Miami received not only a type of financial assistance that Latino migrants to Dallas, Chicago, Lawrence, and other cities did not receive, but the nature of this assistance fundamentally challenged the racial structures of South Florida. This work focuses on a landscape that included the federal government as an active participant in disrupting elements of established racial structures. While federal investment throughout the South led to an embrace of the rhetoric of racial modera- tion during the mid- to late twentieth century for fear of alienating potential investors, the influx of funds was not fundamentally disruptive to established structures, leading only to modest gains by African Americans in the midst of significant growth.[38] There was not an activist state that sought to redress fun- damental economic disparities for African Americans or to advocate for new immigrants, but in Miami, because of Cuban refugees' perceived significance to the Cold War, there was, for a time, an activist state that worked for them and disrupted some of the structures of power related to race in the region.

The structures of race in Florida were made complex by the state's proxim- ity to the Caribbean and the presence of immigrant communities, but in the ongoing struggle between Jim Crow structures, complications due to immi- gration, and the push for civil rights, the post-1959 Cuban influx further com- plicated the racial landscape. Historians have demonstrated the richness and complexity of this history. Paul Ortiz has shown, for example, how labor orga- nizing and an alliance between enfranchised African Americans and Cuban migrants helped stave off the rollback of Reconstruction in Key West before the state firmly entrenched Jim Crow.[39] Others, like Andrew Gomez, have shown the complexity of the landscape for both white and Afro-descended Cubans at the turn of the twentieth century.[40] Chanelle N. Rose's study of Miami and the struggle for civil rights also demonstrates how Jim Crow became a liability for the city as it drew increasing numbers of tourists from Latin America, with Cubans attaining a degree of whiteness as tourists visiting the city.[41]

While these challenges existed by 1959, the economic, political, and social power of the city was concentrated in the hands of the city's white elites, with African Americans being subjected to segregation, economic exploitation, and disruptions of their communities through urban renewal schemes. The investment by the CRP and related institutions into the economic well-being of the Cuban refugee community and development of a path to citizenship presented a fundamental challenge to the continued dominance of white, native-born elites. The programs meant to aid the Cuban refugee community provided them not only with the pathways to power, but with structures of privilege explicitly denied to African Americans and to other groups coming from Latin America and from other parts of the world. While the federal government engaged in these actions without the intent of reshaping race in Miami, these early decisions had unforeseen effects.

Local elites and white Miamians came to realize the effects of these programs within a few years and reacted with racialized portrayals of Cubans as
being unworthy of the avenues to economic well-being and political power
with which they had been imbued. This set the stage for decades of struggle
over local power. Institutions like the *Miami Herald*, which had been inte-
gral in obtaining the attention and assistance of federal policymakers for the
Cuban refugees in the early 1960s, soon adopted antagonistic stances against
the Cuban and Cuban American community in the city, portraying federal
assistance in a negative light and questioning the community's influence on
the city and on federal policy. They were not alone in these reactions. White
Miamians expressed their outrage at the presence and increasing power of
the Cuban refugees and Cuban Americans throughout the period. In letters
to political figures, newspapers, and institutions, they vented their frustration
with the changes they saw and sometimes clearly identified their greatest frustration: that the institutions meant to maintain their own power and privilege
were actively working in the service of a different group. This frustration was
aimed at the federal government's general Cuba and Cuban refugee policy, but
often it focused on the presence of the CRP in the city and its defense of the
refugees.

Because the federal government sought to advance foreign policy, not to
fundamentally challenge the racial structures of South Florida, there were
significant limits to the extent of this challenge.[42] While the growth of Cuban
power and wealth and the support the community received from the federal
government created a competition for the upper rungs of Miami's racial lad-
der, it did little to improve the fortunes of African Americans in the city. This
was, in part, because the Cubans arriving in Miami were not themselves a
racially homogenous group and because they brought their own conceptions
about race across borders. Consequently, the experience of Cuban refugees
coming to the United States were not uniform, and these differences were
often dictated by race. While some Afro-Cuban arrivals used their refugee
status and the support of the federal government to challenge some of the
restrictions that African Americans encountered in Miami in the 1960s, they
often found themselves facing both the systems of racial segregation of the
United States and concepts of race prevalent within their own community,
which were rooted in Cuba's own racial history. Cubans who were not Afro
descended, or were not identified as such, portrayed themselves as outsid-
ers in the struggles regarding race in the United States but used their own
experiences in leaving Cuba to position themselves in opposition to much

of the civil rights activism in the United States. They sought to downplay the history of racial conflict in Cuba, placing themselves as arbiters of legitimate racial grievance. As historian Devin Spence Benson notes, "By re-creating an enclave community composed of mostly white middle- and upper-class residents, Cubans in south Florida constructed an idealized space where racial and class discrimination was an aberration of the distant past."[43]

The Cuban refugee community embraced this narrative of racial innocence, accepting no responsibility for the discriminatory structures of Miami's racial order while also supporting policies and stances that made positive change for the city's African Americans even more difficult to attain.[44] The majority of the early waves of Cuban refugees could move situationally and embrace their own whiteness within their community, while either accepting the structured support of the federal government, and the power and privilege that came with it, or a status as outsider when it came to the negative effects of local racial structures on their African American neighbors. These neighbors, in turn, reacted with frustration to the fact that the structures of aid and empowerment they had long sought for the federal government to provide to them were instead provided to a group of refugees. They did not see why the ordeal of exile held more weight than centuries of oppression starting with the trauma of slavery.

Miami's African Americans were frustrated, not only by the fact that Cuban refugees were granted levels of aid their community had never seen, but also by how the Cuban presence could be used as an excuse for their own neglect and could exacerbate their own hardships. As noted by Marvin Dunn, a chronicler of Black Miami, the era of integration in Miami was complicated by coinciding with the Cuban influx.[45] In 1960, the city considered the presence of the refugees so urgent that it drew attention away from the struggle for civil rights. It forced the city, or perhaps provided the city the opportunity, to dissolve its biracial relations committee in favor of a Cuban Refugee Committee.[46] This work shows how, as the Cuban refugees became the city's Cuban Americans, many Black Miamians in the 1970s and 1980s came to regard them as being deeply ingrained in a system that still excluded African Americans from structures of power and economic success. The influx of Cubans into Miami had fundamentally challenged some aspects of race in South Florida and reinforced others.

This book uses the lived experience of Miamians, both those born in the city and those for whom the city would become a place of refuge and then a home, to make critical contributions to our understanding of several significant issues in twentieth-century history. This history lays bare the intersections between the American welfare and security states, U.S. relations with Latin America, the history of Latinos in the United States, the role of immigration in shifting political coalitions, racial hierarchies and state power, and the significance of the Cold War in shaping American cities. These trends converge in Miami, but the narrative scope of the chapters that follow is not restricted to South Florida as it shows how events in Havana; Washington, DC; or Atlanta, GA, could shift the politics of Miami, and how Miami could affect these places in turn. The Miami metropolitan area is not a curious outlier, as it is often portrayed; rather, its history is essential to our understanding of the trends that have borne out many of the shifts to the current political landscape that befuddle pundits and politicians.[47] The forces behind these changes can be well understood by looking back on the history of the shifting ground by Biscayne Bay.

CHAPTER 1

"Our Unnoticed Neighbors": Cuban Refugees, Community Action, and the Push for a Federal Response

On July 4, 1959, a group of Cubans sympathetic to the recent revolution gathered near Bayfront Park in downtown Miami to participate in a "Cuba-U.S. friendship parade." Members of this group, including Cuban consul Alonso Hidalgo, reported that a car full of Batista loyalists erupted onto the scene and snatched a Cuban flag from a young girl's hands, interrupting the event. Parade participants gave chase to the loyalists. The pursuit ended at the home of Batista-era senator Rolando Masferrer on Southwest Second Avenue, where over fifty anti-Castro Cubans were gathered.[1] Another report, signed by more than a dozen Miami police officers, blamed Hidalgo for what happened next. Looking "disheveled and almost incoherent with rage," Hidalgo arrived on the scene of a minor clash between the prorevolution group and the anti-Castro group gathered for a "Catholic Anti-Communist" rally and started shouting encouragement at the prorevolution crowd.[2] Hidalgo's actions caused the anti-Castro group to surge out of Masferrer's home, intending to trounce him. The resulting skirmish required a force of forty-five police officers driving motorcycles, radio cars, and police wagons to stop an estimated two hundred Cubans engaged in a street brawl on the intersection of SW Second Avenue and Eleventh Street.[3]

This clash was just the latest in a series of incidents occurring in and around the city of Miami. In the months preceding the incident, the *Miami Herald* had published reports of verbal and physical confrontations between Cuban groups, the international intrigue related to the agents of several Caribbean nations in South Florida, and the arms trade flowing through the city. This mounting strife finally led the *Herald*'s James Buchanan to declare in the weeks following the brawl that his city would become a destination for exiles fleeing for their lives and a hub for their political activities. Buchanan compared the recent clashes on city streets to occurrences in recent memory, asking, "Is Miami to be more of a Latin American battleground than it was during Castro's Cuban revolution?"[4] His readers had already lived through a period of clashes between Cuban factions, when the city had served as a staging ground for pro-Castro groups. Buchanan expected that this current round of strife would be worse as the number of exiles in the city had continued to grow. He noted that during the three weeks between June 22 and July 13, 103 new exiles had arrived in South Florida. The scale of the refugee arrivals in later years would dwarf this number, but the article suggested that a few hundred agitators on either side would propagandize the estimated 25,000–30,000 "neutral" Cubans in the city, threatening further unrest. The question was whether the violence that had largely abated in Cuba would become the new reality for South Florida due to the growing exile presence.

The Cuban migration to South Florida in the first two years after the ouster of Fulgencio Batista was a massive humanitarian crisis, but it did not make itself immediately apparent. The flow of refugees was a trickle that became a flood. This growing presence was also masked by the efforts of the city's established Cuban community and its civic and religious leadership, who provided aid to many of the early arrivals. While locals were made aware of the predicament they faced by its effects on their city, federal officials were slow to recognize the scope of the problem and its implications for U.S. relations, not only with Cuba, but with the rest of Latin America and the Cold War world as a whole. Concerned Miamians would play a significant role in presenting those implications to federal officials and in drawing the federal government into what had previously been categorized as a local problem.

Those in local government and in local civic and religious organizations recognized the scale of the refugee influx before federal authorities, and the interactions between city elites—particularly the city's Catholic Church and newspapers—and the federal government shaped the initial narrative of the crisis as they grappled with determining whether the Cuban refugees were a ruinous tide of humanity, a potentially useful group, or both. The growing numbers of Cuban exiles spurred local individuals and institutions to action as they sought help to alleviate the migratory emergency affecting their city. While Miami's established Cuban community was extremely successful in incorporating the first arrivals with the aid of local charitable organizations, the scope of the humanitarian crisis created by the Cuban refugee presence proved too taxing for the city's resources in these early years and drove the calls for federal involvement. Nevertheless, the initial involvement by the federal government in late 1960 was limited in scope. The first encounters between the refugees, local civic and religious groups, and federal authorities set the stage for a larger federal intervention and had long-term effects in shaping this effort. These early interactions undermine the assumptions that often color popular and academic discussions of Miami and the Cuban community, showing that the federal aid that followed was not a natural outgrowth of Cuban migrant anticommunism, but the result of choices made and the actions at the local and federal levels in conjunction, putting the story of Miami into conversation with a growing literature in American foreign relations about how local and nongovernmental actors have significant power to influence American foreign policy at the highest levels.[5]

Miami and the Caribbean Before 1959

Miami's location, on the shores of Biscayne Bay, put the city in close proximity to the nations of the Caribbean from its founding in 1896. The city's boosters made an effort to capitalize on this proximity by promoting it as a gateway to the Caribbean. Historian Louis Pérez Jr. has shown that real estate developers wanted to exploit the early twentieth-century American infatuation with Cuba by shaping Miami's built environment. These developers lifted architectural design ideas from the island, named streets after places in Cuba, and imported construction materials—including weathered roof tiles and fixtures previously used in Cuban buildings—from Havana.[6] Miami, then, was not only a way station to and from Cuba, but also an attempt at reproducing the country's exotic image on American soil. This exotic character enticed investors and vacationers and helped drive the real estate boom in Dade County in the first half of the 1920s. This boom would slow, particularly after the devastating hurricane of 1926, but even as the American economy took a downturn, the city attracted investment from Cuban venture capitalists in the decades before the Cuban revolution.[7]

While significant in its development, Cuba was not the only Caribbean nation to influence Miami. In his study of queer Miami before 1940, historian Julio Capó Jr. argues that while Cuba had a significant role in shaping the city, prior to 1959 the Bahamas was equally, if not more, influential to the city's development.[8] The presence of Black Bahamians in the city, for example, challenged some of the racial structures present in other Jim Crow cities. As historian Chanelle Rose has shown, Black Bahamians were often shocked by the racial bigotry they encountered in the city, and some attempted to use their British citizenship as a defense against it. This led to white elites in the city seeing them as a liability and being more hostile to them than to African Americans, which had the effect of hardening racial lines. While Rose finds that the continued discrimination against Bahamians and other Black Anglo-Caribbeans demonstrated the city's southern character, their presence and that of other groups from the Caribbean complicated the racial landscape of the city.[9]

This complex racial landscape did not, however, prevent the entrenchment of racial power dynamics that disadvantaged the city's African Americans. African Americans in Miami were exploited politically and economically and were often excluded from a significant share of public services. Throughout much of the twentieth century, they lived in the city's congested Central Negro District, also known as Colored Town (and, in time, as Overtown), located "blocks from downtown but a world away from the beachfront where so many blacks worked."[10] While there were other groups with different experiences in the city, for African Americans the patterns of exclusion and white supremacy in Miami were all too familiar. If anything, this diversity simply allowed different actors to invest in these structures. As N. D. B. Connolly argues in his study of real estate and Jim Crow in South Florida, "Americans, immigrants, and even indigenous people made tremendous investments in racial apartheid in the city."[11] Connolly shows that in this respect, South Florida's racial dynamics were "regrettably commonplace and unexceptional."[12]

By the early 1950s, these structures of racial segregation had contributed to a familiar pattern that would actually benefit the Cuban refugees as they began to arrive at the end of the decade. The Miami metropolitan area consisted of the city of Miami and twenty-five suburban municipalities. The central city was growing at a much slower rate than the periphery as the surrounding suburban municipalities enticed commercial and industrial establishments away from the center.[13] By the time the Cuban migration to South Florida began, the loss of jobs in the central city had led to a recession and an economic environment that undermined the previous diversification of the city's economy.

The depopulation of Miami proper was further exacerbated by the embrace of urban renewal schemes by liberal politicians in South Florida.

Self-styled "racial progressives" wanted to tackle the symbolic and material ills of Jim Crow segregation in the decades after the Second World War through slum clearance and urban renewal. They sought to unmake Jim Crow at the spatial level by democratizing Americans' access to suburban real estate and weakening the property rights of urban landlords.[14] The *Miami Herald* supported these efforts, describing slums and blighted areas as "Florida's Shame," and declaring that "Urban Renewal should be an article of hope and faith" in the state's future.[15] In effect, however, the practice of utilizing eminent domain legislation to carry out urban renewal projects served to raze Black rental housing and liquidate Black homes.[16] In spatial terms, the elimination of Black housing in the Central Negro District led to an African American migration from the central city to unincorporated area of Liberty City, a more suburban environment north of Allapattah.[17] Just as many of the city's white inhabitants were following the migration of jobs to the suburban municipalities, African Americans were also moving out of the central city, creating a space for the incoming waves of Cuban refugees.

The depopulation of the city's center set the stage for the arrival of those Cubans fleeing the revolution, but the longer history of U.S.-Cuba relations also prepared members of the Cuban upper and middle classes for their arrival in South Florida. In the aftermath of Cuba's war of independence, the United States used the distribution of its vast resources, including the delivery of food to the hungry, to obtain Cuban compliance with its aims.[18] The material impoverishment of the Cubans in 1898 facilitated the introduction of the Americans' own economic and technical models.[19] American business concerns established deep roots in Cuba by taking advantage of the devastation of the postwar period, and they promoted new economic and social systems that helped to set the stage for both early adaptability by the exiles and familiarity with the city of Miami on the part of moneyed Cubans by the start of the diaspora. Cubans sought to establish a clear standard for what it meant to be a modern Cuban, but these definitions developed in an environment that embraced American business models and connections.[20] Havana's exposure to international business and the heavy investment of American corporations prepared many Cubans to operate in a much more vibrant business environment than that which already existed in Miami—one that they would have to help build.

By the 1950s, Miami held special significance for both exiles and well-to-do Cubans. Miami became a city of refugees in the aftermath of the Cuban revolution, but throughout the 1930s, the 1940s, and especially the 1950s,

South Florida served as a haven for former office holders and political radi-
cals seeking to bring change to Cuba. The city also served as a natural tourist
destination for many in the upper and middle classes of Cuban society. These
groups were familiar with the city prior to the revolution, but scholars suggest
that these segments were predisposed to this familiarity because the American presence in Cuba had transmitted certain cultural forms. The influence of
American cultural forms in post-Spanish Cuba created in many Cubans a significant pro-American feeling, and the United States in general—and Miami
in particular—came to represent a temporary haven for Cuban tourists as
violence once again took hold of their country in the late 1950s.[21]

The city's image as a welcoming refuge for Latin American visitors and
business was also enhanced by certain decisions made by Miami's government and civic organizations. After the Second World War, organizations like
the Miami Chamber of Commerce sought to attract Latin American tourism
by promoting the city as the "Gateway to the Americas."[22] In doing so, however, Miami's business elites complicated the existing system of Jim Crow segregation in the city. Latin American visitors, even very dark-skinned visitors,
were not as clearly racialized as they might have been elsewhere and were
provided with some exceptions to the prevalent structures of race in the city.
Chanelle Rose notes that Latin American visitors, particularly wealthy Cubans,
were afforded an "honorary" white status in the city.[23] She argues that these
concessions began the process of Latinization in Miami two decades before
1959.[24] While this "honorary whiteness" was intended to affect individuals
and groups who were only visiting Miami, this transient access to racial privilege set an important precedent that would later be tested as droves of Cubans
arrived at the city's international airport, not for week-long vacations, but for
periods of exile without a guaranteed end.

Enemies of the Revolution:
The Early Exiles in a Changing City

Later in life, Father Bryan O. Walsh thought back to New Year's Day 1959 and
recalled how it changed his life. On that day, the Catholic priest saw jubilation
on the streets of Miami as news of the fall of Batista swept through the city.
He watched as carloads of Cubans drove around Dupont Plaza and Biscayne
Boulevard in celebration.[25] Although the number of Cubans in the city was
still relatively small, the joy of anti-Batista Cubans was palpable. Like other

residents of Miami, Walsh observed the festivities unaware of the massive changes that were to come for the city or the humanitarian crisis that would involve him, as the director of Catholic Charities, in the affairs of the city's Cuban population for the rest of his life. Even as the focus shifted from the jubilation over Batista's ouster, the initial reporting on the first of the new exiles focused on their ties to the failed regime rather than their numbers.

The appearance of Cuban exiles in Miami early in 1959 led area newspapers to publish several sensationalistic articles highlighting the individual stories of formerly high-ranking members of the regime now hiding from Castro in South Florida. It was not clear if they would stay there for long. When Rolando Masferrer and several of his associates fled Havana on his private yacht on January 1 and set sail for Key West, they were detained on arrival. While immigration officials granted some of the passengers asylum, others flew back to Havana and a group that included Masferrer was transferred to a detention center in McAllen, Texas.[26] After being paroled on January 27, Masferrer went into hiding, living in a "shabby rented house on the fringe of a Negro section of Miami," all the while issuing denials to the press regarding the Cuban government's charge that he had stolen $17 million when he fled the country.[27] Fulgencio's brother, Francisco Batista, was reported to live in Hialeah and to have opened a business with his son Juan.[28] The presence of Batista associates like Masferrer and Francisco Batista made some people speculate on whether the ousted despot would leave the Dominican Republic and seek refuge in the United States. The days of Latin American dictatorships seemed numbered, so the issue of asylum was expected to come up often.[29] This led the *Herald* to ask whether Batista and other Latin American strongmen should be allowed into the country: "Should the U.S. grant political asylum to deposed dictators?"[30]

Miami was not an obvious destination for many Batista supporters. Many members of the Batista regime or those closely associated with it avoided entering the United States through Miami because of the strong support Castro had in the city.[31] These pro-Castro tendencies in the city were, however, weakened by the arrival of each new flight from Cuba. The very planes that brought Batista supporters would often return to the island filled with Cubans who had fled the former dictator and now sought a fresh start back in their home country.[32] The early exiles made their presence known through their activism and their involvement in their new community. By March 1959, exiles allegedly financed by "Batista sources" had established an anti-Castro newspaper in Miami, called *Tribuna*.[33] Many of the early arrivals began to organize and meet at anti-Castro events, such as the one held in Masferer's home. The activism of these first exiles served to foster political unrest and clashes like the July 4 brawl. Observers were concerned about the exiles' presence because of the clashes between anti- and pro-Castro groups and the exiles' influence on the established Cuban community in Miami. There was not yet widespread concern about the volume of arrivals or the length of their tenure in the city.

The exact number of refugees that made their home in South Florida during this period is difficult to ascertain. This was, in part, because the federal government had made a change to immigration policy in 1954, abandoning an older policy of detaining people seeking to enter the United States until admissibility could be determined. The federal government replaced this policy with a policy of "parole," meaning the status of "parolee" was granted to all but those whom they deemed were either flight risks or threats to public health or national security.[34] By the end of June 1959, district immigration director Edward P. Ahrens estimated that the number of exiles in the city had reached five hundred.[35] The lack of consistency in federal policy regarding Cuban entry and registration in the United States, however, obscured this number. The federal government, under Eisenhower, established an open-door policy for Cubans migrating to the United States. As relations with the Castro government deteriorated, Eisenhower hoped a heavy flow of temporary refugees would discredit the new regime in the eyes of the world.[36] Confident that the situation was transient, immigration officials failed to establish a system by which the entry of Cuban migrants could be accurately monitored and quantified. Without such a system, the traditional flow of tourists and visitors between Florida and Cuba obscured the precise scope of the migration as very few of the Cubans entering the United States at this time sought the designation of political refugee.

A majority of those who came to South Florida entered the country on B-2 (tourist) visas. Many Cubans reasoned—rightly or not—that on identifying themselves as refugees, the Castro government would immediately seize any possessions left behind and their remaining family members in Cuba would be in danger. By August 1960, about 4,000 Cubans had adopted official political refugee status in Miami, but this number was dwarfed by the ill-defined mass of Cubans that remained in South Florida on tourist visas. [37] By the end of 1960, the number of "visitors" who had entered the United States using tourist visas and now resided in the Miami area was estimated at 33,000.[38] The number of Cubans who had specifically requested political asylum or who had stayed in the United States for over a year on a tourist visa and were now requesting work permits, numbered about 15,600.[39] As the months went by, Miamians grew less concerned about intra-Cuban conflict and more worried about the sheer volume of Cubans and the looming humanitarian emergency threatening their city.

Several factors served to mask or ameliorate the effects of the developing migratory crisis prior to fall of 1960. The wealth of many of the early exiles, the more relaxed restrictions by the Cuban government regarding the funds that could be removed from the island, the support of the local Cuban community, and the aid provided by local civic and religious organizations prevented the city from being overwhelmed with the needs of the growing Cuban community. The city's history of hosting Cuban exiles and the significant number of Latin American tourists that visited the city each year made the growing presence of the Cubans less disruptive to everyday life than it might have been elsewhere. In time, however, the economic and social needs of the refugees began to tax existing support structures. The sheer number of Cubans became disruptive even for residents of an "inter-American" city. State and local governments managed the crisis as best they could with the aid of civic and religious groups, but the growing problem forced them to call on the federal government for help.

While some refugees had to flee Cuba with little or no money, a segment of the early exiles was able to bring substantial resources with them. In December of 1960, the Federal Housing Administration estimated that ten thousand refugees had been able to leave Cuba with significant funds and had reportedly been purchasing homes in the Miami area and paying for these dwellings in cash.[40] This influx of Cuban funds was a boon to local banks. When rumors circulated in late 1960 that hostilities with Cuba were imminent and the assets of Cubans in the United States would be seized, constituents reached out to Congressman Dante Fascell with concerns that wealthy Cubans would transfer their funds from South Florida banks to banks in Canada or Europe.[41]

Affluent Cubans wanted stability, and there were those who were willing to take that desire and use it to part the refugees with their money. Two Miami-area attorneys, for example, offered Cuban clients the opportunity to participate in a scheme to lobby the U.S. Congress for a bill to grant permanent resident status to those who paid into the venture.[42] Buy-in began at $100 for an individual, and the cost could grow rapidly for families with multiple children.[43] The attorneys collected over twenty-one thousand dollars from Cuban clients.[44] Between April and August of 1960, attorney Jack L. King inundated Dante Fascell and other members of Florida's congressional delegation with agitated correspondence.[45] He attempted to sway members of Congress by focusing on the angle of family reunification.[46] However, Fascell warned the attorney that the bill was unlikely to be brought before Congress, much less passed, as the Department of State and Immigration and Naturalization Services would not support legislation without being able to review the problem as a whole.[47]

Other Cubans thought the push for permanence useless as the revolution was sure to swiftly collapse.[48] Dr. Manuel Antonio de Varona, the former prime minister and president of the Cuban senate, predicted in early November 1960 that there would be a "blood bath" in Cuba within ninety days as the people turned against Castro.[49] This belief differed from that of other recent refugee groups, like the Hungarians who arrived in the United States after the Soviet repression of their revolution in 1956. One official observed that the Hungarian refugees, unlike the Cubans, "knew they could not go home and so they had to make their lives here for themselves."[50] These Cubans were not alone in this belief; many in the federal government also embraced it. Some shared it earnestly, while others found it useful. Regardless of motivation, the idea of an impermanent revolution made officials hesitate on the issue of migratory normalization due to its problematic symbolic implications.

Francis E. Walter, chairman of the House Un-American Activities Committee and the House Subcommittee on the Judiciary with Special Jurisdiction over Immigration and Nationality, warned Fascell against enacting legislative solutions regarding permanent residence for Cubans on the grounds that any rushed legislation granting permanent resident status "would imply that we consider the present situation in Cuba as a permanent one and that we see no hope of that situation changing so as to permit the people persecuted by Castro to return to their own country." Allowing this implication to arise would not be consistent with American foreign policy interests.[51] Walter was rejecting any piece of legislation suggesting that Castro's regime would have any permanence. For the anti-communist Walter, and for like-minded allies within the U.S. government, the humanitarian dimensions of the crisis in South Florida were secondary to the symbolic and practical implications of this crisis in the fight against Marxism in Latin America. Federal officials had not yet been convinced that addressing the problems created by this migration in South Florida could have its own positive implications in relation to the Cold War in the region.

Selling the Crisis: Defining the Problem of
Miami as a Front in the Cold War

As the revolutionary government solidified its power, it placed restrictions on the amount of currency Cubans were able to remove from the country, making the move to the United States all the more precarious for refugees. The Bank of Cuba decreed that Cuban tourists could take $150 a year out of their country. Given that so many Cubans were leaving the island with tourist visas, however, many of the refugees arriving in Miami reported that Cuban authorities usually denied their request for the $150 under one pretext or another. Restrictions on Cubans immigrating to the United States on resident visas were even stricter; they could carry only $5 on leaving the island.[52]

The refugees who arrived in the Miami area with five dollars or less to their name would often seek out family or friends among the established Cuban community in Miami. These personal ties proved lifesaving for many. Because those who entered the United States on tourist visas could not legally seek out jobs in the Miami area, established Cubans were crucial in the feeding and housing of many early arrivals. Local leaders went so far as to report that the effects of the influx were somewhat delayed by the efforts of the Cubans who had settled in Miami before the revolution or soon thereafter.[53] Father Bryan Walsh made a similar assessment of the situation, stating that the resident Cuban colony "had done a commendable job of absorbing their compatriots into their homes and places of business."[54]

Cubans who did not have friends or family in Miami and those who found the resources of their allies in the city taxed to a breaking point sought out help from familiar institutions. As Father Walsh explained in 1966 to the National Council of Catholic Women Convention, "The Cuban turned to the Church for help."[55] As director of Catholic charities in Miami, Walsh was among the first to see the growing problems posed by the increased Cuban presence in the city. A growing number of refugees sought help from the Centro Hispánico Católico, an agency under the Catholic Welfare Bureau that was created in late 1958 and tasked with dealing with the needs of Spanish-speaking new arrivals in the city.[56] This center became even more important as new Cuban arrivals found themselves without work, shelter, or money in a foreign city. By October of 1960, the bread line at a church on Miami Avenue was feeding 300 refugees a day. The diocese had also spent $75,000 to remodel a building on NE Second Street, where it provided English classes, day care services, and a clinic for the refugees, all with an operational cost of

$25,000 a year.[57] Between December 1960 and March 1, 1961, Catholic chari-
ties saw 1,653 patients at its medical clinic, provided assistance for 2,450 families, distributed 6,200 baskets of food, arranged emergency housing for 4,520
exiles, and helped provide hospital care for 512 exiles. The Diocese of Miami
spent $197,065 on these services, nearly doubling their expenditures to date.[58]

The Catholic Church was not alone in trying to aid the Cubans flowing into
South Florida between 1959 and 1960. The Miami Latin Center, chaired by
Reverend Dr. Harold Buell of the White Methodist Church, served as a clear-
inghouse to bring employers together with refugee job seekers. In October of
1960, however, Buell warned that there were not enough jobs to go around.
The resort industry in Miami and the Hotel Employees Union collaborated to
open an office that found jobs for some four hundred Cubans and came to a
similar conclusion. Tony Farinas, a Cuban-born union representative, echoed
Buell's statements and said that the industry simply did not have the capacity
to absorb all those who were in need.[59] The lack of coordination and the scale
of the problem hindered the impact of these different groups and agencies.

The problem, the *Miami Herald* suggested, was one of visibility. When
the newspaper hosted a panel of community leaders including Bishop Coleman Carroll, Reverend Buell, Farinas, Welfare Planning Council president
Dr. Franklin Williams, and Congressman Fascell, they sought to inform the
public in Miami of the growing problem concerning a population they called
"our Unnoticed Neighbors."[60] These community leaders provided statistics
and stories about the challenges presented by the refugee problem to the *Herald's* readers, but also a clear understanding of the origins of the problem and
some prescient policy predictions. Carroll emphasized the uniqueness of the
situation by declaring that Miami was "the first city in the U.S. to ever have
a Communist state as a next door neighbor."[61] Williams agreed, calling it "a
cold war problem," and suggesting that the federal specialists who had helped
during the Hungarian refugee crisis of 1956 could help in Miami.[62] While
the group discussed the possibility of assistance from such organizations as
the Red Cross and the United Nations, Congressman Fascell warned that no
outside agency would want to help Miami until information regarding the
number of refugees in South Florida and the extent of their needs could be
determined. Miami needed to define the problem and try to solve it.[63]

In the spirit of defining the problem and conveying its urgency, both to
the people of Miami and to the world at large, *Miami Herald* reporter Juanita
Greene wrote a series of stories that illustrated the different situations and
shared problems of the refugees in Miami. In a cheap duplex on NW Fiftieth

Street, on the "fringe" between white and African American areas, Greene met the Bequer family. The husband, Napoleón, a former member of Castro's rebel army, had made a dramatic escape from Havana's Morro Castle prison with twenty other former officers in late 1960. His wife and children had soon followed him to the United States. The Bequers had managed to bring two hundred dollars to the United States—gifts from sympathetic friends in Cuba—and on arrival had received one hundred dollars from friends already in Miami. This money had allowed them to obtain a place to live and some used furniture. Napoleón had, just days prior to the interview, obtained a part-time, temporary job as a rug cutter. Even with this economic uncertainty, Bequer considered himself lucky. While his job might have been temporary, he was still doing better than the father of Luis, the neighbor boy who was visiting when Greene conducted her interview. Luis's father had been a lawyer in Oriente but had no job in Miami. "They were a very wealthy family in Cuba," Mrs. Bequer told Greene; "now they have nothing."[64]

Not all refugees were able to live in single-family dwellings like the Bequers. The *Herald* also showed how the refugee influx had created a housing shortage in the city. On NW Seventh Street Greene found twenty-six Cuban men who had converted a house, a small cottage, and a garage on a single property into an impromptu barracks. This was a fairly common practice: groups of single men would band together to rent a dwelling, sharing the space and expenses. During the day, the men would stack their mattresses to clear enough floor space so they could walk inside the house. Of the twenty-six men, only three had jobs, including part-time work as a plumber's helper for $1.25 an hour. Once daily, one of the men would set two large pots on the stove and make rice and beans for the group, their only sustenance for the day. The group from the Seventh Street house had sought help from different organizations in Miami including the Centro Hispánico Católico, which provided the group with sixty dollars.[65] These group dwellings served as a transitory living situation for single men or men who had come to the United States without their families. Once they found more stable situations, the refugees would leave these barracks behind—but there would often be two men ready to take their place.

Greene and the *Miami Herald* editorial staff wanted to expose the refugee problem and spur state and federal authorities into action. The *Herald* argued that unless state and federal officials recognized that they needed to act in resolving the problem, they would prove themselves "exceptionally short-sighted."[66] Not only was the task of managing this refugee wave ill-suited to volunteer groups and local government, but the way in which these refugees were treated in the United States would resonate throughout Latin America. The problem was not simply an emergency for one tucked-away city; on the contrary, it was a problem with serious implications for Americans and American foreign policy as a whole. The man whom the Eisenhower White House appointed to assess the problem would later write that Greene and the *Herald's* articles on the Cuban refugee problem had largely spurred the local response and helped bring the issue to the attention of the federal government.[67]

In September of 1960, a group of community leaders from the greater Miami area formed a committee to determine the scope of the refugee problem and the possible avenues by which to address it.[68] The committee invited William Kirk, the director of the International Social Service, which had helped resettle thirty-five thousand Hungarian refugees throughout the United States, to the city. Before arriving in Miami, Kirk made it clear that the resettlement of Cubans to other areas of the country would be a significant part of any solution to Miami's refugee problem. The city's resources alone would not be enough to handle the problem, which he likened to a natural disaster.[69] In response to Kirk's findings and his assertion that officials in Washington seemed largely unaware of Miami's refugee problem, the temporary committee reorganized with the aim of exerting pressure at the state and federal levels in order to bring refugee aid to Miami. Miami mayor Robert King High joined the committee and declared that the problems it faced were not simply those of one American city. High stated that because Miami was now the "bastion against communism," Washington needed to help the city immediately.[70]

On October 17, 1960, the chair of the newly minted Cuban Refugee Committee, Ira Willard, sent a letter to President Eisenhower directly stating Dade County's need for help. The letter echoed High's rationale regarding the federal government's obligation. "Our community has become a 'front-line' in the cold war tactics of the Communist world, and a point of first asylum for those Cubans who find their present regime intolerable," Willard explained to the president. The missive applauded the Cubans even as it requested aid to stem the drain on resources that they had become. The problem, as Willard saw it, was not in the refugees as people but in the very scale of the crisis; it simply dwarfed the capabilities of a single city. He urgently entreated President Eisenhower to assign federal officials to travel to Miami so they could clearly determine the extent of the problem and direct the aid that the refugees and the community so desperately needed. Willard stressed that the eyes of the world were on Miami and warned Eisenhower that any action taken there to resolve the situation would have "implications or repercussions abroad affecting our entire nation, for good or ill."[71] The committee's letter spurred the federal government into action. The Eisenhower administration engaged the crisis by inviting Florida governor Leroy Collins, Willard, and Mayor High to a conference where they could present their case for broad-scale federal assistance. The Florida delegation met with Eisenhower's deputy assistant for interdepartmental affairs, Robert Merriam. They reiterated the position that while most of the burden had fallen on Miami, the Cuban refugee crisis stemmed from the federal government allowing entrance of these exiles into the country.[72] After the meeting, Merriam had a better idea of the situation, or at least of the dissatisfaction among local and state officials. In order to learn more and to quiet the calls for federal involvement, Merriam reached out to a refugee expert who had previously assisted the Eisenhower administration: Tracy Voorhees.[73]

The Skeptic: Tracy Voorhees and the Early Federal Efforts in Miami

In the mid-1950s, Voorhees had led the President's Committee for Hungarian Refugee Relief, a temporary organization that had dealt with the Hungarian refugee influx.[74] In a meeting at the White House on October 25, 1960, Voorhees urged Merriam to hold off on involving the president personally until he had explored other approaches. A small-government conservative, Voorhees attempted to convince the Red Cross to tackle Miami's Cuban refugee situation instead of the federal government. It was only after Red Cross president Alfred Gruenther rebuffed him that he agreed to become the president's envoy in South Florida.[75]

On November 10, following continued pressure from the Cuban Refugee Committee, the White House formally announced that it had tasked Voorhees with investigating the problem and reporting on its scope directly to the president.[76] To the disappointment of many people in Miami, however, Eisenhower declared that the refugee problem would mainly continue to be dealt with locally. Voorhees would only determine what added measures the federal government should adopt.[77] This restriction of Voorhees's immediate powers was actually a condition set by the envoy himself, as he had asked the president to make his role investigative in order to avoid local pressures for immediate action while he attempted to determine the true scope of the problem.[78] On arriving in Miami, he told reporters that he had no specific answers to the refugee problem because he did not yet know what the area's needs were, but that former president Herbert Hoover, who knew "more about dealing with refugee problems than all of us put together," was advising him.[79]

Once in Miami, Voorhees was bombarded with appeals for help with the refugee situation, but he remained skeptical. "There was no doubt that the problem in Miami was a very real one," Voorhees wrote later, "but it was hard to define and I was not at all sure that it had not been overstated." The Cuban refugee situation was quite different from Voorhees's previous experiences with the Hungarian refugees coming from Europe. In that case, the scope of the problem was easily understood because of the meticulous collection of information throughout their journey to the United States. The Hungarian refugees were fingerprinted in Austria and brought to a centralized location in the United States—Camp Kilmer, NJ—and they were clearly identifiable as destitute refugees. Voorhees saw the situation in Miami as chaotic due to the lack of centralization, which also meant that "no one had the facts."[80]

Shielded from the pressures put on him by local authorities and community leaders by his mandate to investigate but not act, Voorhees began gathering data. The mass of refugees who had come into the United States as tourists made it impossible to determine the numbers and backgrounds of the refugees in South Florida, but estimates suggested that there were 40,000 Cuban "tourists" in the United States, 30,000 of whom were in Miami.[81] When the Immigration and Naturalization Service (INS) failed to give Voorhees solid numbers, he turned to local government and civic leaders, who supplied data on the refugee impact on local services and institutions. The Dade County School System, for example, explained that there were 3,500 refugee children in area schools but only 7% of them were paying the $50 charge that Florida Law required for nonresident pupils.[82] The rest had had the fee waived by Miami school authorities. This led to increased crowding in Miami public schools, something that drew complaints from parents not only because it strained educational resources, but because in a school system that was still segregated, many white parents resented the presence of young Cubans in their children's schools.[83] From religious leaders, Voorhees learned that another 3,000 were enrolled in parochial schools.[84]

Miamians, meanwhile, were putting pressure on the authorities by asking questions about the Cuban presence and its permanence. James Hennessy, deputy director of the INS, dispelled the idea that those who had entered under tourists' visas would be forced to return to Cuba if they registered with the agency and instead encouraged them to regularize their situation.[85] This was good news for the refugees, but local official and city residents took it to mean that the new arrivals were not going anywhere. This prompted some Miamians to suggest radical solutions to the refugee problem. In November, the *Herald* published a letter to the editor suggesting that the solution of the city's problems lay in the deserted Opa-Locka Naval Air Station. The author argued that the Cubans could clean up the base and the thousands of acres of land surrounding it and be housed on the base barracks and fed at the mess halls. He further suggested that there was sufficient land around the base for the refugees to raise some of their own food by starting a dairy and chicken farm and that the boats that brought some of the refugees to the United States could be remade into a small fishing fleet to feed the refugees at the base.[86]

As the year ended, the idea of using Opa-Locka Air Base as a refugee camp gained some popularity. Whether he got the idea from the published letter or came to it independently, a member of the Dade County Board of County Commissioners proposed housing some fifteen thousand refugees at the base.[87] Putting the refugees in the camp, he argued, would make it easier to evaluate the problems and abilities of the individual exiles in an attempt to place them in jobs in other parts of the country. The refugee community resisted this idea. So did Voorhees and his staff. Publicly, Voorhees's deputy, Leo C. Beebe, stated that the idea of the camp did not seem feasible or in the interest of either the refugees or the community.[88] In private, Voorhees saw the need for a refugee center to process the Cubans in need of help, but he was hesitant to use any military facility for fear that the federal government would be accused of preparing to invade Cuba.[89]

Regardless, Voorhees felt that he needed an equivalent to the Kilmer processing center to make an organized effort for Cuban resettlement. His initial focus still placed most of the responsibility for running the center on local authorities and civic groups, and he described it to reporters as a central refugee office operated by a committee of local citizens.[90] This office would serve the same function that Camp Kilmer had, but without housing the refugees. The problem with establishing such a center, and with waiting for a statistically significant number of Cubans to register there, was that Voorhees estimated it would take up to two months to gather the data needed to determine a permanent solution to Miami's problems. In the meantime, his fact-finding mandate was barely allowing him to resist the pressure from Mayor High, the Cuban Refugee Committee, and other organizations demanding he recommend that the federal government take charge of the crisis. This was a recommendation he was still not prepared to make.[91]

The pressure on Voorhees kept mounting. In his own recounting of events, he withstood the pressure from local groups by professionally shielding himself with his mandate. Other people remembered things differently. Voorhees, to them, was harsh and coldhearted. Bryan Walsh recounted making an appeal for greater action on the part of the federal government. The Cuban refugees, Walsh argued, needed immediate help. "Give them a tin can and let them beg on Flagler Street," Voorhees retorted.[92]

It soon became clear to Voorhees that he could not simply wait weeks or months before he started acting to relieve the situation to some degree. Ever the skeptic, Voorhees still wavered on whether he had the justification to request a substantial sum of money from President Eisenhower. After consulting Herbert Hoover again, he sent a preliminary report and a request for funds to the White House.[93] While he felt obligated to explain to the president that there were no adequate figures to determine the scope of the problem, he had determined that the situation in Miami was "most critical." The refugee issue in Miami was one that differed from the crises of previous decades. "The United States is, for the first time in many, many years, the country of first asylum for large numbers of refugees fleeing oppression," Voorhees wrote. This fact, combined with the muddled migratory practices and the sheer number of refugees, created twin problems in Miami: the humanitarian emergency and the potential security threat of infiltration by Castro loyalists. The solution to both problems was the resettlement of a large number of refugees away from the Miami area. He concluded, like those he had consistently rebuffed during his tenure in Miami, that the crisis was greater than could be handled by local or state authorities. Voorhees recommended that he, or someone else, receive up to $1 million and temporary authority to take necessary actions pending his final report.[94]

After receiving Voorhees's report, the White House involved itself more directly in Miami's refugee situation. On December 2, the Eisenhower administration authorized the $1 million grant and made Voorhees the president's personal representative, which broadened his authority to act in Miami.[95] The White House also took a more aggressive rhetorical stance against the Cuban government. The money would aid refugees from what Eisenhower for the first time described as a "Communist-controlled" regime.[96] This rhetorical escalation likely resulted, at least in part, from the origins of the funds. The $1 million to aid the Cuban refugees came from the president's $150 million fund for special contingencies and it had been drawn through a provision of the Mutual Security Act related to the right of self-determination of "peoples who have been subjected to the captivity of Communist despotism."[97] The language chosen by the White House in announcing the funds being allotted to help the situation in Miami provided the justification to use security funds in dealing with a humanitarian crisis centered on an American city and served as a geopolitical chess move. By complying with Voorhees's request, the Eisenhower administration both formally identified Castro's Cuba as a communist state and used the situation in Miami as evidence to both the American public and the world.

On receiving the authority and funding with which to act, Voorhees called in a temporary staff of people who had worked with him during the Hungarian situation. He contacted former aide Leo C. Beebee, who had run the program at Camp Kilmer, and secured his services to oversee the operations of the volunteer agencies that would handle the resettlement of the refugees, including the Hebrew Immigrant Aid Society (HIAS), the Church World Services (CWS), and the International Rescue Committee (IRC).[98] Voorhees secured office space for registration of the refugees and the operation of these volunteer agencies at the Cuban Refugee Emergency Center, which had been established by the city just days before.[99] He envisioned the work of the center as primarily collecting information. Any relief provided for refugees should come from private funding sources instead of government funds. On receiving the $1 million that he had requested from the White House, he made it clear to reporters that he expected to return most of those funds to the federal government.[100] Voorhees worried, however, about directly requesting funds from private sources. His position as the president's personal representative might make it appear that these appeals came directly from the Eisenhower White House. He later recalled with pride that the publicity he and his staff had brought to the issue in requesting the assistance of the American people resulted in several gifts, including a $10,000 grant from the Rockefeller Foundation that went to the Centro Hispánico Católico and a $100,000 gift from the Texaco Corporation that was distributed among multiple charitable organizations in Miami.[101]

Because Eisenhower would be stepping down in January, Voorhees knew that his tenure as the president's representative would be brief, but he sought to advance the resettlement of Cuban refugees past that time. He convened a conference on the matter between January 29 and 31, 1961. Voorhees brought 150 delegates from all over the country to discuss the need for resettlement and the problems facing Miami and the refugees.[102] He saw resettlement as the only viable option for the resolution of the refugee crisis. Many of the Catholic clergy who participated, however, did not see resettlement as the wholesale solution to South Florida's refugee problems. While they agreed that resettlement would serve as an important pressure valve for the community, the Diocese of Miami "never regarded the Resettlement Program as the ultimate solution to the Cuban refugee problem." The diocese believed that the refugees needed to be given free choice to determine whether they wanted to stay in Miami or to relocate and that the federal government and the national resettlement agencies had a responsibility to those who chose to stay in Miami.[103] The resettlement conference did not resolve the issue of whether this policy would solve the refugee problem, but it established the framework for national resettlement and a network of actors across the country who sought to further this agenda.

Two days before John F. Kennedy became president, Tracy Voorhees filed his final report to President Eisenhower. Dated January 18, 1961, the report conveyed his recommendations on the refugee problem and his resignation from his temporary post, effective at the president's convenience. The report stated that in Miami, "an ever-mounting Cuban population quite obviously has overrun the community's capacity to cope with it." The problem, Voorhees informed the president, was now a national one. To illustrate this point, Voorhees utilized the hard data he had obtained from the refugee center. Between November 21 and January 12, some 4,000 Cuban adults in need of help had been interviewed, each representing a family unit of 2.77 persons. Voorhees could now directly address the problem using comprehensive facts on nearly 12,000 Cuban living in Miami between those dates. All the respondents were unemployed, and their material needs were significant.[104]

In the area of housing, Voorhees reported that 43% of refugee families were living in one-room dwellings that were sometimes shared with friends or relatives. Referring to living situations similar to those described by Juanita Greene two months before, the report stated that larger dwellings were often occupied by enormous groups. Dwellings with eleven to thirty rooms were shared by groups ranging from 17 to 127 refugees. This housing situation was compounded by other needs. Over 40% of respondents needed aid in food, clothing, housing, or a combination of these. "In view of the very bad housing conditions above described," Voorhees wrote, "it is a tribute to the courage of these distressed people that the least frequent request made upon the Center has been for Housing assistance."[105]

These problems extended to the younger refugees as well. There were, by this time, sixty-five hundred Cuban students attending Miami's public and parochial schools. About 93% of those attending the public schools had been exempted from the $50 charge for nonresidents due to necessity. Necessity also exempted 18% from school charges for instructional supplies and 6% from the school lunch charge. Cafeteria supervisors reported that many of the Cuban students were getting their one hot meal per day at school. Class sizes ranged up to forty-two students in the public schools and up sixty students per classroom in the parochial schools, with nearly two thirds of the students, in some instances, being unable to speak English. While the public school system was developing special orientation sessions for the students given by Spanish-speaking teachers, the schools needed at least twenty-five more bilingual educators and up to fifty additional teachers in order to cope with the influx of new students. At the university level, Voorhees estimated that as many as nine hundred Cuban students were experiencing financial difficulties and might have to leave U.S. colleges and universities.[106]

Voorhees used the report to reiterate his belief that "the heart of the problem remains in Miami and the crux of it is our ability to resettle refugees from Miami." He advocated a significant push for resettlement, utilizing, primarily, private charitable funds. Voorhees explained the attitude of many Cubans who expected a swift return home after an inevitable fall of the Castro regime. He indicated that a key to successful resettlement efforts lay in "the assurance to the refugees that the United States will be equally interest in giving needed assistance to them to return to their homeland if conditions improve there in a manner to make this possible." If the refugees could be assured that the federal government would provide the means to return to Cuba once Castro was gone, they would be far more likely to brave a language barrier, the separation from the larger Cuban community, and the colder weather of the northern states for a job that better suited their qualifications and needs.[107]

Out of desperation, Cubans had been taking any jobs available in the Miami area. These jobs were often informal service jobs ill-suited to a highly educated and highly motivated migrant community. Voorhees wrote that the problem was not that so many of the refugees were in a professional or highly skilled class. He argued that this was actually a great asset. Out of the Cuban adults who had registered at the center, 55% had completed a high school education, 12% were college graduates, and 7% had advanced or professional degrees, with over three hundred of them having medical degrees.[108] The large proportion of professionals and highly skilled workers drove Voorhees's conclusion that the assimilation of the refugees had to be done on a national level instead of the local level, where their skills would be wasted by sheer overabundance. The refugee situation was a significant problem, but the makeup of the exile population could also serve the United States. Voorhees believed that this situation had to be treated as both "a national responsibility and a national opportunity."[109]

The first two years of the refugee crisis in Miami were characterized by a slow realization of the scope of the humanitarian problem in South Florida and an even slower reaction by the federal government. These early years saw the establishment of patterns that would hold for many years even as conditions changed. The Catholic Church in Miami established itself as an ally to the refugee community and established its role as an advocate for its needs, often pushing the local, state, and federal authorities to do more for the exiles. While a Cold War–fueled sympathy for the new arrivals and a simultaneous concern over their sheer numbers initially dominated in the minds of many Miamians, the fear of how the Cubans would change the city began to take hold. Officials in the U.S. government began to exhibit an interest in the Cuban refugees that went beyond the humanitarian; the refugees might be useful in the larger struggle against communism. And Tracy Voorhees, despite a distaste for the idea of government directly involving itself in the refugee crisis, established an inchoate version of the Cuban Refugee Center and set in motion a resettlement program that would remain central to the federal government's reception of the refugees for well over a decade. As the Kennedy administration transitioned into power, however, it became clear that their response to the refugee crisis, and the effect of this response on the city, would be vastly different from Voorhees's vision.

CHAPTER 2

"The Score": Federal Funding, Refugee Management, and the Changing Economic Landscape of South Florida

On January 18, 1961, an aide to John F. Kennedy contacted Tracy Voorhees, who had recently submitted his resignation to the president-elect. Kennedy wanted to know if Voorhees would continue in his role as envoy to the president until January 31 and if he would be willing to carry on his work within the framework of the Department of Health, Education, and Welfare (HEW) thereafter. Voorhees agreed to the former but declined the latter, informing the aide that he would not be able to work successfully under the proposed conditions.[1] Kennedy was certain that the best approach to the Cuban refugee problem was to centralize the work under HEW and its new secretary, Abraham Ribicoff. As a cabinet member, Ribicoff would be able to coordinate the efforts of other federal agencies in the field.[2] The new president's approach to the refugee influx was decidedly different from Voorhees's own. This was not lost on Voorhees or on his mentor, Herbert Hoover.

In February, the former president wrote Voorhees a letter inquiring of his protégé why he was no longer in charge of the Cuban refugee situation. After Voorhees explained that he had declined to continue serving under a new bureaucratic structure, Hoover wrote again and stated that Vorhees had made the correct choice and that while he had done excellent work, the new administration did not understand the task.[3] Voorhees agreed. When President Kennedy diverted an additional $4 million for direct aid to the refugees, Voorhees was displeased. A decade after the decision, he wrote that most refugees saw this as a way to stay in Miami's warm climate and live at government expense. He believed that in committing itself to direct aid, the

Kennedy administration had undercut the position of the resettlement agencies Vorhees had been working with. He admitted that while some resettlement had taken place, the foundation of the program had been undermined.
"In short," Voorhees summed up, "the Welfare State had taken over!"[4]

Voorhees saw resettlement as the core of a solution to the refugee influx,
but forcing the Cubans to relocate from Miami would have been antithetical
to the implicit and explicit promises made by the United States. This did not
deter the U.S. government from trying to direct the refugees toward resettlement through the promise of jobs elsewhere. However, by increasing the
levels of direct aid to the Miami area, the Kennedy administration was, in
Voorhees's eyes, ensuring that the Cuban refugees would not have need to
seek out colder and less culturally familiar climes. As he saw it, the Kennedy
administration was discounting his work in Miami and his experience from
the Hungarian refugee crisis in favor of a big-government approach that
undermined the only viable solution: resettlement.

Voorhees correctly identified the Cuban Refugee Program as a product
of 1960s liberalism, but he failed to see the extent to which the welfare state
was bound together with the national security apparatus in the program.
The Kennedy administration was responding to continued calls for aid from
Miami, but the development of the CRP also had deep foreign policy implications. Federal policymakers sought to help Cuban refugees, but also to assign
meaning to even the most mundane activities as part of American foreign
policy. As the years wore on, a program intended to provide a medium-term
solution to the problem of Cuba instead had long-term effects on the city of
Miami. As federal action provided Cubans access to structures of privilege
and economic empowerment that were denied to other minority groups and
migrants, Miami was fundamentally transformed. While this transformation
had unique cultural elements, the economic and political structures worked
similarly to other defense-related expenditures that reshaped metropolitan
areas across the Sunbelt.

From 1961 to the mid-1970s, the federal government became more
directly involved in the Cuban refugee crisis. Among the first refugees to
experience this involvement were unaccompanied Cuban children, whom the
Catholic church, with the aid of the federal government, dispersed throughout the country through a program called Operation Pedro Pan. The complex experiences of these children, their parents, and their caretakers in the
United States would shape the narrative of the Cuban diaspora and the role
and intentions of the federal government in this story on both sides of the

Florida Straits. While the initiatives to give aid to the unaccompanied Cuban minors were managed by private parties, this was done with the permission and cooperation of the State Department and with ample federal funding. The experiences of these children were shaped by both the national security needs of the United States and the structures of the welfare state at its apogee.

In its second major intervention, the Cuban Refugee Program, the federal government established a far larger response to the general refugee crisis. The program sought to provide aid to the refugees, but also, despite Voorhees's assessment, to disperse the Cuban exile population throughout the United States. The pressure felt by Cubans to leave the Miami area shows that even as the federal government sought to alleviate the economic pressures on the area, they were also using the refugees as living reminders of the Cold War struggle and exposing them to American life and values. Most significant, however, is the fact that federal officials never forced these refugees to relocate and promised a swift return to Florida and to Cuba should conditions change on the island.

Through these and other programs, federal officials in this period clearly sought to use their influence to shape the refugees into a tool of American foreign policy. Policymakers planned to create the basis for a post–Fidel Castro Cuba by stimulating the economic potential of the exiles living in the United States. As such, despite the desire to resettle the refugees from South Florida, the Cuban Refugee Program pushed for education and vocational training and unintentionally set the stage for the long-term empowerment of the Cuban American community. Within a decade of the program's creation, these "temporary" measures had created a powerful economic bloc in the city.

Parental Rights and Cold War Politics: The Cuban Unaccompanied Children's Program

In early 1961, Father Bryan Walsh, as director of Catholic Charities, was dealing with an ever-increasing number of Cuban refugee children in Miami. Some were in the care of family or family friends, but many were unaccompanied minors who had been sent to the United States by their parents and had no one to care for them but Miami's Catholic Church. By January 14, 1961, when Walsh started a diary of his experiences with these children, Miami's Catholic Charities had forty-one Cuban children in their care.[5] Miami's schools were already overtaxed by the introduction of the refugee children into their classrooms, so Walsh and others sought to find solutions for the problem of overcrowding and the education of the children in their care.

Something that Walsh did not commit to paper in those early days was his role in bringing more unaccompanied minors to the United States. Walsh had become concerned about unaccompanied Cuban children after meeting a young refugee named Pedro. Pedro had been in Miami for a month, sent by parents who expected friends and family to care for him. What Pedro's parents did not know was that these friends and family would have their own trouble subsisting in Miami. The boy was passed from household to household until he was brought to the Catholic Welfare Bureau. When Walsh met the boy, he learned that in the month since his arrival, he had lost twenty pounds.[6] Walsh then secured resources for the care of refugee children like Pedro and convinced Tracey Voorhees to request funds for these children in his report to President Eisenhower.[7]

In early December of 1960, James Baker, the headmaster of the Ruston School, an American school in Havana, came to Miami to meet a group of American members of the Havana-American Chamber of Commerce. Much like many refugees and policymakers, the representatives of the American corporations that had withdrawn from Cuba after the revolution were waiting in Miami for what they expected would be the imminent overthrow of Castro's government. Baker brought to the meeting the concerns of many of his Cuban friends, including members of anti-Castro factions, about the safety and the possible interruption to the education of their children. He hoped to gain the help of the chamber in creating a boarding school for the children.[8] Baker found a partner in Walsh. They agreed on terms and determined that Baker and his contacts would get the children out of Cuba, while Walsh would see to it that these young refugees were met at the airport and cared for in the United States. Baker originally estimated that parents would send two hundred children to the United States.[9] The headmaster and his contacts established what came to be known as Operation Pedro Pan to help Cuban parents get their children out of Cuba. In the United States, Walsh developed the Cuban Children's Program (CCP) for the care and protection of these children.[10]

Baker and Walsh soon found that their original estimate of two hundred children was inadequate as rumors spread quickly through the Cuban middle class. Radio Swan, which was sponsored by the Central Intelligence Agency (CIA), told listeners that the revolutionary government was seeking a transfer of parental authority to the state, removing the *patria potestad* (parental custody and rights) over Cuba's children from their parents.[11] Rumors of revolutionary authorities removing children from their homes were particularly troubling to middle-class Cubans who had emigrated from Spain or were the children of Spanish immigrants. They recalled the removal of children from battlefronts in the Spanish Civil War by the Republican government and their relocation to the Soviet Union. The rumors that the children of those arrested for counterrevolutionary activities would be sent to the USSR as a reprisal against their parents were particularly alarming.[12]

Miami's Cuban community was soon buzzing with reports of Castro's alleged intention to indoctrinate the children, and there was talk of hundreds of Cuban children arriving at Miami's airport each day.[13] Walsh understood the political and foreign policy implications of his actions and those of his agency in housing the children. "No longer were we simply a social agency concerned about a community problem," he wrote; "we were now sharing the worries of families we did not even know, hundreds of miles away in a life and death struggle in the Cold War."[14] Walsh knew how to use these political implications to further his goals. He convinced the State Department to issue visa waivers with the understanding that the Catholic Welfare Bureau was ultimately responsible for the children.[15] An agreement between the State Department and the Catholic Welfare Bureau allowed for the issuance of up to 250 student visas for unaccompanied minors.[16]

The program, now known as Operation Pedro Pan, ran from December 1960 to October 1962.[17] On December 26, 1960, Bryan Walsh welcomed the first two Pedro Pan children to the United States, a pair of siblings named Sixto and Vivian Aquino.[18] In Cuba, a network of parents and dissidents distributed visa waivers to families. Once the children landed in Miami, the Catholic Welfare Bureau placed them with relatives or in the care of the Cuban Children's Program, which had facilities in Florida and thirty-five other states and the District of Columbia.[19] By January of 1961, Walsh was running out of visa waivers. He met with State Department officials and petitioned them to waive visa requirements for the children, arguing that they were in imminent danger of communist brainwashing. The State Department approved the plan and Walsh received the authority to grant visa waivers for Cubans under the age of sixteen.[20] This allowed thousands of frightened parents to send their children to the United States, not knowing when or if they would ever see them again.

Over the nearly two years of Operation Pedro Pan, the CCP helped 14,124 children enter the United States.[21] Walsh estimated that the program placed

50% of the youths with family members on their arrival in Miami.[22] Of the minors taken into the care of the Catholic Welfare Bureau (CWB), 85% were between the ages of twelve and eighteen and 70% were boys over the age of twelve. CWB did not collect statistical information regarding the children delivered to relatives or of those older minors who came of age and became independent soon after arrival.[23] With the cessation of regular flights between the United States and Cuba following the Cuban Missile Crisis in October of 1962, the influx of new unaccompanied minors was significantly reduced. The Catholic Welfare Bureau's own statistics from September of 1963 indicated that of the children it had assisted, 10,611 had been reunited with parents or relatives and 3,438 remained under the care of the CCP. Of these, 1,914 were placed in group care and 1,569 in foster care.[24] In later years, Walsh consistently reiterated that since the program aimed to safeguard the parental rights of Cuban parents over their children, none of the Pedro Pan children was ever placed for adoption.[25]

To fund the care of an increasing number of children, the Catholic Welfare Bureau once again turned to the federal government. President Kennedy charged the Department of Health, Education, and Welfare with the care of the children while in the United States. HEW, through its Children's Bureau, worked with the Florida Department of Public Welfare to disburse funds and contract the services of social service agencies. A total of $138,619,000 was spent for the Unaccompanied Children's Program, and by 1967, the Children's Bureau reported that foster homes and institutions had provided care for 8,331 children.[26] For those children who were relocated to other parts of the country, the federal government reimbursed travel costs incurred by voluntary agencies in charge of relocation.[27]

While thousands of minors were dispersed across the nation, Miami's Catholic Church was still faced with the housing and other needs of an ever-growing group of children. In Miami, the Unaccompanied Children's Program saw its ranks swell to three hundred staff members, including priests, social workers, doctors, office personnel, cooks, social workers, and drivers.[28] The program established several temporary homes in the Greater Miami area. The largest shelter was in Florida City, thirty-five miles south of downtown Miami. Florida City consisted of a series of two-story buildings divided into apartments. The facility was licensed to house seven hundred children in a unique arrangement by which the children lived in apartments under the supervision of Cuban refugee couples, an experience that proved less traumatic than the foster care experiences of other Pedro Pan children. They could bond with the other children in the common areas while maintaining a semblance of family life in their living quarters.[29]

While many of the Pedro Pan children cultivated fond memories of the program, and particularly of Father Walsh, others encountered abuse and heartbreak. A group of Cuban boys sent to Helena, Montana, alleged that Monsignor Harrington, the local director of Catholic Charities, had abused them physically and sexually.[30] One boy recalled midnight visits from sexual predators in the all-boy Camp Matecumbe. There were incidents of hazing and bullying at that camp and at other locations.[31] At St. Vincent's Orphanage in Vincennes, Indiana, caretakers stripped the children of their possessions in order not to differentiate between the young refugees and the local orphans, who referred to the Cuban children as "spics."[32]

Changes in facilities also traumatized some of the children. Following the decline in arrivals after the Cuban Missile Crisis, Archbishop Coleman Carroll and his advisers decided to consolidate the remaining homes into a single facility. Bryan Walsh, who by then was Monsignor Walsh, disagreed. He wanted to move the remaining children into smaller facilities where they could receive foster parent care in the model of Florida City. Carroll over-ruled Walsh and ordered him to open a five-hundred-person shelter at the disused barracks of Opa-Locka Naval Air Station.[33]

Monsignor Walsh was not alone in his discontent with the new facility; many of the remaining minors despised Opa-Locka. At least one boy made his displeasure known to the monsignor. Ángel Wong Alcázar wrote that he felt "betrayed, offended and defrauded." Opa-Locka, according to Wong, was known as la pajarera del welfare (welfare's birdcage). There, he wrote, the boys who had previously been treated for homosexual tendencies had reverted "to such extremes" that one afternoon he had found "a boy exhibiting a pretty woman's hair due [sic], of the latest style, through the whole Camp."[34] The closer supervision the young exiles had received in the smaller homes and which had reinforced heteronormative practices was absent in the larger camp, allowing for freer experimentation regarding sexuality and gender per-formance among the Pedro Pan children. Wong saw this as a betrayal of both the social and religious norms of their Cuban parents, norms that the parents had expected the children's caretakers would maintain.

Wong's Opa-Locka was a place where boys became "cheap gangsters" and where the children of middle-class Cubans lost their manners and ate "like pigs." He felt that the church had abandoned him and the other minors, deliv-ering them into the hands of the monolithic "Welfare." The children raised in this environment would be a disappointment to parents who had "sent their children to a Catholic institution to save them from Communism and they found that they are worst [sic] than if they would have stayed there under Communism."[35] Wong argued that if the children had been sent to the United States to ensure that they would be raised in accordance with their parents' values, that sacrifice had ill served the children at Opa-Locka. For some Cuban minors who remained in the custody of the church for years, the myth of a swift return had proven itself entirely false and a faceless institutional bureaucracy had replaced the face of the kindly priest who welcomed them to Miami.

The children cared for outside an institutional setting, by foster parents, faced their own set of challenges. Some had terrible experiences, but even those who were cared for by good foster parents were still faced with problems such as discrimination and a fundamental desire to understand and live with their parents' decision to send them to a different country. This burning existential question led to both frustration and confusion. One unaccompanied minor explained her exile experience through poetry:

What It Means to Be An Exile

By a Cuban Foster Child

It means to wake up a day and find yourself in a new country and
    home.
It means to remember how just yesterday you left your country and
    home for the first day.
It means to know that your flag is being walked upon and your coun-
    try is being torn apart.
* * *
It means to wake up every morning and wish for time to stop
    because you want to see your sister grow.
It means to remember your parents, and how you thought they were
    wrong, but they weren't.
It means to know that you must try and lead a new life, but you can't.
* * *
It means to wake up and try to remember about that country you left
    so long ago.
It means trying to remember about your country, but you can't
    because your mind wanders farther and farther apart every day.

It means to know that you are forgetting your language and customs
and you try to do something about it, but you can't.
* * *
It means to wake up a day without a mother or father to run to, even
though they are alive.
It means to remember all those things you used to do so long, long
ago.
It means to know that you are becoming an American and on the
outside you are proud.
But on the inside, Oh God, doesn't that matter too?
* * *
It means to say your prayers at night and ask for the Communist
government to fall.
It means that then you will wonder what you do if this happens.
It means to know that you have a dilemma, because you can't choose
between your real parents and foster parents. You love them
both!
* * *
And above all it means to pray:
Oh! God! Please help me to understand your doings, help me to have
faith in You and please help me to have the courage which I don't
have.[36]

Even those children who had positive experiences as unaccompanied minors
did not know if they would ever see their parents again. Those who formed
attachments to their foster parents both dearly wished for and but also
dreaded the news that their families would join them in the United States.
The children were torn between their love for a home country that each day
became more of a hazy memory and their lives in a new environment. In
this way, many of the Pedro Pan children were among the first to face a crisis of national identity that would become more widespread in the 1970s as
young Cubans came of age and many refugees wrestled with the question of
naturalization.

While Operation Pedro Pan ended with the cessation of flights between
Cuba and the United States following the Cuban Missile Crisis, the Cuban
Children's Program continued until 1981.[37] The minors cared for by the Catholic Welfare Bureau in the latter years of the program tended to be Cuban
children who had entered through third countries or who had lost parents

in an attempt to enter the United States. Walsh claimed that, even after the Cuban Missile Crisis paused direct migration to the United States for several years, nearly 90% of the children who remained in the care of the CCP were reunited with their parents by June of 1966.[38] Because there were no follow-up procedures in place for the children who were handed over to relatives or family friends at the airport, it is difficult to ascertain the exact number of Cuban children for whom the temporary dissolution of their families would turn permanent. Despite this lack of exact statistics, the separation of these children from their parents left deep wounds within the Cuban American community.

Cold War Welfare: The Cuban Refugee Program and Cuba's Future

For those refugees in need of financial assistance, 1961 marked a change in the availability of aid in South Florida. The Kennedy administration built on the foundations Voorhees had laid, but it furthered these efforts by centralizing them and bringing them within the formal institutional structure of the federal government. President Kennedy wrote a letter to incoming secretary of Health, Education, and Welfare Abraham Ribicoff on January 27, 1961, directing him to assume the responsibilities for all Cuban refugee activities on February 1 of that year. Kennedy instructed Ribicoff to travel to Florida and investigate the problem within a week. The new HEW secretary was to convey the president's concern and sympathy and to assure the refugee community that the U.S. government would ensure their return to Cuba as soon as conditions allowed. Kennedy wanted to reemphasize to audiences both at home and abroad that the United States would act as a humanitarian sanctuary. The United States could not be a peacemaker if it was "not also the protector of those individuals as well as nations who cast with thier [sic] personal liberty and hopes for the future."[39]

By February 2, Ribicoff had prepared a report for the president based on his experiences over several days in the Miami area. "It is apparent that many of the refugees are now in serious need," Ribicoff wrote. "They are living in extremely crowded quarters; their resources have been used up or have largely depleted; and health and educational facilities are badly overtaxed." He warned the president that many of the refugees were at the point of desperation and that many others were rapidly approaching it. While he stated that the courage and fortitude of the Cubans in the face of such an overwhelming disruption of their lives were "magnificent," he did report that there was widespread anxiety. Ribicoff made a series of recommendations that embraced Voorhees's resettlement push, but which would also create a safety net for those refugees who chose not to resettle.[40]

Under the plan, volunteer agencies would retain responsibility for encouraging and supporting the resettlement of Cuban refugees from South Florida, with the federal government providing supplementary support, including transportation and adjustment costs. Many refugees were wary of resettling in a new environment, and they feared being away from Miami should things change in Cuba. Ribicoff recommended that return transportation to Miami be provided for those who had voluntarily resettled if there were some fundamental changes in the situation on the island. A program of financial assistance was also to be established for refugee families both in the Miami area and elsewhere, to be administered through existing federal, state, and local channels. A similar arrangement needed to be made with established public agencies to provide essential health services to this population.

Ribicoff also proposed a series of measures to aid in the education of the refugees, including loans for higher education, financial assistance for language training, skill refresher courses, orientation and vocational training, and programs, in cooperation with the University of Miami, to provide accreditation to Cuban professionals. He also endorsed the funding of care for the unaccompanied Cuban minors, the distribution of surplus food, and the requirement that the head of each household be registered at the Cuban Refugee Emergency Center in order for a family to be eligible for aid. Ribicoff explained that the remainder of the $1 million allocation made by President Eisenhower the previous December would allow the Cuban Refugee Emergency Center to operate until June 30, 1961. Additional funds would be required to run the larger, more comprehensive program. For that same period, Ribicoff estimated an additional allocation of $4 million would be necessary.[41]

On February 3, President Kennedy approved the creation of the Cuban Refugee Program, which had two central aims. First, it would resettle as many refugees as possible to ease the pressures on South Florida, while still assuring them that they would be returned to Miami if the situation in Cuba changed. Second, the program would establish a system of aid for refugees both in Dade County and in other areas. Kennedy ordered that the program follow nine central guidelines. This more robust federal response was still to be largely dependent on volunteer action. The program was to obtain the assistance of both private and government agencies in securing employment opportunities and to assist those agencies in relief and resettlement. The CRP would also provide supplemental funds for resettlement, give direct financial assistance to Cuban refugees through local welfare departments, distribute surplus food, and supplement health services. Kennedy also made Cuban children a priority by ordering the program to assist unaccompanied children and to aid public schools taxed by the refugee influx. Finally, the program was to help prepare the refugees for financial independence by augmenting the educational and training facilities available to them.[42]

Kennedy's directive did not explicitly state the common conception that Castro's days were numbered and that the exiles' stay in the United States was temporary, but this was the mindset when his administration initially conceived the Cuban Refugee Program. As one study of the program conducted four years later pointed out, until the Bay of Pigs Invasion, both American authorities and refugees considered the program a "brief stop-gap."[43] The new administration was committed to actively managing the refugee crisis, but it believed that the plan for the invasion of Cuba by CIA-trained exiles would make the CRP obsolete.

On February 6, Ribicoff tasked commissioner of Social Security William L. Mitchell with implementing and administering the Cuban Refugee Program. Mitchell's Social Security Administration took the lead of the program with the aid of the Public Health Service and the Office of Education.[44] The program began operating out of what was then called the Cuban Emergency Refugee Center, the former home of the *Miami News*, and which the CRP rebranded as the Freedom Tower (see Figure 3).[45] By the end of the month, the center began distributing assistance checks to those refugees who had registered with the program.

On February 27, Cubans stood in line outside the center waiting to receive their first biweekly check. Officials at the center estimated that the average monthly assistance for each Cuban family would be $75. Refugees spoke to reporters from the *Miami News* about the hardship they had endured. Waldo Rodríguez, a former Cuban senatorial candidate and government employee from Matanzas, had been attempting to sell television sets on commission but had been having trouble making ends meet. Others made it clear that their current situation would not last much longer. Former land developer José F. Viciana spoke of a 125-acre farm he had owned on the Isle of Pines. "When that man Castro is gone," he said, "it will be one of the finest resort areas in the Caribbean."[46] Viciana believed it was only a matter of time before he, his

Figure 3. Entrance to the Cuban Refugee Center, now branded as the Freedom Tower, which served as the central point of administration and distribution of aid for the Cuban Refugee Program in Miami. Courtesy of the Cuban Heritage Collection, University of Miami Libraries.

daughter, and his grandchildren would return to Cuba to rebuild the lives they had left behind.

The refugees' sense that they would be returning home in the near future stemmed, at least in part, from what one historian has called "an open secret" in both the United States and on the island: the planned invasion of Cuba by American trained exile forces.[47] In March of 1960, President Eisenhower had authorized a CIA plan for an exile-led invasion.[48] The CIA began training exile volunteers in Guatemala, a fact publicized in January of 1961 when the *New York Times* ran an article with the headline, "U.S. Helps Train an Anti-Castro Force at Secret Guatemalan Air-Ground Base." The Guatemalan government, according to the story, was training forces to engage in battle with forces of the Cuban government. Guatemalan government officials insisted that they intended the training program to repel an expected invasion from Cuba, but critics claimed otherwise. While the article focused on the training of Guatemalan troops by men who appeared to be American military personnel, it also indicated that the rapidly growing project had brought in foreign trainers who specialized in guerrilla tactics, including Cubans.[49] By the time of this story's publication, Cuban diplomats had requested a United Nations (UN) Security Council meeting to discuss the plot to invade their territory and Cuban intelligence had produced a detailed report on the training facilities in Guatemala.[50]

As the days and weeks went on, speculation only grew on both sides of the Florida Straits. This "secret" invasion became a subject of public discussion. A week before the assault, the *Times* ran another article speculating on what the specific invasion strategy the exile forces would follow.[51] The invasion was even the fodder for jokes in exile publications. One political cartoon entitled "Hombre Precavido" (A man forewarned) showed a toadyish aide informing Fidel Castro that the invasion had begun. A distraught and cowardly Castro then has the aide see to the readiness of his escape submarine, dons armor, starts packing large stacks of cash into a suitcase, and ensures that there is an airplane standing by to evacuate him to Mexico. Castro then goes on television and denies that the Cuban government is at all worried about an invasion and demands that all officials remain at their posts.[52]

The Bay of Pigs Invasion in April of 1961 was an unmitigated military and public relations disaster for both the United States and exile political groups.[53] The failure of the invasion dampened the mood in Miami concerning a swift return, but it did not extinguish the flame of hope in the hearts and minds of many refugees. It also added importance to the Cuban Refugee Program, not only as a relief measure, but as a Cold War propaganda program. This second dimension was clear both in the public statements of U.S. government officials and in documents related to high-level discussions regarding the program's usefulness. Officials like Cuban Refugee Center director J. Arthur Lazell expressed concern that for many Latin Americans, the treatment of the refugees would be "indicative of the extent of United States' determination and effectiveness in combatting Communism in the Western Hemisphere."[54] Cuban refugees would serve as effective propaganda tools so long as they had received a warm welcome in the United States.

It was at this point that the federal government sought to tie Cuban refugees' economic success to a larger geopolitical strategy. Discussions of the
"Cuban Problem" and its national security implications between the White
House and the Department of Health, Education, and Welfare show that, in
the aftermath of the Bay of Pigs Invasion, the federal government considered
placing a greater emphasis on Cuban refugee civilians than on exile paramilitary activities in the planning for a Castro-free Cuba. A confidential memorandum from April 29, 1961, outlined the objectives of a new, revised Cuban
Refugee Program. It suggested that the program's intent was to facilitate the
melding of Cuban refugees into American life in a "useful and self-supporting
role." The memorandum went on to state that the CRP also sought to "pre-
serve or increase [Cuban refugees'] skills and professional attainments to the
end that they as individuals may live more satisfying lives and be a source of
trained manpower available to meet the needs when opportunity arrives to
return to a free Cuba."[55] In essence, efforts to teach new skills to refugees or
to facilitate the ability of Cuban professionals to practice in the United States
served to make the refugees self-supporting, improve their lives, and provide
a postcommunist Cuba with a social and economic force that would help turn
the country into something more acceptable to U.S. policymakers.

The memorandum was part of larger discussion about the potential of
the Cuban refugees in Miami to function outside paramilitary roles. A secret
report from May of 1961 suggested going even further by creating a radically different Cuban Refugee Program that would take an even greater hand
in Cuba's future. The proposed program would "capitalize on the resource
these exiles represent" by identifying and training "potential top leadership
and key bureaucratic personal for a post-Castro government," preparing the
"armed services components of such a government," and providing relief
and resettlement to those exiles who did not fit in those categories. The program would comply with international law and existing treaties by making it
clear that any military training provided was not in preparation for another
invasion of Cuba by exile forces.[56] This version of the Cuban Refugee Program would have carried out the principal duties of the program as it already
existed, but it would have also engaged in the creation of a prepackaged
state-building apparatus.

This version of the CRP did not coalesce. The organizational structure for
such a program would have required a massive bureaucracy and the expense
would have dwarfed the already extensive expenditures of the Cuban Refugee
Program in the 1960s. Some elements of the plan survived in altered forms,

as when Cuban exiles were encouraged to join the armed forces of the United States in the early 1960s.[57] The greatest challenge to this plan was probably the conception its authors had of Cuban refugees generally and the exiled political leaders in particular. The authors of the secret report wrote that most of the exiles believed a swift return to Cuba was contingent on the United States being an active participant in the process and providing leadership for the endeavor. "Therefore," they concluded, "[the Cubans] can be expected to follow and support the U.S. in any venture promising an early elimination of Castro."[58] They made this assessment barely two weeks after the failure of the Bay of Pigs Invasion. American policymakers and intelligence officials did not yet have a clear understanding of the anger that many Cubans felt toward the U.S. government and the Kennedy administration. However, their rancor would soon become apparent.

Despite ongoing plans for a post-Castro Cuba, government officials saw a need to stabilize the CRP. A series of congressional investigations into the Cuban refugee question resulted in a report, issued in April 1962, which concluded that the CRP could no longer be regarded as a temporary or emergency matter.[59] Following these conclusions, Congress passed the Migration and Refugee Assistance Act of 1962 in June of that year, which formalized the Cuban Refugee Program. When the missile crisis occurred the following October and the standoff over Soviet nuclear weapons on Cuban soil did not end with the removal of Castro from power, belief in a swift return to Cuba was further diminished.

The aim of the program remained not only to aid those refugees who could not help themselves, but also to cement the foundations for a new Cuba free of Castro and of Soviet influence. A Kennedy administration insider succinctly stated this when he testified before the Senate Judiciary Subcommittee on Refugees and Escapees on April 13, 1966. "Of course our entire refugee program has in one sense been an investment in the rebuilding of Cuba," Senator Robert F. Kennedy told the subcommittee; "The positive experience in this country of those thousands of Cubans who will choose to return to their native country will make a great difference in the future of the nation."[60] The Cuban Refugee Program, both in public and in top-level discussions, was a cornerstone of American foreign policy toward Cuba. Local activists and officials framed the refugee crisis in terms of the struggle of the Cold War. In turn, the U.S. government sought to resolve it through the creation of a program that both explicitly and implicitly made the mundane experiences of Miamians political actions in a global conflict.

Self-Support and Dispersal: The Push for Resettlement

While the Cuban Refugee Program was far different from anything Tracy Voorhees ever conceived of, one of his original recommendations became a primary function of the program: the resettlement of refugees to other parts of the United States. The CRP sought to ease tensions in South Florida, but many people also argued that resettlement would be essential to imparting a true American experience to the refugees, particularly the younger ones. In his testimony before Congress in December 1961, senior judge for the Dade County Juvenile Domestic Relations Court W. R. Culbreath encouraged the relocation of Cuban families away from metropolitan areas and into small towns. Aid received by the refugees would go further in a small-town setting, but Culbreath also argued that it would also prevent any juvenile delinquency problems from arising in the Miami area and impart small-town American values to the young refugees.[61]

Some officials also believed that the resettlement of the Cuban refugees would serve to awaken Americans "as nothing else has to the oppressions of communism." In a radio interview meant for Spanish-speaking audiences in 1967, director of the Cuban Refugee Center Errol T. Ballanfonte remarked that people in the Miami area were well aware of how articulate Cubans could be about the dangers of communism. "In scattering out to self-supporting opportunities all over this country," he went on, "Cuban refugees have told their convincing stories and alerted Americans by this first-hand information."[62] By sending the refugees to new communities and giving them new audiences for their personal stories, the federal government could also reinforce domestic support for the Cold War.

The Cuban Refugee Emergency Center (CREC) provided office space for representatives of four different volunteer agencies engaged in the resettlement of refugees. Catholic Relief Services, the Protestant Latin American Emergency Committee of the Church World Service, the United Hebrew Immigrant Aid Society Service, and the International Rescue Committee all worked to entice the refugees to resettle in other areas of the country. When a refugee registered at the center, they were interviewed and classified based on several categories: job skills, numbers of employable family members, friend or relatives living in the United States, and whether they desired voluntary agency assistance. After a medical examination, they spoke to one of the four volunteer agencies, based on religious preference or the desire to be aided by the secular International Rescue Committee. Social workers would interview

and screen the refugees and certify their eligibility to receive monthly financial assistance checks for a maximum of $100 per family and $60 per single
adult, and for hospital care for acute illnesses.[63]

To find sound resettlement opportunities for those who registered, the
CREC needed to inform the American public of both the plight of the Cuban
refugees and the resettlement program itself. In January of 1962, the program
made comprehensive contact with daily newspapers around the country. That
month, staff sent more than fifteen hundred letters to the editor with information about resettlement and operations of the center. The resulting news
stories and editorials helped increase consciousness about the Cuban refugee
situation and the need for resettlement. The center's media blitz included over
four thousand envelopes addressed by the National Association of Broadcast-
ers to all its members, providing comprehensive coverage of all radio stations
in the United States. By August of that year, the CREC had also sent ten-
minute interview scripts to be conducted by an announcer and a local official
or influential citizen regarding the program to 117 ABC television stations,
111 CBS stations, and 191 NBC stations.[64] It also engaged civic organizations
around the country like the U.S. Junior Chamber of Commerce (the Jaycees)
by sending telegrams to all its chapters along with "Make Mine Freedom"
cards reminding officers about the Cuban Refugee Resettlement Program
and urging them to "talk it up next meeting."[65]

Seeing the reluctance of refugees to resettle in other areas of the country
for fear of missing a swift return to Cuba, of colder climes, and of culture
shock, officials sought to both coerce and entice the Cubans to consider
resettlement. The Cuban Refugee Program's public assistance aid for refugees in Miami came with conditions. If a refugee who was offered a sound
resettlement opportunity refused the offer without "adequate cause," they
would be removed from the public assistance rolls and become ineligible
for any further cash assistance under the program. The CRP recognized two
types of "sound" resettlement opportunity. A responsible sponsoring organization could offer suitable employment that was within the refugee's capacity
to perform, conformed to fair labor standards and would not expose them
to undo hardship. Sponsoring organizations could also offer a relocation
opportunity that would guarantee their maintenance in decency and health
until they could become self-supporting.[66] When faced with the possibility
of being cut off from assistance and with a seeming lack of employment
options, many refugees chose to accept the offer of transportation to a new
location and a onetime $100 payment meant to sustain them while their new

sponsorship opportunity began.[67] Others chose to stay in Miami and found themselves shut out from the more direct forms of assistance that the CRP provided.

Despite the ebb and flow of Cuban refugee arrivals, resettlement remained central to the Cuban Refugee Program. Following the Cuban Missile Crisis, the rate of refugees arriving in the United States slowed significantly due to the revolutionary government's decision to halt commercial air travel between Cuba and the United States. For a period of three years, ending in fall of 1965, the 30,000 to 50,000 Cubans who arrived in the United States did so by traveling to a third country and applying for a visa, by demonstrating sufficient medical need to have the Red Cross bring them to the United States, or by crossing the Florida Straits by boat.[68] While the rate of migration slowed, the refugee center continued its efforts to relocate as many of the Cubans in the Miami area as they could. When Castro decided, in fall of 1965, to open the port of Camarioca to family members of exiles who wanted to leave the country, some 5,000 Cubans crossed the Straits to Miami. In an effort to control the movement of refugees, the Lyndon Johnson administration signed a memorandum of understanding with the Cuban government that allowed two daily flights of refugees from Varadero Beach to Miami. These "freedom flights" were in operation between December 1965 and April 1973 and brought approximately 340,000 new refugees to the United States (see Figures 4 and 5).[69] The agreement established that 50,000 refugees could migrate to the United States each year. It also allowed both governments to place restrictions on who could make the journey for the first time.

The U.S. government prioritized family reunification, dividing potential new refugees into two priorities. Priority A included immediate relatives and was focused on reuniting children under the age of twenty-one with family members. Refugee parents in the United States could claim their children who were still in Cuba under Priority A and unaccompanied children in the United States could do the same for the parents they had left behind. Priority B also favored close family relations, but it removed any age limit to the process of claiming relatives for entry to the United States.[70] Havana, meanwhile, refused to let men of military age, those citizens deemed essential to the economy, and political prisoners migrate to the United States.[71]

This new influx of refugees and the estimated six hundred thousand requests for resettlement from Cubans on the island only reignited the urgency of the resettlement program.[72] Miami mayor Robert King High appointed a committee of representatives to assess this new phase of the refugee crisis. The

Figure 4. Cuban refugees deplaning from a Freedom Flight, circa 1966. Courtesy of the Cuban Heritage Collection, University of Miami Libraries.

White House responded by meeting with representatives of the State Department and HEW to review and expand the resettlement program.[73] This, in turn, led to a reunification policy that had relocation as a prerequisite. For example, this family reunification focus served to reunite several of the Pedro Pan children with the parents they had not seen in years. In the first month of the Freedom Flights, December of 1965, the parents of 128 Pedro Pan children arrived in the United States, setting the stage for many reunions.[74] Because of the concerns in South Florida, the federal government forced families to leave Miami if they wanted to reunite with their children. Most parents with children living in other areas of the United States sought to have their children brought to Miami, where they might have friends or relatives and where the culture shock would be far less than in other areas. While some parents managed to avoid this, as when the Catholic Welfare Bureau brought children back to Miami to avoid making parents make the choice, many others were relocated so they could be reunited with their children.[75]

Figure 5. Girl scouts visiting the Freedom House at Miami International Airport. As part of the Cuban Refugee Program branding, refugees arriving at the airport would clear customs at the Freedom Gate and those who were not met by friends or family were provided with temporary housing at the Freedom House. Once in Miami, the refugees had the option of seeking assistance at the Freedom Tower. Courtesy of the Cuban Heritage Collection, University of Miami Libraries.

In addition to the more coercive measures they applied, officials at the refugee center also attempted to make relocation seem like an enticing possibility for the exiles. The center regularly released a newsletter entitled *Resettlement Re-Cap*, which provided information on its efforts and included stories about successful resettlements throughout the country (see Figure 6). The November 1962 issue, for example, told the story of Mr. and Mrs. Rigoberto Areces, who had relocated to the small town of Nevada, Iowa. Mrs. Areces gave Spanish lessons to her neighbors as a way to improve her English

Figure 6. Two Cuban refugee workers, identified as Mrs. Carlos Álvarez and Mrs. Reynaldo Pérez, featured in the December 1966 *Resettlement Re-Cap* while at their place of work, Flexsteel Industries in Dubuque, IA. Courtesy of the Cuban Heritage Collection, University of Miami Libraries.

and said of small-town life that she and her husband "never really knew what family life was like here. Until we came to Iowa, we didn't know how nice American people are."[76] The center reprinted stories from local newspapers about the ease with which resettled Cubans integrated into new communities and distributed these stories in both English and Spanish in the Miami area. They also reached out to resettled Cubans in order to get positive statements about their resettlement experience. "The day we left Miami we were a bit scared," wrote Pedro Heng, who had relocated to Kansas City, MO, "but now we feel at home and are very happy to be in this city."[77] These stories never carried negative comments regarding any hardships, discrimination, or isolation that exiles might have experienced after relocating from Miami.

   In time, resettlement became a way for the CRP to measure its own success and publicize it in its literature. The *Resettlement Re-Cap* newsletter carried a text box near its masthead entitled "The Score." For the week ending on

September 28, 1962, the newsletter indicated that of the 2,044 refugees registered at the center that week, 963 had resettled. Since January 1961, 150,544 refugees had registered at the center, and of those, 44,258 had resettled and over 100,000 remained in the Miami area.[78] By May of 1963, a program press release was proudly proclaiming that with the resettlement to Alaska of a twenty-year-old Cuban who claimed not to fear the cold, the resettlement program had touched every state in the Union.[79] Resettlement figures also played a significant role in the weekly fact sheets published by the program regarding its activities. With the increased emphasis on relocation that came with the establishment of the Freedom Flights, the CRP gave particular attention to the ratio of resettlement based on new arrivals.

Between February 1961 and December 1970, the center reported a resettlement rate of 73.1%.[80] What this figure did not convey was that the CRP did not track any statistics regarding the return of resettled Cubans to the Miami area. While officials sometimes estimated rates of return, the structure of the system prevented the collection of hard data on this subject.[81] Cuban refugees knew that if they resettled, they would become ineligible for any further aid on their return to Miami.[82] As such, they had little reason to report to the refugee center or to provide the institution with any information if they returned to South Florida. Another problem with the statistics provided by the CRP is that they were based on those refugees that chose to register at the center. A 1965 study derived from Immigration and Naturalization Service statistics indicated that while 85,465 Cubans had registered at the refugee center, 94,987 had settled in Dade County without assistance.[83]

The Cuban government imposed more restrictions on immigration and caused the educational and social composition of the refugees to change. As Cubans with fewer resources and less training arrived in the area, a greater percentage of refugees must have sought assistance from the center. The center was unable to track these statics due to the lack of information-gathering procedures involving the entire refugee population. They understood, however, that there remained a significant and growing Cuban population in the city of Miami despite the efforts to encourage resettlement. This required a significant investment from the Cuban Refugee Program in the form of economic disbursements, not only in the form of direct aid, but also through subsidies for relocation, medical care, and other services.

These programs were not cheap. The costs of the CRP rapidly escalated after the first six months of 1961. The Kennedy administration allocated $13,560,000 as a budget for the rest of the year.[84] Appropriations for the years

1962–1965 totaled $141,901,869.[85] Ultimately, the Cuban Refugee Program disbursed approximately $2 billion in aid and provided relief for more than seven hundred thousand Cubans in the United States.[86] Direct aid for individual refugees and for families continued at a rate of $60 maximum per individual case and $100 per family until July of 1971, when new maximums of $86 and $246 were enacted.[87] This direct aid helped to revitalize the local economy.

Another federal initiative had an impact on Miami's economy, but its covert nature obscures its full effects. The University of Miami's South Campus was the site of a cluster of office buildings and warehouses, allegedly the site of Defense Department weapons system research, publicly known as Zenith Technological Services. This entity was one of South Florida's largest employers between 1962 and 1968. Zenith Technological Services was actually the front for an operation known to insiders as JM/WAVE, the largest Central Intelligence Agency (CIA) installation in the world outside the CIA headquarters in Langley, VA. JM/WAVE employed thousands of Cuban agents and maintained hundreds of pieces real estate in the Miami area.[88] Operation Mongoose, the Kennedy-directed plan to destabilize the Castro regime was run out of these facilities, involving more than five hundred caseworkers handling over three thousand Cuban exile agents at a cost of over $100 million a year. These funds allowed for the establishment and operation of over fifty-four front businesses.[89] The full extent of the CIA's economic influence over the Miami area in the 1960s is unclear, but by one estimate, projects run out of the station may have employed some fifteen thousand Cubans.[90] What is certain is that the economic disbursements related to the agency's presence in the South Florida further augmented the funds provided by the CRP.

The influence of the Cuban Refugee Program over the Miami metropolitan area went well beyond direct payments issued to qualifying exiles and their families. An essential element of the program was to aid the refugees in securing economic self-sufficiency. Given the socioeconomic makeup of the early refugee waves and the belief among federal officials that the skills of those professional and educated exiles needed to be maintained, particular efforts were made on behalf of those Cubans with the greatest levels of education and experience. Among those refugees who registered for assistance at the center, there were a significant number with professional and semiprofessional occupations. As of March 1963, the registered refugees with professional occupations broke down in the following categories (see Table 1).

The potential economic benefit for the United States represented by the comparatively high education and experience contained in these early waves,

Table 1. Professional and Semiprofessional Occupations

Occupation	Total	Percent of Registration
Accountant—Bookkeepers	2,009	2.3%
Architects	208	0.2%
Chemists	115	0.1%
Dentists	283	0.3%
Engineers (all types)	556	0.7%
Lawyers	1,770	2.0%
Pharmacists	542	0.6%
Physicians	1,051	1.3%
Professors (university level)	498	0.6%
Teachers (elementary and secondary)	2,937	3.4%
Total Professionals and Semiprofessionals Registered	9,969	11.5%

Source: Cuban Refugee Center, "Socio-Economic Characteristics of Refugees Registered at the Center" [presumably 1963], Folder 13, Box 1, Series I, Cuban Refugee Center Records, CHC.

which brought the so-called Golden Exiles, was tremendous. Federal officials and the refugees themselves understood this clearly. "No other country in the world has ever been so fortunate to receive the cream of the crop from another society," stated Manuel González-Mayo, a Cuban veterinarian, when questioned by a researcher in 1969. "It takes $85,000 to produce a new doctor—a green beginner in this country," González-Mayo went on, "but the United States has got more than 2,000 experienced M.D.s from Cuba, as a gift."[91] In order for the United States to receive this gift, the CRP had to take steps to ensure that the training of professional Cubans was not wasted.

Keeping the Skills Sharp: Professional Certification, Refugee Vocational Training, and Avenues for Entrepreneurship

Starting in early 1961, federal authorities began working with the University of Miami Medical School to create a program that would allow refugee physicians to practice their profession in the United States. Faculty from the University of Havana School of Medicine joined with the faculty of the School of Medicine of the University of Miami (UM) to establish a program tailored to meet the group and individual needs of these physicians. The program included English-language courses for the physicians established by special arrangement with the UM School of Languages and Barry College. Explaining their aspirations, the initiative's creators said they hoped "that as a result of helping them continue their education, they will be exposed to the most lasting and valuable impression of Democracy that is possible."[92]

By the time of the fifth course of the program, starting on January 3, 1963, the medical school saw an enrollment of 130 physicians from twelve Latin American countries, 114 of whom were Cuban refugees. These doctors, who represented fourteen medical specialties, hoped to take the course and pass the Emergency Council for Foreign Medical Graduates' Examination (ECFMG). The ECFMG certificate was necessary for foreign-trained physicians to practice medicine in the United States and each subsequent course of the University of Miami's program saw growing success in the percentage of students who obtained this certification. The first course, which was held from January to March of 1961, had a success rate of 67%. By the fourth course, held between July and October of 1962, the graduates obtaining the ECFMG certification reached 80%. By March of 1963 the faculty expected that 110 physicians from the program would obtain their certification, be qualified to work in American medical institutions, and would share with their friends "knowledge of how education was used to advance the cause of democracy."[93]

The program began as a University of Miami project and was largely funded through private donations.[94] After the establishment of the Cuban Refugee Program, the university began working with the federal government on this project and received a grant from the Department of Health Education and Welfare to fund its operations. Over twenty-five hundred Cuban doctors would make their way through the program, with the majority obtaining the certification to practice medicine in the United States.[95] This allowed for the accreditation of well-educated, and often very experienced, medical doctors in the United States for a cost of $384 per physician.[96] By 1963, even with federal authorities pushing for resettlement, at least 18% of the newly accredited physicians had found work in the Miami area.[97] Not only did this benefit the area, allowing for a greater concentration of medical professionals locally, but it often provided great successes for the resettlement program to tout in encouraging the relocation of Cubans from the area. This was the case when the CRP reprinted a November 1967 story from the Kansas City *Kansan* about how Dr. Alfredo L. Hernández, a Cuban psychiatrist, became the new chief of the main section at Osawatomie State Hospital.[98] Accreditation allowed refugee physicians access to work in their field and to further opportunities, as organizations like the American Medical Association established revolving funds for loans to Cuban physicians attending postgraduate programs.[99]

Not all Cuban professionals had the same opportunities to work in their fields. In February of 1961, after having laid the groundwork for the training of the Cuban physicians, the University of Miami planned to offer the same type of training opportunities to Cuban lawyers.[100] There was an obstacle for the refugee lawyers in the English system of common law prevalent in the United States. This is significantly different from the codes that served as the basis of Cuban law. In March of 1961, the American Bar Association sought to help the refugee lawyers by establishing a special committee to help Cuban lawyers, judges, and legal scholars to find employment as teachers, librarians, and legal counsels in corporations. Unfortunately, if a Cuban lawyer wanted to enter private practice in any state, they would be required to start their legal education over in an American law school. The University of Florida and the University of Miami eventually created an intensive training program for Cuban lawyers that allowed them to graduate with an American law degree in eighteen months, but this did not happen until 1973.[101]

The Cuban Refugee Center sought to find employment for these refugee attorneys in alternate fields. The center urged Cuban lawyers who were sufficiently qualified in English and who could not use their advanced university training in jobs related to the law to take up teaching.[102] Starting in January 1963, the University of Miami's School of Education established a new program with financial support from the welfare administration. Programs to teach English to Cuban refugees so they could become Spanish educators were founded at Indiana University, the College of Great Falls, MT, and Pacific University in Forest Grove, OR, among others. A significant number of the refugees who participated in these programs were former lawyers.[103]

Officials in the program proposed similar initiatives for refugee dentists.[104] Cuban dentists faced greater difficulties than did medical doctors. Cuban dentists had to return to dental school and be evaluated by the school in regard to what standing they would be allowed. If a dentist entered dental school with a third-year standing or better and they were residents of Miami, they were eligible for maintenance grants from the Cuban Refugee Program, in addition to student loans.[105] This is indicative of the difficulties faced by Cubans in certain professions. It also illustrates the availability of student loans under the U.S. Loan Program for Cuban Students, which used funds made available by the Migration and Refugee Assistance Act of 1962.[106]

Figure 7. Adult Cuban refugees receiving English language instruction as part of the Cuban Refugee Program's push for self-sufficiency, as featured in the February 1965 *Resettlement Re-Cap*. Courtesy of the Cuban Heritage Collection, University of Miami Libraries.

Access to educational opportunities for refugees went beyond the program's profession-specific initiatives and the subsidies paid to Dade County public schools. The push for refugee self-sufficiency was particularly important in the Miami market. One of the most significant obstacles for Cubans attempting to find work was the language barrier. To address this, English language courses were established and made available to any adult refugee in the Miami area who chose to participate (see Figure 7). The refugee center made card-sized fliers to hand out to Cubans visiting the facilities that asked in Spanish, "Are you improving your English?" The center advertised free extension classes, available both day and night, and listed several junior and senior high schools and educational centers where adult refugees could work to attain a greater grasp of the English language. At the bottom of each card, the recipient was reminded that "opportunities come more quickly to those refugees that help themselves."[107] English-language training was positioned as a cornerstone of financial self-reliance and independence from the program.

The center also provided training that would allow professional and semi-professional Cubans to enter the marketplace, either in their own fields or in fields where they could use some of their skills. It sought to do the same with skilled and unskilled laborers who had come to the United States as refugees. The first step in this process was to sort out the exiles' skills and aptitudes for placement in industrial and service jobs. The center was the site of seventy-five weekly aptitude tests administered by the U.S. Employment Service to identify "men and women whose manual dexterity and fast reactions can be directed toward a variety of skills." This allowed center personnel to offer enticing candidates to manufacturers providing paid training courses, and thus ideally setting the refugees on a path to a well-paying job and self-sufficiency. The staff also reached out to out-of-state manufacturers, noting that refugees had already obtained jobs at shoe factories in New England, clothing makers in New York State, and electronics producers in Texas. Despite this dispersal, many of refugees wound up using these skills and aptitudes to get jobs in local manufacturing concerns.[108]

The center also offered new skill sets to individuals who had never held jobs in manufacturing or in the service industry. While many of the refugees were successful, the Cuban Refugee Program established an initiative for refugees who had been left behind. This was particularly important for the significant number of Cuban women who were the heads of their families in the United States. The "Training for Independence" program started in July of 1964, when 1,475 women started intensive English classes as a precursor to vocational training aimed at ending their dependence on public assistance. During the eight to nine months of the course, each student received two and a half hours of intensive English instruction five times a week before they could proceed to further training. Cuban Refugee Center officials had found that female heads of household generally had low levels of education. In fact, 71% of these women had less than a high school education. A similar percentage had no knowledge of the English language. Among this group, 33% were married but without a spouse in Miami: most of their husbands were still in Cuba or in some country other than the United States, leaving the women as the only source of support for their children.[109]

While the stated aim of the Training for Independence program was to establish "a new approach to the problems of dependency," the official attitude of the program registered a heavy dose of paternalism in its description of the women interviewed to participate in the program. Officials in the program directly compared them to the American mothers served by the Aid to Families with Dependent Children program and found their reactions to their situation similar. "Many were unable to face reality and, while unhappy in their ghetto slum," read a report on the program encased in a glossy booklet, "had only vague and improbable dreams of how their lives might ultimately change for the better." In order to ensure that these women would participate in the program, they had to enroll in the project or they would cease to be eligible for financial assistance from CRP. While the program described the way in which many Cuban women actively and enthusiastically sought out participation in the Training for Independence initiative, they also gave examples of refugees who had been coerced into it. This was the case with a woman whom the program referred to as Mrs. H., a thirty-year-old Cuban refugee with three children under the age of ten who had been on public assistance for three years when she was brought into the program. Mrs. H. was described as "an obese, slatternly-looking woman, with only two years of formal education," who lived in a grimy bedroom equipped with a gas plate and a refrigerator. According to the program's narrative, Mrs. H. was far from interested in the slow and arduous process of gaining independence by learning English and a trade. "It would have been difficult to enable her to become employable," the program's writers went on, "even if she had been genuinely interested in achieving independence."[110]

The report went on, playing up a sort of pathology in Mrs. H. that set her apart from the established narratives of Cuban refugees, but which was coded to be understood by an audience reading for the possibility of wider welfare reform. Caseworkers reported that Mrs. H. was frequently absent from the program despite being provided with childcare during class hours. The narrative claimed she had attempted to "buy" her way out of the program multiple times. On one occasion, she wrote President Johnson a letter requesting he send her an automobile as a present, explaining not having a car that kept her from earning a living for her children. When her caseworker questioned her about the letter, Mrs. H. "admitted that she did not know how to drive a car and had no plans for using it, but she still felt that if the president would give her one, all her problems would somehow be solved." Ultimately, Mrs. H. was able to complete the language training and a course in laundry work but kept missing job opportunities until her caseworker forced her to meet a prospective employer. The story's happy conclusion, as explained by the program, was that a few months later the agency received a letter from the employer lauding Mrs. H.'s work and asking if any other workers of her caliber were available.[111]

The officials of the Cuban Refugee Program wanted to illustrate the effectiveness of their plan to bring the destitute out of a state of dependency and into self-sufficiency. The program's narrative of the Cuban exodus had been that it was "a top flight migration" of people with "special talents, ambition and initiative."[112] This was describing how the upper classes of the Cuban refugees had integrated themselves into American society with relative ease. Other refugees portrayed in the narratives of Training for Independence fit well in the long-established mold of the "worthy poor," who actively sought to escape their situation.

The program likened Cuban women like Mrs. H. to U.S.-born women who received assistance through the Aid to Families with Dependent Children program. This comparison was intentional. The program's publication, "Training for Independence: A New Approach to the Problems of Dependency," claimed that the project had been successful in "virtually eliminating the problem of hard core poverty among the individuals in this group" (see Figure 8). Their study of the initiative was meant to provide ideas and encouragement to community leaders, welfare officials, and employment specialists in dealing with problems of extreme poverty because Cuban Miami served as a social laboratory where they could conduct experiments to understand larger societal issues. "In this Cuban group," wrote Cuban Refugee Program director Howard H. Palmatier, "all the complexities of the problem of hard core poverty are reduced to a scale which facilitates study and comprehension."[113] By instituting an initiative that used government funds to provide childcare, education, and work placement, the Cuban Refugee Program sought to provide for the larger Department of Health Education and Welfare and for officials and activists throughout the nation a model by which to tackle one of the major issues of the larger War on Poverty. The hybrid nature of the CRP allowed officials to serve American foreign policy aims through welfare programs that they believed could be replicated and used to address problems facing the welfare state.

The Training for Independence initiative produced tangible successes for the Cuban Refugee Center beyond an attempt to influence the rest of the HEW structure. Of the 3,800 women who initially qualified for the program, 2,103, approximately 55%, had been removed from the financial assistance rolls by June of 1965. A small, mixed-gender group of Cubans ages fifty-six through sixty-four was also included in the program, and by that month,

TRAINING FOR INDEPENDENCE

A New Approach
To The Problems
Of Dependency

U. S. CUBAN REFUGEE PROGRAM
Social and Rehabilitation Service
Department of Health, Education, and Welfare

Figure 8. Cover of the Cuban Refugee Program (CRP) pamphlet, "Training for Independence: A New Approach to the Problems of Dependency," which proposed broader changes to the U.S. welfare system based on the CRP's experience in refugee training. Courtesy of the Cuban Heritage Collection, University of Miami Libraries.

nearly 20% of them had been removed from the rolls.[114] The vocational schooling provided by Training for Independence allowed women to receive training in the hotel industry, childcare, and upholstery work. It also had clerical courses that included lessons in typing, filing, bookkeeping, and general office practices, and it provided training in industrial power sewing machine operation.[115]

This last form of training was particularly important because it allowed the women who pursued this work to become part of a larger trend that saw Cuban women enlivening Miami's garment industry. Miami's garment industry was not as large as that of other manufacturing centers, but by 1951, fashion was the single largest industrial employer in Dade County. While this industry had already actively recruited labor from Puerto Rico and from several Caribbean nations, the influx of trained Cuban labor further fueled its growth.[116] By November 1967, there were some 350 clothing factories operating in the Greater Miami area, ranging from large industrial plants to small, sparsely equipped family shops. Operating in two garment districts located in Northwestern Miami and Hialeah, this industry employed more than 12,000 workers. That same year the *New York Times* reported that 85% of these workers were Cubans who worked in the manufacture of a great variety of garments, principally women's and children's wear. For the fiscal year ending on June 30, 1967, the value of garment production had exceeded $120 million. This annual output had been growing at an annual rate of 15% for the previous three years, and it had made Miami the third largest garment center in the nation; moreover, it was rapidly approaching a position in which it would challenge California for second place. One Miami garment executive told the *Times* that the only time he could thank Fidel Castro was when he thought of what an asset the Cuban refugees had been to his industry. Another spoke to the almost magical skills of Cuban women working in the manufacturing of clothing, stating that his company had operators who had never worked a day in their lives yet immediately adapted themselves to industrial work. He then went on to list the reasons that made South Florida so appealing to the garment industry, the first of which was the ample Cuban labor supply. While it was an industry still seeking stability, the presence of the Cubans was credited with its explosive growth.[117]

In the early days of the refugee crisis, many people feared that the influx of the refugees would only exacerbate the economic recession in the city, but this fear proved unfounded. An economic study published by the University of Miami in 1967 attributed the economic stagnation from 1960 to 1964 to two earlier sharp declines in economic activity in both the tourist and building industries, which were related to the national recession in 1958. The study found that the refugees did cause a significant amount of economic dislocation. When the Cuban refugees moved into areas with large number of vacancies and improved the lagging rates of housing occupancy, they changed the consumption patterns for local businesses, causing some of them to fail or move. The researchers also found that the refugee community had a significant impact on the city's economy through their entrepreneurial activities. "With the passing of time," the researchers found, "methods for establishing credit for business and business loans in the absence of credit records and references from Cuba have been developed and Cuban participation in the business community has been increasing."[118]

The loans obtained through references from Cuba was known as "character loans." Carlos Arboleya, who had been a banker in Cuba before coming to the United States, claimed to have started this practice. Arboleya's story was reminiscent of those of other Cubans who were highly educated or highly experienced. Arriving in Miami in late 1960, he became frustrated that no bank would give him a job and instead found work at a shoe factory. After a year and a half at the factory, he obtained a position at Boulevard National Bank, where he rose to the position of executive vice president. Arboleya would go on to become the first Cuban president of an American bank, Fidelity National Bank. When he came to positions of authority within these financial organizations, he engaged in the practice of character loans. When a Cuban refugee would come to him seeking a loan to start a business, Arboleya based his decision on the man's character and reputation. If he knew that the applicant had had a business of the same type in Cuba and that he was a man of good character, he felt compelled to aid the exile. "Their financial state did not warrant a loan," Arboleya later recalled, "but this person's character, and experience, and life did warrant it."[119] Most professional refugees had lost their wealth in fleeing from Cuba after the revolution, but as members of the community attained wealth and the clout to aid new arrivals, they found they had carried with them an asset in the form of the history they shared with other refugees of the same class.

Entrepreneurial Cubans also received aid from the federal government in establishing new businesses through loans from the Small Business Administration (SBA). Statistics on the loans granted by this organization between

1968 and 1979 show that Hispanics received 46.9% of available funds, totaling $47,677,660. By comparison, "Euroamericans" received 46.6% of the available funds, while African Americans received 6.3%.[120] While there were fluctuations in the composition of Miami's Hispanic population over the years, by 1970 this population was estimated to be 87.3% Cuban.[121] If Cubans were the recipients of a comparable percentage of the total funds that went to Hispanics, this suggests that this group received approximately 41% of the total available funds.[122] But regardless of whether the funding came from the SBA, a character loan, some other privately secured loan, or another source, Cuban entrepreneurs opened a significant number of new businesses in the Miami area. By 1966, five years after the creation of the Cuban Refugee Program, the Miami area had close to two thousand Cuban owned businesses.[123] Five years after that, in 1971, that number had increased to six thousand.[124]

In the early 1960s, the Cuban refugee influx added thousands of new Hispanic residents to Dade County, most of whom had been in need of aid from the established Cuban community or the federal government. By the latter half of the decade, research firms were engaging in market studies to measure the spending power of this market in Dade County. A study conducted by First Research Company in 1970 found significant growth in the total annual income of the county's Spanish language–origin households. When carried out for the third consecutive year, the survey found that the annual figure of $588 million represented an increase of about $246 million in the period from mid-1968 to the end of September 1970. While the number of Hispanic households increased by 37.3%, from 59,500 to 81,695, in the same period, total income increased nearly 72%, outpacing the growth in population. By the start of the 1970s, the Hispanic population in Miami had high levels of car ownership and 38.9% of Hispanics owned their own home.[125]

These economic indicators suggest a massive change from the first two years of the refugee crisis. Within ten years, what had been a largely destitute population gained a significant share of the economic power in Dade County. They accomplished this through access to structures of privilege usually denied to minority groups and migrants and through their social composition, education, experience, and entrepreneurship. By serving the needs of the U.S. national security apparatus, the CRP set the Cuban refugees and Miami on a path toward economic growth. This, however, does not mean that either the national security officials who began the program or the Cubans themselves felt particularly satisfied with the way this arrangement unfolded. On a local level, the empowerment of the Cuban community challenged the established social order, and prompted confrontations between the exiles and Miami's African American and white residents. As the refugee community navigated international, national, and local politics, the stage was set for a political transformation of Miami that rivaled the demographic and economic metamorphoses that came about because of the intersection between national security and the welfare state in South Florida.

CHAPTER 3

"Second Class Citizens": Race, Citizenship, and the Politics of Exile at the National and Local Levels

n July of 1972, the *New York Times* ran a story on how Miami's "long-passive" refugees were becoming active in local political life. The *Times* estimated the Cuban population in Miami at around 300,000 people. Some eighty thousand Cuban Americans were eligible to vote, but only about half of them had registered. There was, however, a drive to register as many eligible Cuban Americans as possible in time for that year's presidential election. The piece portrayed this drive for registration as a problem for Dade County's Democratic Party, given that 80% of Cuban Americans who registered to vote registered as Republicans. The *Times* contrasted several Cuban civic groups that had sprung up in the city to the "now moribund anti-Castro organizations of the 1960s," stating that the new groups focused principally on participating in community affairs. The *Times* informed its readers that a younger group of exiles who had come of age in the United States now led the Cuban community; men like Manolo Reboso, the first Cuban-born member of the Miami City Commission. Another young leader, Armando Lacasa, stated that Cubans were the largest minority in Dade County and that in a brief span of time they had attained economic power and now had to unite with the goal of attaining political power. This union, however, was far from assured as differing Cuban factions competed for power and influence over a united Cuban voting bloc. Regardless, these struggles were framed as a new, local political force coming into being; one which had forsaken the counterrevolutionary struggle of the past to focus on their present in Miami.[1]

While the *Times* correctly identified the growing influence of the Cuban community in South Florida, it mistakenly equated the Cuban American embrace of local politics with a turn away from anti-Castro politics. The author not only prematurely declared the death of paramilitary exile organizations as a political force, but also failed to identify that the change in political direction by Miami's Cubans in the late 1960s and early 1970s was a new manifestation of the same worldview and the same desire for a Fidel Castro–free Cuba. The access to economic opportunity created by the federal government allowed the Cuban community to harness increasing social and economic power in South Florida. The troubled history of the exiles' political organizations with the federal government in the early 1960s set the stage for a new approach to Cuban politics in South Florida, one that used the community's local power as a springboard to influence American policy.

The event that permanently married the politics of exile with local politics in Miami was the passage of the Cuban Adjustment Act in 1966. This piece of federal legislation solidified Cuban access to the structures of power and privilege offered by the federal government: a path to citizenship through permanent residency in the United States. Exile politics were complex and divided in the 1960s, but the experience of the refugees on the local and national levels informed how individuals and groups made the politics of the Cold War as local as they were global. Local Black and white communities, in turn, had their own reactions to the Cuban presence and the federal intervention in their city. These were both transgressive to the established social order and to the hopes for a more equitable order held by many African Americans in Miami. Once a path to citizenship was open, this transgression became a new and unstable social order. It also created a larger Cuban American community that sought to influence American foreign policy not as a refugee group making demands of a host state, but as a voting bloc that could mobilize influence for friendly candidates in local and legislative elections.

This process led to the public association of the growing Cuban American community with the Republican Party. Some scholars and commentators have portrayed the rapport between these two groups as being based on some natural conservatism inherent in the Cubans or being due to some unbridgeable chasm between the community and the Democratic Party that followed the failure of the Bay of Pigs Invasion and other perceived missteps by Democratic administrations.[2] While there were some very vocal conservative elements in the Cuban American community, both major political parties in the United States were invested in anticommunism in the 1950s and 1960s. Likewise, while John F. Kennedy's "betrayal" of the Cuban cause was a significant obstacle to future relations between the Democratic Party and many exile political groups, it did not end their working relationship. As they grew increasingly frustrated, however, exile organizations continued to clash with the Kennedy and Lyndon Johnson administrations as they sought free rein in their struggle against Castro's government. Leaders of both major political parties in Dade County would ultimately accept the narrative of the Democrats and the Cuban Americans being permanently at odds, leading to an institutional abandonment of Cuban Americans as a Democratic constituency and the creation of a superior Republican recruitment effort in the late 1960s and early 1970s.

In the 1960s and early 1970s, the federal government's policy choices empowered Miami's Cubans economically, but exile organizations and politically minded Cubans with local ambitions negotiated with both federal authorities and the city to build their political power as well. Cuban American politics were shaped by interactions between the federal government, Cuban exile political organizations, the city's institutions, and its Black and white communities. Poor relations between exile political groups seeking an end to Castro's government and the Kennedy and Johnson administrations helped set the tone for Cuban exile politics at the national and local levels, which was characterized by the fierce independence of many factions. Of equal importance to the formation Cuban American politics were the often-fraught relationships between Cuban refugees and Miami's African American and white communities. In this way, opposition to Castro's government shaped, not only the community's relationship with the federal government, but also their dealings with groups at the local level. This is most apparent in the final section of the chapter, which chronicles how the Cuban American community became increasingly involved in local politics after the passage of the Cuban Adjustment Act. While this push for political participation was tied to a desire to solidify the community's economic gains, the Cuban American opposition to Havana influenced the approach and substance of the community's push for political power. Cuban American politics in this period are a clear example of how local, national, and international politics often overlap to the point where it becomes difficult to see where one sphere ends and another begins.

Divided in Common Purpose: Cuban Exile
Politics, the Federal Government, and
Divergent Visions of Anti-Castro Action

Early on in their engagement with Cuban exile politics, federal policymakers walked a fine line in balancing their desire to see Cuba's revolutionary government toppled and concern over the risks they were willing to take in this pursuit. The fear of another fiasco like the Bay of Pigs or a direct confrontation with the Soviet Union made it even more difficult to contend with the impatience of Cuban exile organizations. Although American policymakers could sympathize with the refugee population and saw exile groups as comrades-in-arms in the global struggle of the Cold War, Cuba was a single battleground in a larger conflict and not a dream that drove them. Policymakers also had to contend with a fractured and often contentious landscape of exile political organizations.

Walking this line often meant strategically disappointing some exile groups in favor of others or of long-term plans. In late 1959, the State Department, spurred by reports of a political faction preparing to set up a Cuban government-in-exile on American soil, publicly warned Cubans in the United States that they would not tolerate such an action.[3] In doing this, the Dwight Eisenhower administration aimed to keep its future options open. By openly rebuking one group, the U.S. government wanted to ensure that whatever de facto government-in-exile ultimately combined the Cuban exiles' efforts would be compatible with long-term American policy in Latin America and would not be resentful of the federal government first favoring another faction. When, in fact, the federal government went on to work with a preferred group, this exacerbated the exiles' factionalism. In the lead-up to the Bay of Pigs Invasion, the Kennedy administration endorsed a government-in-exile in everything but title in the guise of the Cuban Revolutionary Council (CRC). José Miró Cardona, who was formerly the first prime minister of the revolutionary government, was elected as head of the CRC. This infuriated many on the Cuban exile right who claimed that the CRC's platform was "Fidelismo without Fidel."[4]

While the Kennedy administration meant to unify the exile organizations, it ran into the problem that the exiles did not have unified political aims outside a general opposition to Castro. In the fractured landscape of Cuban exile politics, the Cuban Revolutionary Council was one of the most ambitious attempts at unifying the anti-Castro Cubans living in exile. The

CRC, however, was not up to the task. By May 1962, the CIA reported that over two hundred anti-Castro organizations had been formed in Cuba or among Cubans in exile. "The exile community, divided and quarrelsome," explained the agency's report, "forms into groups and organizations, breaks up, disappears and reforms in a kaleidoscopic picture which varies from week to week."[5] In October of that year, the CIA provided national security advisor McGeorge Bundy with a handbook "designed to provide an abbreviated read reference to pertinent available information concerning known Cuban Counterrevolutionary organizations." This abbreviated guide, with one-page descriptions of each organization, was 102 pages long.[6]

The lack of Cuban unity was not the determining factor in the failure of the operation for which the CRC had been created: the Bay of Pigs Invasion. American intelligence officials and the members of the exile organization had expected the invasion to bring about a national uprising, or to allow the exile force to move into the countryside to carry out guerrilla tactics against Castro's government. Castro had made military preparations, and in the weeks prior to the invasion had shattered the local resistance's ability to organize any support for the invasion by capturing several of its leaders.[7] The invasion force, called Brigade 2506, which was comprised of 1,400 exiles accompanied by three Catholic priests, found itself at a massive tactical disadvantage. By the end of the battle, 114 exiles had been killed; a few were executed shortly after falling into the hands of the Cuban military, and 1,189 were captured. Some 150 brigade members were not able to land, were never deployed, or barely managed to retreat and make their way back to the United States.[8]

In the wake of the failed invasion, the federal government offered those members of Brigade 2506 who had not been captured the possibility of serving in the United States military. Meanwhile, the larger refugee community campaigned to have the captured members of Brigade 2506 returned to the United States. The U.S. government officially refused to participate in the negotiations, but it did allow private individuals to try to secure the release of those invaders who were still alive. Ultimately, all but seven of the brigade members imprisoned in Cuba were returned to the United States in December 1962. On December 29, President Kennedy addressed the members of the brigade at the Miami Orange Bowl, and after receiving the flag of Brigade 2506, he told the cheering crowd, "I can assure you that this flag will be returned to this brigade in a free Havana."[9]

Kennedy had plans for Brigade 2506. Prior to the rally at the Orange Bowl, the president had met with the Joint Chiefs of Staff in Palm Beach.

Kennedy was looking for a group that might become a "focal point" in Miami. The Joint Chiefs again brought up the issue of a government in exile, but the president was not ready to take that step. They all agreed that something needed to be done about the lack of direction among the exiles. "Right now," summarized an aide, "these various groups sit down there, stew in their own juice, elect committees, become emotionally upset, and then finally call upon somebody in Washington to let off their steam." A "focal point" would direct and focus the energies of the various groups.[10] The Kennedy administration had already attempted to establish a focal point in the Cuban Revolutionary Council, which had been meant to be the basis of a new government following a successful invasion. It continued to exist in the wake of the Bay of Pigs fiasco, when the White House designated the CRC its point of contact related to any refugee issues.[11] In October of 1961, the U.S. government tried to solidify the power of the CRC over other Cuban exile organizations by having the aid provided to those organizations flow through the council.[12]

This central position gave Miró Cardona the role of U.S.-backed spokesperson of the Cuban cause. He served in this role, for example, when he testified before the House Committee on the Judiciary in December of 1961. As part of his prepared statement, he outlined exactly what he saw as the mentality of the Cuban refugee population. Every exile man, woman, and child, had "but one wish, one idea, one obsession—to go back to his country as soon as possible." Miró Cardona reinforced both the desire of the exiles to return to Cuba and the intent for a brief stay in the United States.[13] By March of the following year, Miró Cardona and Antonio de Varona asked McGeorge Bundy to give the CRC "the wherewithal to invade Cuba and overthrow the Castro regime." Bundy replied that should the United States support any military action against Castro's Cuba, such action had to be both decisive and complete. Bundy informed the CRC's leaders that Cuba's military capabilities were sufficient that decisive action against Castro's regime would require the open military involvement of U.S. armed forces and that the United States was not prepared to wage open war against Cuba.[14] Frustrations only mounted as the resolution of the Cuban Missile Crisis in October of 1962 did not bring about the removal of Castro from power in Cuba.

By late 1962, Miró Cardona and the Cuban Revolutionary Council were in a difficult position. They were the official point of contact for the U.S. government, but they were not allowed to carry out the type of operations that they believed would result in a victory over Castro's government. Miró Cardona, like Kennedy, attempted to ally himself with Brigade 2506. Those attempts backfired when, on January 3, 1963, the members of the brigade received $250 bonus payments for their service. The combatants were not against the bonus payment, but rather against receiving it publicly from Miró Cardona. A Central Intelligence Agency report indicated that the members "were enraged by the humiliating publicity and pictures appearing in the press and on television of them lined up to receive cash from 'Miro, Benefactor of the Brigade.'" Brigade members were furious over being used for Miró Cardona's political gain, and they held that the publicity was ultimately harmful both for the United States and for the brigade because it followed the Castro propaganda line of the brigade being mercenaries.[15]

The CRC's head was unable to recast himself as the leader of all exile political organizations and became an object of ridicule and scorn among many in the Cuban community. As one refugee wrote of him, "we felt Miro Cardona was the instrument of U.S. policy among exiles."[16] Miró Cardona remained mostly silent about his own discontent with the federal government, only expressing his displeasure when the United States refused to allow exiles to conduct raids against Castro's Cuba.[17] This changed on April 18, 1963, when Miró Cardona resigned from his post at the Cuban Revolutionary Council and ended his silence on matters of U.S. foreign policy, becoming increasingly vocal about what he saw as American failures. By the end of his life in the early 1970s, Miró Cardona wrote that, "one American, Teddy Roosevelt, helped Cuba's Independence; another, John F. Kennedy, handed her to Russia."[18]

The Cuban Revolutionary Council soon disbanded. Cuban exile politics were completely bereft of a "focal point" through which the United States could deal with refugee issues. Miró Cardona's resignation also stoked the anger of many in the Cuban community toward the U.S. government for not giving the refugees the full military and intelligence support to which they believed they were entitled. The *Miami Herald*'s editorial board took offense to the fact that the exiles appeared to feel entitled to determine American foreign policy. "Our foreign policy is our own to control," declared the *Herald*, "it is not subject to changes determined by how loudly a troublesome ally shouts his own contrary policy."[19] The *Herald*'s editorial board, already presenting a more antagonistic view of the Cuban community than they had previously, made it very clear to the exiles that they were the tail, not the dog.

Others tried to fill the vacuum left by the disappearance of the Cuban Revolutionary Council. In early 1964, Cubans in several countries voted in a nonbinding referendum. The organizers of the referendum presented a group of five candidates. This group was meant to represent Cubans in the United States and abroad and to continue to work against Castro's government. José M. Bosch, chairman of the board of the Bacardi Corporation, had financed all the preparations for the referendum. Bosch wanted twenty-five thousand Cubans to vote positively in the referendum, despite a reaction among Miami's Cubans described as "indifferent and skeptical" by the State Department. The organization created by this referendum, RECE (Cuban Representation in Exile), did not have a major impact. While RECE facilitated covert operations and attempted to advance the cause of a post-Castro Cuba, its most notable feature was the participation of a twenty-four-year-old member of Brigade 2506 named Jorge Mas Canosa. Mas Canosa would go on to accrue significant political influence and wealth, but at the time he was described by the State Department simply as a good speaker who was "politically ambitious."[20]

By the time RECE entered the scene, there was a new president in the White House and the federal government was no longer actively seeking a "focal point" for exile activities. In a 1965 memo on whether to support RECE, Gordon Chase, an assistant to McGeorge Bundy, wrote that he did not think that exile organizations had much to offer the United States in relation to solving the Cuban problem. To start a program of support for RECE would cost the United States money and time and might "cause us a Pandora's Box–full of typical exile problems."[21] Chase's statements are representative of the remorse expressed by many national security officials who found that their investment in the militant wings of the Cuban exile community had not paid off. They had also found that their conception of a docile, easily controllable refugee population that would fall in line with American foreign policy needs was less than accurate.

Despite the problems in dealing with exile political organizations, the U.S. government continued work on issues related to the well-being of Cuban refugees in the United States. One issue that drew particular attention in Congress was the issue of status normalization for the Cuban refugees. As parolees, the Cubans remained in a sort of legal limbo. A refugee who wanted to change status from parolee to permanent resident of the United States had to leave the United States and then apply for an immigrant visa at an American consular office.[22] Normalization would allow refugees to apply for permanent residency without having to leave the borders of the United States. In the midst of the legislative conflicts surrounding passage of the Immigration and Nationality Act of 1965, the Johnson White House had come out in favor of status normalization for the Cubans but had not pressed the issue.[23]

In October of 1965, President Johnson received a letter from New York Democratic congressman William F. Ryan. Ryan had introduced legislation aimed at allowing status adjustment by the Cuban refugees in the United States. Ryan's discussions with the Department of Health, Education and Welfare revealed to him that the lack of permanent resident status was one of the most difficult problems that Cubans faced in the United States and that status adjustment would lighten the welfare rolls of many of these refugees. "If we are going to admit them, then we should admit them with as much help as possible," he explained to the president. "We must not admit them, then hold them at arm's length from many of the privileges of living in our society."[24] The Cuban Adjustment Act of 1966 solidified the access of Cubans in the United States to the very privileges alluded to by Congressman Ryan.

The Cuban Adjustment Act allowed Cubans who had entered the United States after January 1, 1959, to apply for permanent resident status and set them on a path to citizenship. Instead of having to wait an additional five years after attaining permanent resident status in order to apply for citizenship, the Cuban refugees were allowed to count up to thirty months of time spent in the United States toward satisfying the five-year residency requirement. This cut the wait time between a successful adjustment to permanent residence and the ability to apply for citizenship, allowing refugees to become citizens in two and a half years.[25] Permanent residency and a path to citizenship would be crucial for the development of the Cuban community in Miami. Not only did the community secure the economic gains made in the 1960s, but the Adjustment Act provided access to new forms of political power that were not dependent on exile organizations courting the patronage of a presidential administration. This more permanent power helped the Cubans further transgress the established social order. It is no wonder, then, that the legislation was strongly opposed by leaders in South Florida's Black community, a group that felt it had been negatively affected by the advantages being given to the Cuban refugees now living in their area.[26]

Whose Freedom? African Americans, Aid Structures, and First-Class Citizenship

In the early evening hours of Wednesday, August 7, 1968, a group of three hundred frustrated Black Miamians gathered at the intersection of NW Sixty-Second Street and Seventeenth Avenue, in the predominantly African

American area known as Liberty City. Urban renewal schemes had forced many of Liberty City's forty-five thousand African American residents into the crowded municipality. Anger, meetings, and rallies in reaction to the Republican National Convention being held in Miami Beach had characterized the preceding days. That August night, the crowd had already begun to throw stones and gravel at passing cars when a white man driving an automobile with a "Wallace for President" bumper sticker approached the intersection. The driver soon found himself in the middle of a rain of rocks. He panicked and attempted to flee, driving around two other cars, speeding through a red light, hitting a truck, and ultimately seeing his vehicle stall. The driver waited for police intervention as members of the crowd pelted his car with rocks and bottles amidst cries of "Get Whitey!" When the authorities failed to arrive, he fled from his car and a group of African American spectators pulled him into the safety of a nearby bar. Teenagers from the crowd then proceeded to overturn his vehicle and set it ablaze. This began two days of disturbances that pitted the community against the Miami City Police, the Dade County Public Safety Department, and members of the Florida National Guard.[27]

The Liberty City Riot was a minor event when compared to the other urban uprisings of the decade, but it still warranted investigation by the National Commission on the Causes and Prevention of Violence. The commission's investigators concluded that many of the same causes that had set off similar incidents across the country had driven participants in Liberty City: chronic unemployment, poor access to public services, and bad relations with city police.[28] The task force's report did note several characteristics unique to the disturbance in Liberty City. Most Miami-specific among these was the widespread feeling among African Americans that jobs in the city were being kept from them and instead being awarded to the Cuban refugees.[29] Many of the city's Black residents saw the ongoing issue of refugees and jobs as another obstacle between them and first-class citizenship. One report noted that twelve thousand jobs previously held by African Americans had gone to Cubans. Even the increasing participation of Cubans in Miami's garment industry, which was heralded as a triumph elsewhere, had an impact on the city's African American community. While white workers saw their share of the garment industry's labor force decrease most, African Americans also felt the impact as their share of garment work went from 6% to under 4%.[30]

The loss of jobs and potential advancement was starker in relation to the city's tourism industry and the deep gulf between African American neighborhoods and the city's tourist areas. Some Black Miamians felt that the Cuban presence exacerbated divisions in the city and took up tourism jobs previously available to African Americans. In his interview with the task force, disk jockey Milton "Butterball" Smith recalled Muhammad Ali's remark that in Miami the division between heaven and hell was the railroad tracks. On one side of the tracks were crowded, impoverished African American communities; on the other were the playgrounds of affluent white residents and tourists. Smith contended that the Cubans made this division even starker. "So the argument is that not even is the white man going to let us live in Heaven, over there," Smith stated; "They won't even let us work over there—they give the jobs to Cubans."[31]

African Americans feeling excluded from the economic opportunities associated with living in a Sunbelt city was common, but the inclusion of the Cubans in Miami complicated established understandings of race relations and economics in the area. While the flow of federal funds related to the Cold War and the national security state changed the economy of the Sunbelt, it generally did not challenge ingrained power structures established along lines of race and class.[32] The influx of federal funds aimed at helping the Cuban refugees, however, changed power relations in the city of Miami. The Cuban challenge to the racial order, aided by the unprecedented access to welfare state structures of power and privilege that this group had received, drew anger and confusion from both whites and African Americans in Miami. The reactions of both groups shaped politics in the city and the Cuban responses to their fellow Miamians.

Much of the conflict had its roots in how African Americans received the news of the Cuban refugee influx and of the federal response. Miami's Black press was receptive to the idea of providing shelter for Cuban refugees, but it also welcomed the idea of resettling as many of them as possible from Dade County in an effort to ease unemployment in the area.[33] By late 1961, the *Miami Times*, the city's African American weekly, reported on complaints that employers were giving Cubans preference for jobs. In some cases, refugees replaced Black workers. "While we sympathize with the unfortunate Cubans we feel that charity should begin at home," the newspaper's editorial read, "or in other words, American citizens should at least stand an equal chance of getting employment."[34] The *Times* questioned the logic of providing such levels of aid to a foreign group while American citizens were suffering from high unemployment numbers and a lack of access to welfare programs that would aid the unemployed. This narrative arose multiple times in the newspaper's editorial page, particularly after each increase in size of refugee presence. After a new wave of refugees started to appear in Miami in 1965, the *Times* once again suggested that while it was "an act of Christianity to help those in need," the burden of this act fell on the taxpayers and it was hard paying taxes without employment.[35]

When *Miami Herald* reporter Juanita Greene testified during Senate hearings on the problems caused by the refugee influx, she conveyed the general anger and frustration among Miami's African Americans. "Resentment in Miami appears highest among our Negro population," Greene wrote in a statement submitted to the Senate Committee on the Judiciary's Subcommittee to Investigate Problems Connected with Refugees and Escapees.[36] Despite the fact that Black refugees also experienced discrimination in the United States, Greene related to the senators the discontent of many of Miami's African Americans, who saw children of Afro-Cuban descent attending public schools that their own children could not because of segregation.[37] She also told the story of an African American minister who told Black parents that teaching their children to speak only Spanish might be the only course to save them from compounded inequalities. Greene referred to those leaders in the African American community who were trying to gain equal opportunities for their community in a southern city, indicating that many of them were outspoken about how "in the name of freedom and democracy [there is] is a group of foreigners that is given not only more assistance but more dignity than their own American group."[38]

While Greene had the ear of the Senate subcommittee by virtue of her profession and her whiteness, Miami's African Americans were perfectly comfortable advocating for themselves. There were many voices in the Black community who decried this inequity in the years before the Liberty City disturbances. Attorney Donald Wheeler Jones, president of the local National Association for the Advancement of Colored People (NAACP), wrote a letter addressed to several public officials, including President Johnson. He stated that the federal government had a responsibility not just to the politically oppressed of Cuba, but also to the economically oppressed of South Florida. Jones stated that each African American who had lost a job to a Cuban had "borne his burden in silence as a sacrificial lamb for the extension of freedom and democracy to refugees from another land."[39] For Jones, as for many other African Americans in Miami, full access to the welfare state was a zero-sum game that they had lost before even taking a turn.

Many African Americans wanted the airlift from Cuba ended, but some thought the program was evidence of Washington's subtler, but ultimately more scarring, discriminatory practices against Black citizens. In April 1970, *Miami Times* writer Ricky Thomas started an installment of his column, "Out of the Dark," by stating a common belief among Black Miamians: "Being a Cuban ain't bad." Thomas questioned the fairness of providing such largesse to refugees while his people, who were already burdened by centuries of oppression, were denied any relief to help overcome the effects of that injustice. He suggested that a Cuban could get one hundred dollars or sometimes more with only one condition set upon him: that of need. "How many black families do you know," he asked, "that have the condition called NEED, but still have to go through rigid restrictions and requirements to get their monthly checks?" Thomas's column took on the fundamental differences in access to multiple benefits between African Americans and Cubans and recoiled at the imbalance. He asked why the federal government could not create such a program for African Americans and poor whites. He argued that this was particularly frustrating for the city's Black population because the Cubans had been, under Batista, "as prejudiced, clannish, and had imbedded in them as much hatred towards the poor as any Mississippi Whites."[40]

Many Cubans actively sought to challenge any portrayal of their community as racist, but statements made by some members of the community regarding race relations in Cuba and the United States added fuel to the fire of African American anger. In 1969, journalist John Egerton visited South Florida to draft a report on race relations in the city after years of Cuban migration and in the aftermath of the Liberty City Riot. Over several days, he collected data on the complex racial landscape of the city of Miami. He concluded that Cubans and African Americans were not at each other's throats, arguing instead that the resentment over the loss of jobs was more directed toward white decisions makers. He also reported that the refugees thought themselves more racially progressive than white Americans.

Egerton believed that Afro Cubans had integrated well into the larger Cuban communities in the area. One Cuban he spoke to claimed "there was no racial discrimination in Cuba. Class discrimination, yes, but not race."[41] This admission of class divisions was more than many Cubans were willing to make. As historian Devyn Spence Benson has shown, many refugees held to a narrative that there had been no racial tensions in Cuba before Castro came to power. Some even argued that the revolution had created not only racial division but also class divisions in Cuba. Others accepted that Cubans of African descent had been discriminated against before the revolution but suggested conditions would improve in a post-Castro Cuba.[42] The complex transnational landscape of Cuban racial politics led many refugees to down-play their own racial attitudes, which carried over into their interactions with African Americans. While Egerton met with scholars who suggested that racial and class discrimination in prerevolutionary Cuba could not be divorced from one another, most of the Cubans he met acknowledged no part in the repression of African Americans.

Egerton interviewed some Cubans who were keenly aware of the structures that created racial discrimination, as when one group told him white Americans were responsible for the ghettos. "They are free to move when and where they choose, but Negroes are not," they told him, adding, "Cubans don't feel any ani-mosity toward Negro Americans, like the white Americans do." These Cubans could identify racial exclusion, but not within their own community. The same group then turned around and told Egerton that the civil rights movement was a communist ploy. Castro, they said, was pitting African Americans against whites and Cubans, planning and inspiring Black unrest. "We have seen this protest against authority before," one Cuban told Egerton; "It is how our trou-ble started. It should not be allowed to happen here."[43] This conflation of the civil rights movement with communism was not rare in Egerton's interviews, nor was it a recent phenomenon among Cubans. American conservatives often used these types of assertions as confirmations of their fears of the movement.[44]

The African Americans and Cuban refugees saw one another and the role of the federal government in their lives very differently. The refugees wel-comed the federal aid they received, but they believed that their success in the Miami area had little to do with these privileges and everything to do with their own actions. African Americans were able to identify the structures of privilege provided for the refugees and how they were parallel to those that had been denied their community. Many also saw that their well-being had no tactical value for American foreign policy goals. Still, they saw that there was access to privilege and asked why they, as citizens, were still denied what was being given to refugees.

A Transgressive Presence: White Miamians
and the Challenge of Cuban Permanence

Other Miamians were also unhappy with the role the Cubans were now play-ing in Miami. In late 1967, an article in the *Miami Herald*'s local feature, "The Cuban Beat," featured a complaint from Dr. Bernardo Benes, a Cuban banker.

Benes, who was the director of the Welfare Planning Council of Dade County and the vice president of the Washington Federal Savings and Loan Association, decried the fact that Cuban refugees were treated as "second class citizens" when it came to the services they received from local and state job agencies. Upon reading this, Harry L. Tyson, the metropolitan area manager for the Florida State Employment Service, wrote a letter to the editor of the *Herald* seeking to clear up what he saw as a fundamental misconception on Benes's part. "The Cuban refugees are not second class citizens," Tyson stated; "They are in fact, not citizens at all, but refugees on parole." Tyson declared that it was the responsibility of his agency to seek out jobs for citizens first and for refugees second. He also pointed out that there were plentiful jobs available throughout the country, if only the Cubans were willing to relocate away from South Florida. He finally asked the *Herald* editor and his readers how much more of the refugee population Miami could absorb in the current labor market.[45] While there was significant statistical evidence suggesting that the refugees were not a consistent drain on Miami's economy or labor market, this perception persisted, even in the minds of local officials.

Like the African Americans and like local and state officials, many white Miamians complained about the Cubans almost from the moment of their arrival in the United States. Most Miamians were quick to repeat the view that the Cubans were allies in a larger struggle and that their exile was tragic, but many also questioned the benefit of the migration and its effects on their city. In August of 1962, for example, Congressman Dante Fascell received a letter from a constituent who was irate about the effects of the Cuban migration. An attorney named Effie Knowles informed Fascell that "too many Cuban refugees" lived next door to the home she had owned for thirty-eight years. Knowles claimed that one of her neighbors had phoned her home early one morning and threatened to break every bone in her body. She stated that she was outraged because the Cubans got "free money, free food, free clothing out of our tax money." Knowles called into question the veracity of the refugee claim to political asylum, suggesting, as others did, that many of the exiles were in fact coming to the United States to seek better economic opportunities. If the Cubans wanted to come to the United States and enter the public welfare rolls, could they not at least behave?[46]

Fascell and his staff forwarded the complaint on to the Cuban Refugee Program and received a response stating that the type of behavior described by Knowles was out of line with the generally good behavior of refugees in Miami and elsewhere.[47] CRP staff adviser A. A. Micocci contacted Knowles and suggested she take her neighbors to court, which prompted her to write Fascell again. She was livid at the suggestion that she, a decent, respectable, law-abiding American citizen, should have to "stoop to go to Police Court with Cuban prostitutes and procureers [sic] who have invaded our good neighborhoods." The language Knowles used clearly reflected that used by other white Americans when faced with racial and class transgressions in what had been previously homogenous communities. Knowles differentiated herself from the Cuban "invaders" not only by her nationality, but by her class and her distance from their perceived criminality. She went so far as to use a property rights argument against the Cuban presence in her neighborhood by stating she did not know "why my peace and property values should be disturbed by the scum of Cuba."[48]

Knowles's rage against her Cuban neighbors not only stemmed from the conflicts she was having with them and their racial and class transgression of the social order, but also from another outrage: she believed that her government was far more interested in the well-being of the Cubans than it was in her own. Moreover, other institutions, like American churches were straining their resources to help the refugees. The social institutions long tasked with defending her racial and class interests were failing Knowles. Instead, they were supporting the refugees. The national security argument provided little comfort for Knowles. She believed officials were being duped. She sought desperately to open the Congressman's eyes by asking him if "*any of you realize that Castro is letting out his friends too?*" She concluded by telling him that she did not want her second letter sent to Micocci and that all Fascell needed to do to see ill-behaved Cubans was to take a walk on Flagler Street.[49]

Knowles was not the last white Miamian to criticize the Cuban exiles and their effect on South Florida. In August of 1970, a woman named Violette McCrary attempted to call Fascell and complain about the continued Freedom Flights, her plummeting property values, and the recent increase in her property taxes.[50] Another constituent stated that Miami was "ruined already." "Our downtown is a pollution of street-walkers," wrote Mrs. Samuel J. Constance in a letter addressed to a group of politicians including Fascell and President Richard Nixon, "mostly brazen 50¢ whores who approach our teenagers male and female . . . wallowing in their dope-wealth."[51] One man called into question Fascell's stance on not immediately ceasing the airlift from Cuba and promised not to vote for him again. "You are supposed to represent us," wrote Fred C. Oakley, "*not Cubans*."[52]

By 1963, some in Miami's journalistic community had also become critical of the Cubans, a fact made particularly clear by the opening song to a

90-minute show performed by several journalists to a sold out crowd of 650 at a fundraiser for journalism scholarships at the University of Miami. Sung to the tune of "South of the Border," the full cast began:

South of the border,
By way of Key West,
They sneaked out of Cuba's isle, the rank and file
To be our guests,
Right here in Miami,
Where everything's free
And here's where they'll stay, bub,
Till eternity.[53]

The scene then shifted to the Cuban Refugee Center, where the roasters portrayed Cubans waiting in line for relief checks while they smoked expensive cigars and sported diamond stickpins. The "refugees" then took up their own song: "Oh, resettle us not on zee cold prairie / Where zee men must work, and zee dough ain't free."[54] This satire allowed the journalists to openly portray the Cubans as undeservedly privileged freeloaders, a far cry from the early articles that portrayed their bravery in the face of tragic adversity. More drastic, in light of their part in the 1960 drive to obtain federal aid for the refugees, was the publication in 1970 by the *Miami Herald* of an editorial entitled, "Cuban Airlift Simply U.S. Aid to Castro."[55] The *Herald* had been critical of exile attempts to control U.S. policy toward Cuba, but voices within the paper were growing increasingly concerned about the long-term effects of the influx on Miami's economy and its politics. A decade had decidedly changed the perspective of Miami's press in regard to the refugees.

There were also voices in local and state government that were growing increasingly impatient throughout the 1960s and into the 1970s. Some people had already suggested using the Opa-Locka Naval Air Station as a self-sustaining Cuban community, but in March of 1963, former governor LeRoy Collins went further and suggested the creation of a new nation of Cuban exiles. Collins, who had been part of the push for federal involvement in the refugee situation, was one of the most prominent proponents converting an uninhabited West Indies island into "a new Cuban homeland."[56] Many people were quick to point out flaws with this plan, however. Officials in the Bahamas explained that the uninhabited islands were in this condition because they were uninhabitable.[57] The refugee community decried this idea as ridiculous, with one Cuban calling it an exercise in land development instead of nation building. In a piece written for the *Herald*, former *Prensa libre* editor Humberto Medrano counseled Collins, "Please do not confuse your plans of urban development with the birth of a nation, because a nation is not born by building on an empty lot."[58] While this idea did not make serious headway into policy circles, it remained popular among those Miamians who were opposed to a continued Cuban presence. One letter sent to Fascell and Nixon years later simply asked "WHY NOT CLEAN THIS PLACE OUT AND PUT THE MAJORITY OF THESE PEOPLE ON AN ISLAND OR TWO . . . AND LET THEM BUILD THEIR ECONOMY, BUILD THEIR WAR SUPPLIES, as Free China has done?"[59]

The Cuban community in Miami was not without allies. While exile politics lacked unity and influence at the national and foreign policy levels, the growing economic power of the Cuban community in Miami ensured the growth of their political power at the local level. This made for overt intersections between local politics and the transnational politics of exile. This was the case when, in September of 1969, the City Commission of Miami passed Resolution No. 40983. This resolution condemned the treatment of political prisoners in the "foul, pestilence ridden jails of Communist Cuba," where these prisoners were incarcerated "solely because they are patriots who were engaged in a death struggle to keep the world from being enslaved by Communist Masters."[60] The resolution itself did not mention the Cuban community in Miami, but it is clear that their growing power was becoming a factor in the politics of Dade County.

No Politics Is Local: Cuban American Political Activism and the Shifting Electoral Landscape of Dade County

When the U.S. Congress passed the Cuban Adjustment Act in 1966, it did more than establish a path to citizenship for the refugee community; it also provided a path to political power for Cuban Americans in South Florida. This did not mean that Cubans started flocking to the polls immediately. Many Cubans were reluctant to apply for American citizenship, seeing it as a signal that they had given up on returning to Cuba.[61] Cuban Americans were not yet a powerful voting bloc in South Florida in the late 1960s, but as early as August of 1967, they were mobilizing at a local level in an attempt to gain influence. In that month, Democratic representative Claude Pepper introduced Concurrent Resolution 492, which called for the government of the

United States to formulate and present a plan of action to the members of the Organization of American States for the elimination of the Castro regime in Cuba "by whatever means necessary." The U.S. government was to undertake this task with the cooperation of other governments, or alone if necessary.[62]

The resolution, which would have committed the United States to an active, public plan to eliminate Castro's revolutionary government, did not pass, but it did spur the Cuban community in Miami into action. Congressman Pepper's friend Bernardo Benes held meetings with other prominent Cubans seeking their endorsement and support of the resolution. He was able to obtain the cooperation of RECE leader Ernesto Freye Varona and financial support from José Bosch Lamarque of the Bacardi Company. Working together with Luis Botifoll, Benes and Freye created the Sponsoring Committee in Support of Resolution 492 in September of 1967 after a private meal with Congressman Pepper to which nearly sixty prominent Cubans were invited.[63] This organization mobilized its lobbying capability, inviting members of Congress to a luncheon with Jorge Mas Canosa at the Capitol Hill Club less than ten days after the creation of the committee.[64] The committee met several times until October 12, 1967. Factional infighting had once again destroyed any semblance of a united front as U.S. government sources reported that Freye had attempted to dominate the committee and present it as an effort of RECE, most likely in an attempt to revive the dormant organization.[65]

For the election of 1968, Republicans in South Florida attempted to court the Cuban community and change the electoral math of the traditionally Democratic Dade County. A pamphlet entitled, "¿Por que los Cubanos-Americanos respaldan a Mike Thompson para el Congreso?" (Why do Cuban Americans endorse Mike Thompson for Congress?), was circulated by the campaign of Dante Fascell's Republican opponent.[66] The pamphlet charged Fascell with pandering to Cuban voters after having also embraced the position that refugees were taking jobs away from African Americans. He was also portrayed as an enemy to the cause of Cuban liberation because of statements he made in Congress, where he stated he did not believe an invasion from the outside would attain the desired objectives. The pamphlet contrasted Fascell with Mike Thompson, describing the latter as a "genuine anti-Communist" and claiming the Republican candidate had identified Fidel Castro as a communist in his writings and speeches as a student leader at the University of Miami in 1959.[67]

Thompson fell short of convincing Fascell's allies in the Cuban community to shift their support to him and ultimately lost the election to the

veteran Democrat. Despite Thompson's depiction of Fascell as an enemy of
Cuban freedom, the Congressman was a valuable ally to many Cuban organizations. In 1966, for example, the founder of the Truth about Cuba Committee, Luis V. Manrara, sent Fascell a letter describing how the congressman and
some of his colleagues kept "the torch of freedom for the countries enslaved
by the international socialist/communist conspiracy" as heartwarming. Manrara held Fascell up as an example of the type of good man who would make a
difference in the fight against communism.[68] It is not clear whether Manrara
truly felt that Fascell was so stalwart and steady an ally of the Cuban exile
cause or if he was simply maintaining a relationship with the existing power
structure until a stronger ally could be found. It is clear, however, that many
among the most fervently anti-Castro exiles did not see a direct challenge to
Fascell as feasible in the 1960s.

Fascell also actively courted the Cuban American vote. In the lead-up
to the 1970 midterm election, Fascell and his campaign sought to bolster
his anti-Castro bona fides. On May 20 of that year, the congressman made
a statement on the floor of the House of Representatives regarding the sixty-
eighth anniversary of Cuban independence and attacking Castro for making
a mockery out of the very concept.[69] Fascell and his staff then contracted a
booth at the Fourth Annual Cuban and American Exposition Fair, which was
held in July. The show was meant to demonstrate the commercial, industrial,
and artistic achievements of the "USA, Free Cuba, and Latin America."[70] Fascell's staff saw this as an opportunity to distribute material about the Congressman's work and he ultimately approved the use of five thousand copies
of his May 20 speech for distribution at his booth.[71]

Fascell was more active than many of his fellow South Florida Democrats at courting the Cuban American vote, in part because he sought out
literature on the effect of the Cuban presence in Dade County. In 1971, the
congressman actively corresponded with political scientists Paul S. Salter and
Robert C. Mings. Fascell noted that their report, "The Projected Impact of
Cuban Settlement on Voting Patterns in Metropolitan Miami, Florida," filled
a void in political intelligence on the region and was a cause for concern.[72]
The authors predicted that the Cuban influx would have consequences for
local, state, and national elections.[73]

Salter and Mings identified three areas of high Cuban concentration
in the Greater Miami area: the Center City District, the Hialeah-Miami
Springs District, and the Edison District of Northeast Miami. The researchers reported a strong Democratic leaning in all three districts in presidential

elections between 1948 and 1964. In the election of 1968, there was a change in there, given that it was the first "real, if limited," opportunity for Cubans to vote in a presidential election. While the Democrats carried Miami with 48.4% of the vote, compared to 37.0% for the Republican Party and 14.6% for George Wallace's American Independent Party, these three areas saw the Republicans gain a slight majority over the Democrats, 40.1% to 39.9%. Salter and Mings noted that 70% of the Spanish-speaking population in Miami were not citizens and had not applied for naturalization. They attributed this to the five-year residency requirement and still-prevalent belief that the exile was temporary, and they would soon return to their homeland. They cited numerous studies that divided Cubans in Miami between a temporary "exile type," who fully expected a return to the island, and what they considered to be a more realistic "immigrant type," who had begun to think of South Florida as home.[74]

The research team sought to gauge where the Cubans fell within the American political spectrum by conducting interview surveys with refugees at major street intersections in the Cuban districts during July of 1970. The survey requested opinions on political party preference and three societal issues facing the United States. The responses showed a strong preference for the Republican Party at 73%, compared to only 16% with a preference for the Democratic Party. When respondents had to rank three topical issues by order of importance. they chose "law and order" as the most significant problem of the day by 78%, with only 10% selecting "civil rights" and 6% choosing "pollution and the environment." Salter and Mings believed that classifying Cubans as prospective adherents to "right wing" politics was an overstatement, but they observed that an ample antiradical feeling was prevalent. They also explained that much of the distaste for the Democratic Party among the exiles came from its association with the Kennedy and Johnson administrations and that the "extremely unpopular handling of the bay of Pigs Invasion [sic] has created seemingly 'permanent' hostility" toward the party, comparing it to the distrust toward the Republican Party in the South following Reconstruction.[75]

The authors argued that the Cuban vote could turn Miami from a Democratic stronghold to a source of Republican electoral power. While they conceded that many factors would affect that pace of this transition and that predicting voter behavior without complete data could be hazardous, Salter and Mings made a prediction about the electoral patterns in Dade County starting in the mid-1970s, stating that if Castro's regime did not fall by 1976, then the presidential candidate who, in that election, "champions conservative ideals and proclaims a militant anti-communist international policy should be able to speculate with some confidence that he will receive a large proportion of the Cuban vote and probably carry Miami, Florida in his victory column."[76] As the Cuban American community gained political influence, it seemed possible that it could serve as the lynchpin of a presidential election. The price of victory for the candidate courting them would be an embrace of a specific set of foreign policy objectives regarding Cuba.

Mings and Salter's predictions were disconcerting to those Democrats who paid attention to their report, and in the lead-up to the 1972 presidential election, Fascell received evidence that the Republican Party was actively recruiting Cuban Americans. Bernardo Benes wrote Fascell in May of that year. Benes pointed out that between 1965 and 1970 Democratic registration in Dade County had dropped by eight thousand while Republican registration had increased by twenty thousand. Benes, a registered Democrat, credited the change to the close to eight hundred Cubans who were becoming American citizens each month. "While the Republican Party has been active in seeking the support of the Cuban-American in Dade County," Benes wrote, "the Democratic Party doesn't show any sign of being alive." Benes disliked the "over simplistic" reasoning by Republicans that the Cubans were in Miami because of Kennedy's handling of the Bay of Pigs Invasion. In contrast, the GOP had recruited a group of Cuban Republicans to fundraise for Richard Nixon's reelection and it had already accumulated eight hundred thousand dollars. Benes encouraged Fascell to work with Dade's Democratic leadership to be more proactive about courting Cuban Democrats in the county. He had never heard anyone from the Democratic Party challenge the Republican assertions regarding the Bay of Pigs Invasion, despite his belief that the Democrats had traditionally been more responsive to the needs of minority groups in Dade County and that Latin America, including Cuba, was always better treated when the United States had a Democratic administration. Benes did not have any simple solutions, but he encouraged Fascell to work with him or other Cuban American Democrats.[77]

Fascell shared Benes's frustrations with the party. He had urged the county and state Democratic committees to engage in a campaign of active registration and outreach to the Cuban American community, but neither the county nor the state parties had mounted a significant, continuing campaign. Fascell tasked his office with sending a letter to people who became a citizen in Dade County giving them basic information and "at least letting them know that one Democrat was interested in them and anxious to maintain contact."[78] Other individuals in the Democratic Party, like Congressman Claude Pepper, had also engaged in this tactic.[79] As early as 1968, Pepper had expressed awareness and concerns about the "determined effort the Republicans are making among Cuban-Americans in our area and throughout the country," and had declared that the Democratic Party needed to combat this effort.[80] As Fascell pointed out to Benes four years later, the efforts of individual Democrats were "no substitute for a well-organized, highly visible Democratic Party effort." The congressman vowed to work with Benes and other Cuban American Democrats and to discuss the matter with Pepper, Senator Lawton Chiles, Governor Reubin Askew, and any other Florida Democrat who would listen.[81]

Benes was not the only Dade Democrat sounding the alarm about the vast organizational superiority of Dade's Republicans in recruiting Cuban Americans. A manager of the International Ladies' Garment Workers' Union in Miami, Mayer Finkel, contacted Fascell about the issue of voter registration two months after Benes. Given the large number of Cuban women working in Miami's growing garment industry, Finkel had significant contact with the Cuban American community. He informed Fascell that when Spanish speakers in the Greater Miami area were sworn in as citizens of the United States there was a delegation of Spanish speakers from the Republican Party at the swearing-in ceremony. They were there to "greet and congratulate these new citizens and to assist them to register to vote, and indoctrinate them to the views and aims of the Republican Party."[82] Finkel included a Spanish-language leaflet distributed by the Republicans at naturalization ceremonies encouraging the new citizens to make their opinions heard on issues including taxes and busing. The leaflet explained that at the end of the ceremony the new citizens could register as members of the Republican Party at the tables located at the entrance of the precinct to avoid having to take another trip. "New citizen," the leaflet read, "the Republican Party congratulates you, and needs you!"[83]

By the early 1970s, most Cubans in the United States were well aware that there was no magic bullet to get back their country. No single political victory would bring about an end to the revolution. This did not mean that hope for a return home in a post-Castro era was lost among Miami's Cubans. As more refugees embraced American citizenship in an effort to influence policy on both a local and national scale, others still refused to take this step for fear it was an admission of defeat. Despite the prediction that the organizations of anti-Castro exiles were dying out, they continued to be a presence in Cuban

American politics. However, they were no longer the only approach to influencing the United States and the situation in Cuba. There were new, local
approaches that made the politics of Miami as potentially important as those
of Washington or Havana.

The political divisions among Miami's Cubans remained and deepened as
variables related to party affiliations in the United States came into play. These
divisions would come to the surface more fully in the wake of the cessation of
the Freedom Flights in April of 1973. The large-scale refugee influx that had
started in 1959 was, seemingly, at an end. The years that followed would see
many among the Cuban community focus their energies on solidifying the
gains they had obtained in Miami since 1959. The relative calm that set in
after the end of the Cuban airlift would not last, as different factions within
the community began to turn on one another over the issue of diplomatic rapprochement with Castro's government and the conflicts between the Cubans
and other groups of Miamians intensified. While the 1970s in Miami lacked
the urgent eventfulness of the decade that had preceded it, the city's residents
would discover that the calm at the eye of the storm would be short-lived.

CHAPTER 4

"At Home, but Homesick": Bilingualism, Local Politics, and the Divided Politics of Cuban Miami

B y the time the Freedom Flights ended on April 6, 1973, the airlift had brought 297,318 refugees to the United States.[1] While some refugees still entered the United States from third countries, the large-scale migration from Cuba appeared to have ended. With much of the Cuban community in the United States already resettled or in an economically stable position, the need for the Cuban Refugee Program began to wane. Over the next two years, the Department of Health, Education, and Welfare planned to phase out the CRP only to meet with significant resistance from Florida's governor and congressional delegation. In 1975, Howard Palmatier, director of the program, died unexpectedly. The vacancy led several rival groups of Cuban Americans to pressure President Gerald Ford's administration to appoint a member of their community as director. White House staffers supported the idea, but they expected that any candidate named to the position would invite the ire of one or more groups of politically connected Cuban Americans.[2] The Ford administration appointed Dr. Ricardo Núñez as director of the Cuban Refugee Program, a candidate supported by the Inter-American Chamber of Commerce of Dade County.[3]

The concerns of White House staffers proved justified when Núñez was immediately attacked by rivals and members of the Cuban press as a detached, possibly corrupt millionaire who had been absent from any anti-Castro activity in the United States.[4] The attacks on Núñez led administration officials to question the new CRP director's fitness. While his work was adequate, there was "sufficient controversy and criticism about him" to cause the

Department of Health, Education, and Welfare to conduct a major program review and a federal audit of the Cuban Refugee Program.[5] Given that the mass migrations from Cuba were apparently over, the federal government used this investigation to justify the elimination of the CRP. By the end of the decade, the program ceased to exist.

The controversy over the appointment of Núñez to head the CRP is illustrative of the political moment that the Cuban refugee and Cuban American community was experiencing between the end of the Freedom Flights and the Mariel boatlift of 1980. The end of the Cuban Refugee Program meant that while the federal government still privileged them over any other group of migrants, Cubans in South Florida no longer had a powerful federal agency consistently advocating for them on a local level.[6] The work of the CRP, which was aimed at helping the refugee community and shaping them into a tool of policy had ended, but the decisions made by policymakers had reshaped the politics and economy of South Florida, empowering the Cuban community to effectively advocate for itself. South Florida's Cubans would now be expending their own political capital to attain advancements like bilingual services and greater inclusion into local power structures. The fact that over the course of fourteen years, Cuban Americans had gained the influence to pressure the White House to appoint one of their own as head of the CRP spoke to their rapid accumulation of power.

The Núñez incident is indicative of where the Cuban community found itself in during the 1970s: they sought to solidify the economic gains they had made through politics but were met with resistance from other groups or had those efforts undercut by infighting. This chapter focuses on the relationship between the Cuban community with elite institutions in Miami, but it also examines the rifts within the community and their relationship to the U.S. government and to the Cuban government. These dynamics crystallized during the push for bilingualism. The Cuban community tried to use their economic power to get Spanish language-service in both public services and private businesses. Many native speakers of English in the city opposed these efforts, particularly in relation to a successful ordinance to declare Dade County bilingual and bicultural and a failed push for universal bilingual education in the county's school system. The push for bilingualism generated increasing polarization between Anglo communities, including city elites, and the Cuban community, and the Cuban community's relationship with the *Miami Herald* serves as a salient example. Where once the *Herald* had advocated for Cuban refugees, its stances on the Cuban American community grew increasingly confrontational over time.

There were also significant internal cleavages within the Cuban community over what it meant to be Cuban in the United States and whether there could be any form of significant engagement with Havana. While some Cuban Americans used their growing political power to pressure the Ford administration to remove administrative roadblocks for permanent residency and citizenship for Cuban refugees, others in the Cuban community continued to debate whether naturalization was an admission of defeat in the fight against Fidel Castro. These intra-Cuban struggles came to a head in the 1970s around the issue of dialogue with Castro's government. When an ideologically diverse group of Cuban Americans, with the support of Jimmy Carter's administration, chose to engage in a limited dialogue with the government in Havana, others in the Cuban community in the United States reacted angrily and sometimes violently.

Space, Place, and Economics: Placing the Cuban Community in 1970s South Florida

After more than a decade of Cuban arrivals in Miami, many in the city were taking stock of the changes caused by the exodus, the further changes it would bring, and the status of the Cubans in Dade County. A 1971 article by Juanita Greene predicted that by 1975, Cubans would constitute one quarter of Dade County residents. Estimates of the Cuban population in the county that year ranged between 225,000 and 261,000. Cubans represented between 17% and 22% of Dade County's population of 1,268,000 people, a number already surpassing the 15% of the population made up by African Americans. Within the Miami city limits, the concentrations of these two groups were more pronounced. The Cuban cluster around the Little Havana area accounted for about 80% of the population in the city's southwest. Of Miami's 335,000 residents, about 120,000 identified as Hispanic and most of this group was Cuban, constituting 36.3% of the city's population. The African American population constituted 23.7% of the population within the city. Greene noted that although together these populations made up 59% of the city population, the possibility of developing a coalition to control the city was remote because there was "poor communication" between the two groups. Another roadblock to this possible collaboration was the fact that relatively few of these Cubans had become American citizens. Between 1959 and June of 1970, 50,505 Cubans in the United States had become citizens. This number was set to increase rapidly, however, given that more than a third of that group had become citizens between 1969 and 1971.[7]

The following year, reporter Roberto Fabricio outlined the results of a survey that the *Herald* had conducted among Miami's Cuban population. The Cubans, the headline read, were "at Home, But Homesick" in Dade County. The survey of six hundred Cuban-born residents showed that 79% of respondents indicated that they would like to return and live permanently in Cuba, but only 59% believed that the political climate would change enough to enable them to do so. An overwhelming majority, 94%, stated that Castro would have to be overthrown and socialism eradicated before they would even consider returning.[8]

The survey also showed that while most Dade County Cubans had yet to naturalize, those who had naturalized were very active in electoral politics. Of the 25% of Dade County Cubans who had naturalized by 1972, 89% were registered to vote, compared to 71% of the general population. Among Cuban registered voters, 53% were registered Republicans and 40% were Democrats, with 7% remaining independents. Despite the fact that this was a much more even split than the internal conversations among Dade County Democrats suggested, the survey indicated that 84% of respondents were planning to vote for Richard Nixon. One respondent indicated he would be voting reluctantly for George McGovern, whom he held as an extremist, out of loyalty to the Democratic Party. This respondent refused to identify himself in the article "because it is a touchy thing in the community."[9]

Another "touchy" subject in the community was the division between those who wanted to see the United States reestablish diplomatic relations with the Cuban government and those who vehemently opposed any sort of engagement. Only 20% of respondents wanted to see the American embassy reopen in Havana, either to surveil Castro's government or to get humanitarian aid to their loved ones more easily. The overwhelming majority of respondents, 75%, opposed reopening the embassy.[10]

The survey also provided evidence that resettled Cubans were returning to Miami after spending time elsewhere. Of the 70% of respondents who indicated that they had been in the United States for six years or longer, only 60% of them had been in Miami the entire time.[11] Social scientists were also studying this phenomenon. Writing for *Ideal* magazine in 1973, sociologist

Juan Clark estimated that 24.7% of the Cuban population in Miami Metro had returned from resettlement. Entitled "¿Donde viven los Cubanos?" (Where do the Cubans live?), Clark's article utilized data from the 1970 census and showed that close to 91% of the Cuban population of the Greater Miami area lived in three discrete areas: Little Havana, the area surrounding Little Havana, and Hialeah. The greatest concentration was within the city limits of Miami, specifically in Little Havana and this area accounted for 56% of the Cuban population. The areas surrounding Little Havana were home to close to one fifth of the Cuban population in the Greater Miami area, while Hialeah was home to 12% of the Cuban population. Of those Cubans who had returned to Miami from resettlement, the greatest concentration settled in the area around Little Havana, where returnees constituted almost one third of the area's Cuban residents, compared to 26% in Hialeah and 25% in Little Havana.[12]

Clark's data also suggested that an outward migration from Little Havana was a product of increased stays by Cubans in the United States. Over 80% of the Cubans in the peripheral area had arrived in the United States prior to 1965, comparted to 70% in Hialeah and 63% of those in Little Havana. The greatest concentration of post-1965 Cubans lived in Little Havana. Economic pull factors likely played a part in drawing Cubans away from that region. In the case of the returnees, 22.7% of those living in the periphery of Little Havana reported that the creation of a business or some other economic opportunity had drawn them to that area. There was also a level of correlation between the spatial placement of the Cubans and their immigration and naturalization statuses. Those Cubans in Little Havana's periphery had the greatest proportion of citizens, at 48%. In Hialeah, 54.5% of Cubans were residents but only 23.4% had become citizens, and in Little Havana almost half the Cubans were residents but only 26% had become citizens.[13] The available data suggests that as refugees transitioned into residency and citizenship and into greater affluence, many moved away from the immediate vicinity of Little Havana's ethnic enclave without straying too far from the rest of their community.

By the mid-1970s, the economic fortunes of Miami's Cuban population continued to improve despite the shifting economic climate in the nation. A 1974 study by the Strategy Research Corporation found that Dade County's Latinos and Latinas had nearly doubled their annual income in four years and had become a "dynamic force in promoting the [county's] economic health." The total annual income of this population had increased from $612.7 million in 1970 to $1.1 billion in 1974. The median income for Latino and Latina families had also increased from $7,200 to $9,912 a year, and the unemployment rate for male household heads was 1.1% compared to the 4.9% countywide unemployment. While the study was not specific to Miami's Cubans, the city's Latino and Latina population remained largely Cuban. The report also noted a population increase of almost 50%, from 299,217 in 1970 to 448,200 in 1974. The Freedom Flights had stopped in 1973, and the Strategic Research Corporation attributed a major part of the population increase to the return to Miami of families that had previously resettled to other areas of the country.[14]

Even as the economic fortunes of the general Cuban population and the other groups from Latin America that called Miami home were improving, the community's economic elite were also growing more formidable. The 1970s were a particularly pivotal moment for power brokers such as former RECE member Jorge Mas Canosa. When he joined RECE in the mid-1960s, Mas Canosa was a veteran of Brigade 2506 and of the U.S. Army and had been working in Miami as a milkman.[15] After gaining experience in fundraising, lobbying U.S. lawmakers, and funding anti-Castro paramilitary groups, he returned to Miami in 1968 to pursue new business ventures. In 1969, the owners of a Puerto Rican telephone infrastructure company operating in the continental United States under the name Church and Tower offered Mas Canosa half the shares of their operations there if he could improve the outfit's performance. Mas Canosa agreed and was successful enough that by 1971 he bought the remaining shares from the original owners. In doing so, he became the sole owner of what would become, in time, a multibillion-dollar technology and telecommunications company.[16]

Mas Canosa's rapid rise in economic circles was not, by any means, typical of the Cuban refugee experience, but neither was it unique. Cubans had so ingrained themselves into Miami's business and financial communities that by mid-1973, editor Luis Fernández Walpole was running a new periodical, a magazine called *Bancos y Economia* (Banks and economy). While the magazine described itself as "The Interamerican Economics Magazine," Fernández Walpole chose stories that positively portrayed the economic contribution of the Cuban community to South Florida. The first issue of the publication, dated June 1973, contained articles that drew attention to successful Cubans. The articles had titles such as, "Banks Run by Cubans Make Way in Dade County" and "Manuel Balado: An Exemplary Cuban," and the magazine was supported by advertising from multiple Cuban-owned businesses including radio station WFAB, "La Fabulosa."[17]

The staff of *Bancos y Economia* sought to serve the larger Spanish-speaking community of South Florida and showed clear ambitions of finding an audience among Latin American investors, but it always maintained a heavy interest in Cuban American affairs. In November of 1974, for example, the magazine ran a cover story endorsing the candidacy of Puerto Rican businessman Maurice Ferré, who would become Miami's first Hispanic mayor and the first U.S. mayor born in Puerto Rico. This was immediately followed by a story entitled. "Cuban Bankers in Miami's Wall Street."[18] Another issue included a full-page pictorial of Carlos Arboleya, Jorge L. Martínez, Orlando Baro, Carlos García Vélez, Daniel Loris, and Rafael Quintana with no other information save for their professional affiliations and the title, "Six Cuban Bank Presidents."[19] While the focus on Cubans who had reached high levels of success in Miami's banking industry might seem self-congratulatory, the profiles of these figures and even the pictures of the Cuban bank presidents also served a purpose for aspiring small business owners. While many refugees had had time to establish a work and credit history in the United States, the practice of character loans, which had been so crucial in the 1960s, had left an impression on the Cuban community. While it was never stated outright in the pages of *Bancos y Economia*, these profiles could serve as signposts to Cubans reading the publication to learn which banks to patronize and which might be more sympathetic in providing a loan. The focus on the top-earning Cubans in South Florida's finance sector could be useful to refugees as individuals and small business owners in the area.[20]

Gobierno, Negocios, y Educación: Bilingualism, Representation, and Polarization in Miami

The economic contributions of the Cuban community, along with the needs of all Hispanics to navigate government services, would become significant factors in one of the most divisive issues of the 1970s in South Florida: bilingualism. In 1972, a group of Cuban residents began a movement to have Dade County officially declared bilingual to help the more than one hundred thousand Dade County residents who spoke only Spanish. Cuban banker Bernardo Benes, one of the movement's advocates, charged that local government had failed the needs of this group whereas private businesses had met them. Another member, Luis Botifol, stated that the possible legalization of two languages would be a positive addition and not an imposition on any other group.[21]

The *Herald* tested the assertions made by bilingual services advocates by calling 83 taxpayer-supported agencies and asking in Spanish "Do you speak Spanish, please?" Reporter Chuck Gomez found that 13 of those agencies had bilingual personnel who could be of assistance, 17 had personnel who spoke Spanish but were "of no real help," 28 had personnel who spoke English but tried to help as best as they could, and 25 had personnel who were curt and hung up. When Gomez called Hialeah City Hall, he found no Spanish-speaking operators despite the high number of Cuban families in the area. He had the following conversation with the operator who answered his call, as published in the *Herald*:

"City Hall, May I help you, please?"
"Si, senora usted habla espanol [sic], por favor?"
(Indignant) "Speak English."
"Me no speak English."
"Well don't call here if you can't . . ." Click.

While the Hialeah operator might have been particularly rude, the most worrying exchange occurred when Gomez called the South Miami Fire Department and was told, "I'm sorry, you don't understand me and I don't understand you. There's nothing I can do for you." Gomez contrasted these interactions with the steps taken by for-profit entities, mentioning the Spanish-language information hotline set up by Eastern Airlines and the bilingual crew of sales associates at Southern Bell's business office. When he questioned a Southern Bell representative about the establishment of this team, the company's spokesperson declared the practice to be "good business."[22]

The establishment of this good business practice had required some prodding. Just the previous year, Benes had contacted Southern Bell's Florida management to address a company policy that prohibited their staff from speaking in Spanish.[23] Benes and other Cubans addressed the shortfalls of Southern Bell's practices often to pressure the company into the changes it would eventually make. They pressured not only Southern Bell, but also other companies and entities in South Florida to increase the availability of bilingual services. By January of 1973, some in Miami's Spanish language press were decrying any restriction on the use of Spanish as a violation of the equal protection clause of the U.S. Constitution.[24] This emphasis on bilingualism illustrated not only the powerful drive toward local activism of many of Miami's Cubans but also their growing economic and political power. The solution they sought from local government would be the recognition of that influence.

On April 16, 1973, the Dade County Board of County Commissioners passed Resolution 502-73 declaring Dade County a bilingual and bicultural county. County Commissioner Harry Cain called on Bernardo Benes to present the resolution after having worked with the commission for almost a year in its creation.[25] Benes addressed the commissioners and clearly stated that voting for the resolution did not support any sort of progressive agenda but rather reflected Miami's reality, that Dade was already a bicultural county.[26] The resolution declared Dade County "legally, morally and historically obligated to aid our Spanish-speaking population in achieving the goals they have traveled so very far to share," specifically citing the difficulties the county's Spanish-speaking population had in communicating with government agencies and their staff. While the resolution stated that many among this population had retained the language and culture of their native lands, the drafted language made it clear that this was not just a humanitarian gesture, but recognition of something owed to the city's Hispanic community. The resolution recognized that the county's Spanish-speaking population had earned the right to be serviced and heard at all levels of government through its "ever increasing share of the tax burden, and active participation in community affairs." The Board of County Commissioners, which did not include a single Latino or Latina, then voted unanimously, with one absence, to declare Dade County bilingual and bicultural. The county would adopt Spanish as its second official language and create a department called the "Division of Bilingual and Bicultural Affairs" under the office of the county manager to implement the resolution.[27]

A significant crowd of Spanish-speaking residents attended the vote. They celebrated the passage of the resolution, rising to a standing ovation when Commissioner Harvey Ruvin answered "si" to the roll call vote. While the attendees were excited about the vote's outcome, the officials were not certain what the ramifications would be of the resolution they had just adopted. When asked what the resolution meant, its sponsor, Mayor Jack Orr, confessed he really did not know. "But we'll almost certainly have all (street and office) signs printed in both English and Spanish," Orr continued, "and have bilingual people in all the government offices." Many suspected that the resolution would be largely symbolic, but it was a positive step for those who had campaigned for it.[28] County officials embraced the vote in good faith and took steps to carry out the resolution. By late May, a task force of county employees had been created to plan and monitor the resolution's implementation. This

task force consisted of five employees representing some of the major Hispanic groups in Dade County: three Cuban Americans, one Puerto Rican,
and one Mexican American.[29]

Not all Dade residents welcomed the passage of the resolution. The *Herald's* editorial board, having grown increasingly confrontational with the
city's Cuban community, came out against the resolution two days after its
passage. The board expressed concerns about the cost to taxpayers and the
effect it would have on community cohesiveness. *Herald* reporters had covered the difficulties of Spanish speakers in obtaining public services, but the
board now suggested that residents speaking either Spanish or English had
been "getting along well for years." They argued that the issue of bilingualism
should not be addressed through legislation as it risked "translating the de
facto situation into a de jure complication."[30] The piece drew a rebuke from
Bernardo Benes, who argued that the resolution would change the minds of
those who were supposed to be serving the population as a whole, but who
had failed the county's Spanish speakers.[31]

While the bilingual ordinance appeared to be a decisive victory for
Dade's Spanish-speaking population, Cubans and other Hispanics reported
that its passage had inflamed anti-Cuban sentiment. They listed the reasons
for this animosity as "the increased militancy Cubans are assuming in local
matters especially when faced with discrimination; a greater awareness that
their presence is no longer temporary; envy or resentment over their economic success and fear of being displaced by bilingual people." There was
also a belief that Dade County's liberals and Democratic political power
structure were also threatened by a population they saw as more conservative and more likely to register Republican. When reached for comment by
a reporter, Benes cautioned that polarization was so bad that it might reach
a point of open confrontation. Even as he made this dire prediction, Benes
highlighted the positive steps taken by Miami Metro's government, noting
that the percentage of Hispanics hired by the county had almost doubled in
two years, from 6% to 10%.[32]

Not all Cuban Americans were as conciliatory as Benes, particularly when
it came to the Metro's government and school systems. Seeing a need for
activism on behalf of Miami's Spanish-speaking community, several community activists created the Spanish American League against Discrimination
(SALAD) in 1973 to stop "slanderous attacks" against Miami's Hispanic community and ensure greater participation in local politics and society. In 1975,
SALAD formally accused the two largest employers in the area, the public

school system and Miami Metro's government, of unfair hiring practices. The slow increase in hiring by these two entities, when compared to the significant growth of Miami's Spanish-speaking minorities, led SALAD chairman Javier Bray to the "inescapable conclusion" that the public sector was "systematically excluding and discriminating against Latins." SALAD members pointed to the Dade County School System's own figures, which showed that while 27% of the county's students were of Hispanic origin, this group accounted for only 12% of school administration staff and 7% of teachers.[33]

Miami's Anglophone residents had their own grievances against the city's Hispanic community generally, and toward the Cubans, who still represented close to 90% of that population, specifically. One of the most significant grievance regarded the hiring of Spanish-speaking people in Miami's tourist industry. The growing need for Spanish-speaking employees to work in department stores, restaurants, hotels, and airlines resulted in claims of "reverse discrimination."[34] These businesses, however, sought to hire those employees out of a concern with their bottom line. In 1978, the chairman and chief executive officer of the Burdines Department Store chain, Richard McEwen, wrote a letter in support of the implementation of bilingual education. There he explained that several of his stores did "extensive business" with Spanish-speaking tourists, noting that some days the Burdines in downtown Miami did 50% of its business with tourists buying in high quantity. He remarked that Costa Rica Airlines had, in the past, had three daily flights to Mexico City for shoppers, but in the aftermath of the Cuban influx, those flights had been diverted to Miami. Affluent tourists could now come to the city and shop in their own language.[35] McEwen did not offer exact figures in his letter, but the year he wrote the letter, Miami saw five hundred thousand Latin American visitors who spent, on average, over a thousand dollars each in the city.[36]

Despite the increasing importance of trade and tourism from Latin America to Miami's economy and the calls from business leaders for more bilingual staff, one of the most cited wedge issues between the Spanish-speaking communities and the English-speaking communities in Miami was bilingual education in Dade County public schools. Opponents complained about having to subsidize a program primarily for Cuban children through their taxes. In 1962, Miami's Coral Way Elementary School was the site of the first federally funded bilingual program in the postwar era (see Figure 9).[37] However, by 1975, of the over one hundred public schools in Dade County, only four were fully bilingual. Students at these schools took half their classes in Spanish and half in English. Eight other schools were nearly bilingual, and

Figure 9. Children attending a bilingual education program at Riverside Elementary School in 1965. In the 1970s, the Cuban American community sought to make this type of bilingual education standard for all children in Miami. Courtesy of the Cuban Heritage Collection, University of Miami Libraries.

the remaining schools had some manner of bilingual program. Most had classes including English for Spanish-speaking students, Spanish as a foreign language, and Spanish for Spanish-speaking students. In late 1974, a member of the Dade County school board named Linton Tyler had put forth a motion that would have stopped any further expansion of the bilingual program and instead would have intensified the English instruction of Spanish-speaking students. Tyler's motion failed, but the controversy over bilingual education did not cease.[38]

Tyler continued to argue that the bilingual education program was both expensive and inefficient and that any expansion would simply compound the program's failure. Miami city commissioner Manolo Reboso wrote Tyler and suggested that there was a greater enthusiasm for the program than its critics suggested. Given that enrollment in Spanish classes in the first through sixth grades was voluntary, an enrollment of thirty-two thousand American children spoke to the interest and enthusiasm of English-speaking parents. He also cited statistics showing that continued Spanish-language instruction helped native speakers of both Spanish and English score higher in English-language reading comprehension tests. Reboso conceded that there were costs associated with the program, but the demographics of Dade County made it essential. This was true not only for the 54% of Miami's population that was Hispanic, or for the 516,000 Spanish speakers in broader Dade County, but also for native speakers of English. Bilingual education would allow English native speakers "to compete on an equal basis with bilingual Latins on the job market and cultural differences will not be the source of friction, misunderstanding and hostility."[39] Miami's economy had changed so fundamentally that the lack of Spanish language skills was potentially a greater obstacle for employment than not speaking English.

Despite the support of the city's business community, the advocates for bilingual education were ultimately unsuccessful in persuading the school board to make Spanish instruction mandatory for all students. Many among Dade's Cuban Americans saw this as a slight against their community. Others were less troubled. The *Herald*'s editorial board had supported Tyler's proposal from the outset, deeming it "A Sane Approach to Bi-Lingualism."[40] This opinion did not help the widening rift between the city's largest newspaper and Dade's Cubans. The *Herald* fully recognized the reality of the changes to Miami's demographics and the importance of the Spanish-speaking market. This led to the creation in 1976 of *El Miami Herald*, a Spanish-language newspaper under the *Herald*'s corporate umbrella. The newspaper's editorial direction, however, left much to be desired according to many in the Cuban community and *El Herald* remained largely an appendage of the parent publication.

Open Letters, Unbearable Insults: Cubans, "the Establishment," and the *Herald* in Polarized Miami

The increasing animosity between the Herald and the Cuban community is representative of the ongoing struggles between traditional power structures in Miami and an empowered group now demanding that their needs be prioritized by those groups and institutions that had traditionally held power in the city. In 1978, the *Miami Herald*'s executive editor, John McMullan, attempted to address the animosity between his newspaper and the Cuban community in Miami when he wrote a piece entitled, "Open Letter to My

Cuban Friends." McMullan referred to the cultural and economic contributions of the Cubans to Greater Miami before addressing an August meeting
of Cuban American leaders on several "unbearable insults" to the community. Such insults included the failure to make bilingual education mandatory
and the increasingly confrontational stances of the *Herald* itself. McMullan
invoked an anonymous Cuban friend who impugned other Cubans who had
forgotten that they came to the city as refugees and that they had been granted
significant opportunities. This unnamed Cuban charged that these ungrate-
ful members of the community now sought to exploit polarization. McMullan pushed this critique further, arguing that it was time for his anonymous
friend and others in the "silent majority of decent law-abiding family-loving
Cubans" to counter these opportunists by getting involved in community life
beyond the area's economic and cultural life.[41]

McMullan not only accused Cubans of being insular and congregating
exclusively in Cuban organizations, but he charged them with now being discriminatory to other groups. He argued that the community, once discriminated against, had grown discriminatory once they had integrated into the
city's power structure. McMullan defended the *Herald* by claiming it was not
discriminatory or anti-Cuban, but rather that the paper's staff was trying to
carry out a responsibility to the total community, "to our black, Anglo, Wasp,
and Jewish populations and to you new Latin members as well." If a problem
existed, it was not with the *Herald*'s fair and fearless work, but rather with the
"silent majority" of Cubans, who let the "opportunists" have too much sway.
The responsible Cubans who failed to run for public office or engage with the
community needed to step up and face the part of the community that felt
that "the only way to achieve desirable goals is through polarization."[42] This
would, presumably, produce more positive coverage by the *Herald*, or at the
very least, a less contentious Cuban leadership.

McMullan's piece, not surprisingly, drew rebukes from the Cuban community. One letter writer declared that the assertion that it was the Cuban community that was causing the polarization required "a great deal of bad faith at
best and naiveté at worst." The author, Julio Castano, wrote that naivete would
be novel as he was accustomed to bad faith from the *Herald*. Castano, however, had little interest in defending the Cuban leaders McMullan impugned.
In fact, he blamed their presence on people like McMullan who represented
"the Establishment."[43] Regardless of whether Castano was referring to the
city's establishment or the federal government, he had a point. The advocacy

of the city's elites, including the *Herald*, had set the stage for a federal intervention that had bolstered the fortunes of many of those in Cuban politics. McMullan had a reason to dislike some Cuban American voices, but his piece was largely intended to excuse the reluctance of traditional power structures to share power with the Cuban community.

Other Cuban voices denounced both McMullan and the perception of an attempted Cuban takeover of Miami. In a scathing editorial, radio station W-QBA, "La Cubanisima," declared McMullan's letter nothing more than a way to cover up the *Herald*'s past and future mistakes. The editorial denied the existence of "Cuban-only" organizations, claiming that even the most militant Cuban exile group would welcome U.S.-born members. If, however, such organizations did exist, it was because the Cuban community had suffered years of isolation and discrimination at the hands of "the Establishment," which here was defined as a collective group of Americans who had antagonized the Cuban community because of the "absurd thesis of 'take over,'" referring to the idea that the Cubans sought all political power in Dade County for themselves. The editorial then charged that members of the Establishment did not reflect the reality of the city of Miami and neither did the *Herald* as this group's mouthpiece. Miami was a city where 60% of the population was Spanish speaking, and a majority of those Spanish speakers were Cuban. How could the newspaper call itself the *Miami Herald* if it had no Cubans in its upper echelons?[44] "La Cubanisima" was calling out an entrenched city establishment by asking how much they represented the city at all.

McMullan almost certainly expected such reactions, but he also likely hoped to make use of the cleavages within the Cuban community. The *Herald* been seen by many Cubans as an antagonist for a long time. McMullan, as a member of a secret "Non-Group" of Cuban and Anglo leaders hoping to address polarization in the city knew this reputation well.[45] Nevertheless, as a member of this group, he also understood the divisions within the community as well. McMullan had hoped the cleavages in the community would make certain Cubans receptive to his message and that it might possibly draw out leaders with whom older groups and institutions could work more easily. The problem of polarization was not resolved in the 1970s and it grew worse in the 1980s. McMullan's call did not bring about any easy solutions. While political and generational divides existed within the Cuban community, they drove significant battles within the community and did not fuel the groundswell for which McMullan hoped.

Embracing Citizenship: The Cultural and
Policy Battles over Naturalization

The growing number of Cubans choosing to naturalize as American citizens drove one of the significant divides within the community in the 1970s. Despite the passage of the Cuban Adjustment Act in 1966, the number of Cubans in Dade County who had become citizens remained relatively low. In 1973, Juan Clark found that U.S. citizens constituted 36.4% of the Cuban population, while permanent residents made up 45.2%, and those with refugee status came to 18.5%. When he polled those Cubans who had not become American citizens, his respondents fell into three categories regarding plans to become naturalized citizens:

No plans to become a citizen	20.6%
Does not know	35.3%
Planning to become a citizen	44.1%[46]

Becoming an American citizen allowed Cubans to have a say in the politics of their adopted home and allowed them greater agency in solidifying the economic and social gains made by their community. A majority of Clark's non-citizen respondents, however, did not know if they would become American citizens or had absolutely no plans to do so. This was part of a larger debate among Cubans, both in private spaces and in the media. Those who were opposed to becoming citizens often complained about schools making their children pledge allegiance to the U.S. flag.[47] For many Cubans, to become an American citizen meant to abandon the cause of a free Cuba in favor of their adopted home.

As the 1970s wore on and more Cubans chose naturalization, the divide between those who embraced citizenship and those who did not was often generational. When questioned about the greatest challenge to the Cuban community in Miami, Bryan Walsh suggested that it was the fact that Cuban children were not "Cuban in the sense that their parents were Cuban. Neither are they American in the sense that American children are. They are a mixture of both cultures." He warned that the reaction of the Cuban community to this fact would determine if there would be conflict or a drawing together of the best of both cultures.[48] This did not always mean that Cuban children were more inherently Americanized than their parents. The debate on whether to become an American citizen was part of a larger debate about what it meant to be Cuban. The work of historian María Cristina García shows how college students wrestled with issues of identity and national allegiance. Many of them had left Cuba as teenagers and they were keenly aware of how they inhabited a liminal space between cultures. Some elected to adopt a stauncher Cuban nationalism than that of their parents and they castigated older members of the community for forfeiting their ideals.[49] Others saw no intrinsic problem with becoming American citizens. Some professionals saw immense benefits in becoming citizens, which was often a necessary step in returning to their chosen fields, while others simply had resigned themselves to a lengthy stay in the United States and had developed a loyalty toward their adopted home that they did not see as incompatible with their loyalty to Cuba.[50]

The tension between parents and children in the Cuban community over citizenship and the opportunities it presented was a common enough situation to be portrayed in the popular, Miami-produced situation comedy ¿Qué pasa, U.S.A.? Premiering in 1977, ¿Qué pasa, U.S.A.? was the first situation comedy produced for the Public Broadcasting Service (PBS) and the first bilingual situation comedy produced in the United States. Set in Little Havana, the show portrayed the everyday life and struggles of a multigenerational Cuban family in the United States. The series won six regional Emmy awards and nine special awards from the Association of Critics and Commentators on the Arts, and it was named "Freshest T.V. Series" for 1978 by *Nuestro* magazine. Despite being about a Cuban family and entirely bilingual, the program's appeal went beyond South Florida. ¿Qué pasa, U.S.A.? was shown by 126 PBS stations in thirty-four states, covering most major television markets and several smaller ones. The program was successful enough to warrant a limited partnership between showrunner Luis Santeiro and United Cinema Enterprises in the early 1980s to explore the possibility of producing a film entitled *Family Secrets*, which would have had a similar storyline and would have used many of the same actors from the show in new roles.[51]

Between 1977 and 1980, ¿Qué Pasa, U.S.A.? detailed the comedic adventures of the Peña family, composed of the Spanish-speaking grandparents, the bilingual parents, and the mostly English-speaking children, living in the United States and facing situations common to immigrants from Latin America and specific to the Cuban community. The show's pilot, "La Fiesta de Quince," introduced the show's format, whereby the characters communicated with one another freely using both English and Spanish. To make the show accessible to English speakers, the creators gave Carmen, the Peñas' daughter and the only member of the household to be born in the United States, a friend named Sharon. Sharon spoke no Spanish and could be counted on to ask questions about what was going on in any Spanish-language exchange. The program illustrated the way in which the Peña children straddled both cultures. In the pilot, Joe, the Peñas' son, expresses his frustration over how his sister's "fiesta de los quince" might hinder his plans to join the popular clique at school. He explains that he feels pushed and pulled between American and Cuban cultures: he is Cuban at home but American at school.[52]

This push and pull became a running theme in the show. In the eleventh episode, "TV Interview," the Peñas excitedly gather to watch a television reporter interview Joe for a story on Cuban students and how they feel about living in the United States. Joe speaks about having lived in the United States. since the age of three and about how he feels "pretty American" but also "very Cuban." Joe's comedic blunders begin as he explains the culture shock of going from interacting with his classmates to interacting with his grandparents, who not only are having trouble accepting life in the United States, but also with accepting "life in this century!" Joe then portrays his parents as both thankful to be in the United States and critical of the country's problems. He then gets his family into trouble with the rest of their community by declaring his parents relatively progressive in relation to most Cuban parents, who keep repeating themselves "like broken records" when talking about how much better everything was in Cuba. After a neighbor tells Pepe that the Cuban community has declared his son is a disgrace, Pepe threatens to sue the television station. The reporter offers a follow-up interview to the whole family and to a suspicious Sharon, who rightly notes that the reporter just wants her to be the "token Anglo" for his "inter-cultural pals" angle. The rest of the episode uses cultural and generational shenanigans to look at issues like the Cuban focus on an idealized memory of Cuba and the backlash from U.S.-born neighbors before resetting the status quo in classic sitcom style.[53]

Not all conflicts were so easily resolved, as when the show tackled naturalization. The program's fifteenth episode, entitled "Naturalization," starts with Pepe explaining to Carmen that the home improvement projects he is engaging in are not meant to signal any permanence in Miami. "Nosotros estamos en Miami de pasada" (We are just passing through Miami), he tells her. Juana, Pepe's wife, finds a bottle of champagne as she cleans out the kitchen cabinets. Pepe explains that he had purchased the bottle in 1962 and is saving it for their return to Cuba. Conflict arises when Joe comes home and recounts how he has learned that many college scholarships require U.S. citizenship.

As a minor, he needs one of his parents to become a citizen first, which Pepe refuses to do, saying he is not ready to become a "gringo." Carmen notes that she is an American citizen, but Pepe insists that her birth in the United States was an accident; she was meant to be born in Cuba. Father and son clash over the desire to become an American citizen until Pepe tells Joe that he is "a traitor to the name of José Manuel Peña," which is his name as well as that of his father, grandfather, and great-grandfather before him.[54]

Pepe becomes even more agitated when Adela and Antonio, his wife's parents, reveal that they have also decided to naturalize in order to gain the vote. Joe notes that Pepe is always pontificating abut the fact that people have no say under communism, but as long as Pepe cannot vote, he does not really have a say in the United States either. Juana informs Pepe she will help Joe get a scholarship, even if it means becoming an American citizen. Later Juana and Joe write and perform a song titled, "Y Vamos Caminando" (And we walk on), which encapsulates the conflict:

JUANA: A donde van las costumbres
me tengo que preguntar,
supongo que el tiempo las cambia
como cambia la orilla del mar,
los viejos las cultivan,
los jóvenes buscan razón,
y lo que una vez fue exilio
se convierte en emigración.

(Where do customs go?
I must ask myself,
I suppose time changes them
as the shoreline changes,
the elderly cultivate them,
the young seek a reason,
and what was once exile
becomes immigration.)

JOE: How can I yearn for what I hardly knew?
How can I feel the same way you do?
I don't remember what I didn't live.
What I never had I cannot give.

JUANA: Y vamos caminando
el tiempo va pasando
los niños van creciendo
los viejos muriendo
y los soñadores—se van cansando.

(And we go walking
and time goes on
children grow
the old die
and the dreamers—grow tired.)

JOE: You miss the past and want a world that's gone.
There's nothing there for me and I must move on.
and try my best to find a way
to live in the world we have today.

BOTH: Y vamos caminando
el tiempo va pasando
los niños van creciendo
los viejos muriendo
y los soñadores—se van cansando.[55]

The episode closes with a discussion between Pepe and Juana during which she asks him if he really means that he will never become an American citizen. Pepe replies that he never said that, but as he holds his champagne bottle, he states that if he ever becomes an American citizen he will buy another bottle, as the one he has is for Cuba. The original script called for Juana to lightly knock on Pepe's head to indicate that he's *cabezón* (stubborn), before ending the episode with a kiss between the couple. The version that made it to air, however, saw Pepe leave the room after telling his wife that the bottle of champagne was for Cuba and Juana watching him leave before moving to a different part of the house herself.[56]

The broadcast ending reflected the more somber tone of ultimately making the decision to become an American citizen. Naturalization was central to the tensions within the Cuban American community, between embracing an exilic dream of a post-Castro Cuba and becoming full members of American society. It could become a source of division between families and friends.

Between those Cubans who sought an investment in their immediate future and those who clung to an idealized past and a hoped-for future on the island. Even those who chose to naturalize often had doubts about the decision and experienced nostalgia for Cuba. On July 4, 1978, 2,141 new citizens took the Oath of Allegiance of the United States in a mass naturalization ceremony at the Miami Beach Convention Center. Following the ceremony, one Cuban woman explained the mixed feelings that the ceremony elicited. "This is a day of great joy, but also of great sadness for me," Normal Suárez de Alvariño told a reporter; "But in the end, we have to think of the future, because the past is gone." These new Cuban American citizens sought to fully participate in and embrace their adopted country while still holding on to their roots. Another new citizen expressed her joy at becoming an American but also remarked sadly that during the ceremony, she thought quite a bit about her homeland. When asked why they became American citizens, respondents provided largely practical reasons. Some explained that citizenship brought about full rights and participation in American society, with the right to vote coming to the forefront.[57]

A significant portion of the Cuban community was ambivalent toward citizenship or was actively antagonistic to the choice, but others sought to make the naturalization process easier for Cubans. Despite the passage of the Cuban Adjustment Act almost a decade earlier, by the mid-1970s some politically powerful Cuban Americans had grown concerned that bureaucratic roadblocks were slowing down the process of exile stabilization, often by years. In advance of a meeting in December of 1975, the Florida chair of the Republican National Hispanic Assembly, José Manuel Casanova, wrote a letter to President Ford regarding the plight of these refugees. Casanova stated that Cuban refugees that hoped to become citizens had been delayed by periods of three to four years. Casanova assumed that "reduced staffing and some feet dragging" by the Immigration and Naturalization Service were to blame. It was in the best interest of the United States and of the Cuban American community that the refugees "be absorbed at an accelerated rate into the mainstream of the American system." The Republican National Hispanic Assembly recommended that the president issue an executive order to the Immigration and Naturalization Service to expedite the method of processing U.S. residence applications of Cubans living in the United States as well as those of Cuban U.S. residents seeking citizenship. They also asked the president to promote legislation to move Cuban refugees already living in the United States to resident status with minimum paperwork.[58]

The Ford administration was under pressure from the Republican National Hispanic Assembly (RNHA) on other issues at the same time, including greater participation by Hispanics in positions of authority in the federal government.[59] Casanova was also seeking a firm statement that would "end speculation on coexistence [sic] with the Cuban communist government within the foreseable [sic] future."[60] With an election year looming, President Ford instructed his staff to investigate the exact nature of these delays and what could be done through executive action. The problem lay in obtaining Permanent Resident Alien visas. Despite the passage of the Cuban Adjustment Act, refugees were still subject to the limitations on such visas that had been established by Congress. Each year a maximum of 120,000 visas were available to people born in Western Hemisphere countries, which were provided on a first-come, first-served basis.[61] This limitation was creating a backlog among the refugees attempting to establish their residency of seventy thousand applications.[62]

President Ford was eager for a solution he could enact to gain the solid support of RNHA, but officials in the administration were skeptical about the power of the executive branch to affect the backlog.[63] By February 1976, the administration had planned to issue an executive order to ensure that Cuban adjustments did not count against the Western Hemisphere quotas and requested a legal opinion from the assistant attorney general at the Office of Legal Counsel, Antonin Scalia.[64] While awaiting the Office of Legal Counsel's opinion, the president instructed the attorney general to take any necessary action, administrative or legislative, to assure that Cuban refugees could attain permanent resident status without the delays caused by the immigration quota system.[65] In August of that year, Scalia produced a twenty-three-page legal opinion stating that it was within the law and the powers of the executive to order a change of policy by the Department of Justice.[66] The Immigration and Naturalization Service announced in September that Cuban refugees would no longer have to compete for places within the Western Hemisphere quota.[67] Coupled with the removal of the policy-level obstacle, the Ford administration also provided additional workers to the Miami offices of the Immigration and Naturalization Service (INS). Other INS offices handling a backlog of Cuban cases would not immediately receive an increase in labor, despite similar backlogs.[68] This is unsurprising, given that the original request had come from politically powerful and well-connected South Florida Cubans.

The Ford administration was particularly keen on courting the Cuban American political leadership in South Florida in the run-up to the 1976 presidential election, given the actions of the man challenging him in the GOP primary. In December of 1975, within a week of Casanova's request to the White House, Ronald Reagan publicly met with deposed Panamanian president Arnulfo Arias and members of the Cuban American community. He wanted to build up his foreign policy bona fides and potentially win the support of the Cuban American community in Florida.[69] Ford had some cause to be concerned about Cuban American support after Secretary of State Henry Kissinger declared his support for lifting the Cuban embargo if the rest of the Organization of American States voted in favor of this action.[70] While Ford would win the nomination in 1976, he lost badly among Cuban Americans in Florida's Republican primary, obtaining only 29% of the vote to Reagan's 71%. By April of 1976, Ford's campaign was concerned about the fifty thousand votes Carter could take from Ford because of a lack of attention to the Cuban community.[71] Ultimately, Ford lost Dade County, the state of Florida, and the Oval Office in the 1976 presidential election.

Diplomacy or Treason?: The Thaw
and Backlash of "El Dialogo"

During the campaign, Jimmy Carter had exacerbated tensions in the Cuban American community by stating that he might improve American relations with Cuba "on a measured reciprocal basis."[72] There had been discussions of coexistence with Castro's regime during the Ford administration. Casanova had written a position paper on behalf of the Florida members of the Republican National Hispanic Assembly and the Dade County Republican Executive Committee arguing against any sort of coexistence with Cuba. Casanova argued that if, in spite of the Cuban Republican arguments against it, the federal government decided that coexistence was to be enacted, it should "only be on our terms." Those terms were tantamount to a capitulation by Castro:

1. If Castro frees all political prisoners under supervision of the Red Cross (including 1,000 U.S. citizens).
2. If Castro declares himself publicly against all subversion in the Continent and vows not to support guerilla groups.
3. If all Russian, Chinese and foreign troops leave Cuba.

4. If free elections nationwide are conducted, with participation of Cuban refugees, and supervised by a satisfactory international body.
5. If free exit and access to Cuba by nationals as well as citizens of foreign nations are guaranteed.[73]

Casanova took it on himself to claim that Cuban Americans would not consider any sort of rapprochement with Castro's government. This sentiment had long been mutual. Since the start of the exile, Castro had taken every available chance to loudly denounce the *"gusanos"* (the worms), as he called those Cubans who had left after the revolution. As late as 1975, he had indicated that the exiles would never be forgiven for deserting their homeland and would never be allowed to return to the island.[74]

The extreme positions represented by Castro and Casanova did not encompass all Cuban Americans or all Cubans. For some young exiles, the tension between their adopted home in the United States and the need to assert their Cuban roots led to new directions in Cuban exile politics. In the mid-1970s, the Cuban government removed the visitation restriction from the exiled Cubans who had been under the age of eighteen when they left the island and granted visas, first in small numbers and then in larger blocs, to allow for visits by Cuban exile youth groups. These visits were controversial in both countries. Cuban American parents often vehemently opposed their children's return to Cuba, and visiting students were told to tell Cuban locals they were Puerto Rican because of the high politicization of the exile in the revolutionary discourse.[75]

The issuing of these visas was a sign of a measured, gradual thawing of relations between the United States and the Cuban government that had begun during the Ford administration. After Carter became president in 1977, the United States and Cuba took a step toward the resumption of normal diplomatic relations through the establishment of interest sections in Havana and Washington.[76] Both governments approached the establishment of relations cautiously. Federal officials were also concerned about the possibility of upsetting the Cuban community in the United States. Soon after Carter's inauguration, officials sought out Miami mayor Maurice Ferré and a Cuban American Democrat, Alfredo Durán, and asked them for advice on the issue. Durán made it clear that the Cuban community would be divided on the issue.[77]

Durán further cautioned them that a normalization of relations with Cuba could cause an increase in the already existing problem of terrorism in Miami.[78] While paramilitary organizations had remained active in their attempts to disrupt Castro's government through raids in and around Cuba, the years after the end of the Freedom Flights saw a marked increase in the violence perpetrated by exile groups upon those who they saw as enemies to their cause. Between 1973 and 1977 Cuban exile organizations and individuals, including Alpha 66 and Omega 7, had attempted or successfully executed ninety-two bombings.[79] In January of 1977, Dade County mayor Steve Clark and other local government officials signed a letter to President Carter asking for immediate investigation into the terrorism occurring in Dade County. While the people of South Florida saw this as a significant problem, the Justice Department indicated that FBI involvement was unlikely due to the lack of jurisdiction.[80]

The White House needed to shore up community support for any potential normalization and took any opportunity that presented itself. In late 1977, Alfredo Durán and the White House attempted to organize a meeting between national security advisor Zbigniew Brzezinski and "several younger and more progressive Cuban-Americans."[81] The administration also received news from Bernardo Benes that members of the special forces of the interior ministry of Cuba had approached him while he was in Panama in August of 1977.[82] Benes had links to the White House due to his close ties with the Carter campaign, for which he had served as Latin coordinator.[83] Benes was unsure as to why the interior ministry had approached him, but he made a logical contact for these agents as he had ties to the White House and was highly visible in Miami.[84] With the approval of Washington, Benes began a series of behind-the-scenes negotiations, returning to Cuba after eighteen years in exile and meeting with Fidel Castro several times.

Benes's trips and other back-channel negotiations led to serious discussions between the Cuban and American governments about greater rapprochement. In 1978, the Cubans wanted to appeal to Carter's interest in human rights by suggesting that their government should release political prisoners in exchange for certain concessions from the U.S. government. American officials were cautious but also hoped to obtain a reduction of the Cuban presence in Angola. They saw Castro's eagerness to negotiate as stemming from multiple concerns, ranging from economic problems to a psychological desire for the United States to acknowledge the revolution.[85] However, by September of that year, Castro's commitment to operations in Africa had slowed negotiations to a crawl.

Castro sought to outmaneuver the reluctant American officials by holding a press conference in front of Cuban American journalists in which he

invited the exile community to enter into a dialogue with the Cuban government on issues including the fate of political prisoners and a possible family
reunification program. Castro was careful to avoid the label of gusanos,
instead referring to "the Cuban community abroad." He asked Benes to bring
a group of Cuban Americans to Havana to discuss those issues in November
of 1978. Castro was eager to tap into the significant economic resources of the
exile community and to offset the international criticism of Cuba based on
its human rights record. The Carter administration was careful not to publicly involve itself with the dialogue beyond what was necessary, but it was
pleased with Castro's release of several political prisoners before the arrival of
the dialogue group.[86] Castro's invitation was unexpected. Most of the Cuban
American community was not aware of the secret negotiations between the
United States and Cuba and the sudden conciliatory gesture was both surprising and controversial, causing significant strife.[87]

Some people were supportive of the news and its possibilities. Alfredo
Durán spoke to administration officials, conveyed his enthusiasm about the
prisoner release, and urged them to move forward with normalization to
increase American influence over Castro. He also suggested to them that Carter's policy on Cuba was having a positive effect on the shift in support from
the Republican to the Democratic Party for the Cuban community in Florida.[88] Others were eager to go further. The members of the Antonio Maceo
Brigade, a group of young Cuban Americans who had previously visited the
island through the easing of visa restriction, pursued a more radical agenda,
which included the right of repatriation, the right to study in Cuba, and the
release of political prisoners.[89] Many others were eager to see the results of the
negotiations, hoping to see family members they had left behind years before.

However, many people directly opposed any possibility of negotiating
with Castro. Groups like Alpha 66 declared that any negotiation with Castro
was antithetical to the cause of a free Cuba. This caused some division, even
among Alpha 66 supporters. One woman wrote the leaders of the organization and explained that if the exile community refused to enter into a dialogue
with Castro, then it was giving him the entirety of the power in making the
decision on whether to release the political prisoners held in Cuban prisons.
To refuse to negotiate would create a vacuum that would necessarily then be
filled by the U.S. government, which would act in its own best interests to
enact a normalization with Cuba and with less regard for the Cuban American community and the political prisoners. By refusing to negotiate, they
were playing right into Castro's hands. "I want to state here," she wrote, "that

to refuse to negotiate with Castro at this moment is equivalent to POLITI-CAL SUICIDE by the exile." It was easy to deny Castro the dialogue in order to retain one's dignity, she argued, but that dignity would be better served through political action in the service of the larger cause.[90]

The trip was controversial, but it went on as scheduled. The dialogue took place over two sessions held in November and December of 1978 as 140 Cuban exiles returned to Havana for the event. Political scientist María de los Angeles Torres, then a member of the Antonio Maceo Brigade, met Cubans from throughout the United States representing a broad range of political leanings and social backgrounds.[91] Where Torres remembers diversity, Benes saw a delegation divided into factions that were suspicious of one another.[92] Benes was already feeling pressure for his role in the *dialogo* (dialogue) before he went to Havana and before the extent of his involvement in back-channel negotiations with Castro was revealed. He carried with him to Cuba pho-tographs of a group of about twenty organized picketers, including Alpha 66's Andrés Nazario Sargén, who began to protest daily in front of his bank, Continental National Bank of Miami. Castro laughed hysterically when he saw the photos, but Benes was not amused. He told Castro that it might seem funny in Havana but it was far less humorous to have the spectacle in front of his office every day.[93] The talks resulted in an agreement for the release of over three thousand political prisoners, for the authorization for current and formers prisoners to migrate to the United States with their families, for permission for those with family members in the United States to leave the island, and for approval for those who had left to visit Cuba.[94]

Although these developments seemed promising, they enraged a signifi-cant section of the Cuban American community. Many of Little Havana's *periodiquitos*, newspapers published by the community in exile, lashed out at the possibility of any form of normalization of relations with Cuba. In early 1979, a new *periodiquito* launched and declared itself to be "with Cuba and against the traitors." *Látigo* (The whip), declared that Cuba was not negotia-ble, and that between the exile community and Fidel Castro there was "a sea covered in bodies, a prison full of pain and a national slavery, that no one can erase."[95] In February, *Látigo* denounced the "infiltration" of the Cuban exile community by Castro sympathizers and agents who sought the dialogue with Castro. It also castigated President Carter as the "champion of 'human rights,' who sees traits of kindness and generosity in the Beast of Birán."[96]

Upon returning to the United States, many of the *dialogueros* (members of the group engaged in the dialogue) found themselves ostracized from the

communities and groups they had helped build. Bernardo Benes's role in dealing with Fidel Castro was revealed in a *Washington Post* article that recounted
how Cuban officials had approached him in Panama and how he and Castro
had worked behind the scenes before the announcement in September of that
year. Benes had already received death threats before the article's publication.[97] In March of 1979, Benes sent a plea in English and Spanish to all Continental National Bank customers asking for employment accommodation
for the arriving political prisoners. He expected cooperation, but instead he
was met with backlash. He was called a traitor and a communist, had his life
threatened, and found that none of his powerful friends in Miami stood up
for him. He was, suddenly, a pariah.[98]

Organizations like Alpha 66 aided in ostracizing Benes on the part of
Miami's Cuban community. Alpha 66 founder Antonio Veciana had publicly
identified Benes as a de facto agent of the State Department and not an infil-
trator employed by Castro before the dialogueros traveled to Havana.[99] This,
however, was too fine a point of distinction for the organization. In an interview given much later, Veciana's cofounder Andrés Nazario Sargén stated that
he did not personally dislike Benes and that he was acting in the interests of
the U.S. government, yet regardless, he was the enemy. Domingo Moreira,
who would become a founding member of the Cuban American National
Foundation in the following decade, stated that the shunning of Benes was to
be expected. "His motives could have been humanitarian, but he was authorized by the Carter administration to suggest there would be policy changes
that would alleviate tensions with Cuba," Moreira indicated, and "this was
unacceptable."[100]

Benes was even the target of an assassination attempt in 1980, but unlike
many others he survived.[101] Throughout 1979, the exile organization known
as Omega 7 claimed responsibility for more than twenty bombings of the
homes and businesses of dialogue members and the assassination of Carlos
Muñiz Varela, a twenty-six-year-old member of the Antonio Maceo Brigade.
María de los Angeles Torres recalls that the members of the brigade lived in
constant fear that their sponsored events would be bombed.[102] Even under
the threat of death, however, a second group of 168 dialogueros returned to
Cuba. Little of consequence was accomplished, however, due to mutual mistrust and a lack of follow-through on the part of the Carter administration.[103]

Benes remained undeterred in trying to facilitate the arrival of the political prisoners that Castro had released to the United States. In September
of 1979, he and Alfredo Durán again contacted the Carter White House to

secure five thousand parole visas for the former political prisoners. Despite the agreements reached during the dialogo, the U.S. government had been proceeding very slowly in processing the political prisoners' entry. Benes and Durán insisted that the United States had a moral responsibility to the prisoners because most of them had served long sentences as a result of their involvement in anti-Castro operations sponsored by American intelligence agencies in the 1960s.[104] Officials within the Carter administration saw value in the proposal; it was "a way for the Administration to 'declare victory' on the human rights issue."[105]

The handling of these prisoners also provided the Carter White House with a largely cost-neutral solution to a new influx that set the stage for neoliberal programs adopted by Carter's successors. With the Cuban Refugee Program winding down, the administration was not eager to take on the charge of these new arrivals. Durán and Benes committed the Cuban American community to finding jobs for the released prisoners and to handling their resettlement.[106] Future administrations embraced new iterations of this arrangement.

Within months, however, the Carter administration and the Cuban American community were faced with a much larger refugee challenge. After years without any large-scale migrations from Cuba, a massive new wave of refugees would soon be landing on the coasts of South Florida, once again testing local, state, and federal authorities. This new wave would also test the Cuban American community in new ways, exposing even more divisions within the community, forcing them to defend their accomplishments to the city and the country and putting many of them at odds with a new generation of refugees who did not resemble them or the Cuba they remembered.

CHAPTER 5

"Will the Last American to Leave Miami Please Bring the Flag?": The Mariel Boatlift, Backlash, and the Politics of Image in Miami

An article published in *Reader's Digest* in December of 1982 described the situation on the streets of Miami in apocalyptic terms. "They were like wolf packs running loose in the streets—hordes of crazy men with tattooed arms, and loaded guns in their belts," wrote Peter Michelmore about members of the newest group of refugees from Cuba who had arrived during the Mariel boatlift of 1980. The piece, titled "From Cuba with Hate," claimed that the vast majority of Cubans called them "*escoria*, scum."[1] *Escoria* was the very word that Fidel Castro had used for these refugees, the Marielitos, during the most intense period of refugee migration from Cuba to the United States. Michelmore fully embraced this characterization by graphically recounting the murder of nineteen-year-old Claribel Benítez, a "well-brought-up Cuban American girl" shot during an attempted carjacking. The mortally injured Benítez gave a description of the strangers who attacked her. "Three *Marielitos*," said Benítez before her death, repeating the word several times. "To those who heard her," Michelmore went on, "the word needed no explanation."[2] He then blamed Jimmy Carter's administration for the situation, for having been duped by Castro into setting a "vicious new criminal force" loose into an open society.[3]

The *Reader's Digest* article was the latest blow to the Cuban community's reputation in the United States following the Mariel boatlift. Three months earlier, public polling on incoming refugees had shown that of all nationalities, Cubans were ranked at the bottom.[4] The *Miami Herald*'s editorial section commented on the negative press the refugees of the Mariel boatlift were receiving across the country and described how, "like a festering sore, the black legend of Mariel continues to spread across the United States."⁵ It was not surprising, then, that when news of the *Reader's Digest* article broke in Miami, many Cubans reacted with anger. Michelmore defended himself by claiming that the article made it clear he was writing about a small group among the refugees, but others were concerned about the overall effect. "People will draw an image of all Cubans from this description," said Lucrecia Granda, secretary of the Spanish American League against Discrimination.⁶

Not all Cuban Americans had this reaction to the article. *Herald* columnist Roberto Fabricio found that the reaction to the piece by many leaders in the Cuban American community had been unjustified because they had not read it. While Fabricio had shared the concerns of these leaders about a negative portrayal of part of the community reflecting badly on the whole community, he found that in the *Reader's Digest* piece Michelmore had simply stated the facts. Fabricio believed that the estimate that 20% of the nearly 125,000 refugees who came to the United States during the boatlift were criminals was an exaggeration, but he credited Michelmore with squarely laying the blame of the crime wave on Castro and the criminals themselves. For this, he thought Cuban Americans should have applauded Michelmore.⁷ Honest Cubans should not be concerned with the portrayal of lawbreakers sent to the United States by Castro to sully the larger community.

The response of the Cuban American community to the Marielitos' reputation in the national media and in Miami must be understood in the context of respectability politics. After twenty years of being perceived as a model minority, the arrival of the Marielitos threatened to destroy that reputation. Cuban Americans in South Florida and throughout the United States had worked to establish themselves for two decades. They had faced challenges to their economic well-being and had the certainty of their victory shaken in the 1960s. By the 1970s they had helped reshape Miami and had sought to solidify their individual and communal gains through activism and a recognition of their economic contributions. The Mariel boatlift, to many Cuban Americans, threatened the wholesale erasure of two decades of struggle and made the possibility of a Cuba without Castro seem even more remote. This led to an inherent tension within the Cuban American community, between the desire to welcome most Mariel entrants and the fear-driven impulse to repudiate the worst among them and possibly to write off the whole refugee wave, if necessary, to ensure the survival of the established community.

The challenge to the collective image of Cuban Americans also illustrates how the community's importance to foreign policymakers had changed over the course of two decades. Where the Cuban refugee community was once a Cold War asset, the Mariel boatlift presented the federal government with a more severe humanitarian problem than any previous wave of migration from Cuba. These new refugees were arriving in greater numbers and neither their professional and educational backgrounds nor their public image were of use to policymakers. While previous arrivals were portrayed as Cuba's best and brightest who were seeking the promise of freedom in the face of communist dictatorship, the Marielitos were burdened by an image of criminality and deviancy that the Cuban government had originated and the U.S. media was all too happy to promulgate.

The Marielitos, particularly in their portrayal by the American media, were also marked as different because of their perceived disability. Disability studies scholars and scholars of immigration have long shown how the exclusion of disability was central to immigration law, starting in the nineteenth century.[8] The contrast between the perception of the Marielitos and that of previous waves of Cuban refugees went beyond established desires to exclude people with mental and physical disabilities, but it also struck at ways in which Cuban refugees had traditionally been portrayed by the U.S. government and the media, as well as how they portrayed themselves. At the core of their portrayal had always been skills, self-sufficiency, and the idea that even those receiving assistance should receive training and be given the opportunities to be independent. To add to the overblown fears of criminality, the homophobia experienced by LGBTQ Marielitos, and the racist and xenophobic concerns, many people feared that vast numbers of Marielitos would become permanent public charges. Disability served as one more way in which this population was unworthy of the welcome previous refugees had received and the federal government's carelessness with disabled and mentally ill Marielitos led to situations of harm and trauma for some of the most vulnerable refugees within the boatlift.

Where the early waves of refugees were credited with having a miraculous effect on South Florida's economy, the Marielitos would not be lauded the same way. The Marielitos came from a different Cuba than earlier refugees and arrived in a different Miami. They had either come of age during or lived through the two decades that followed the revolution. The significant minorities of professionals and entrepreneurs upon which the federal government had previously seized gave way to a more solidly working-class and racially mixed group.[9]

The most significant difference, however, was that this wave of refugees was not provided with the same opportunities as those that had arrived throughout the 1960s and into the early 1970s. Federal officials were desperately trying to manage a more intense flow of refugees than they had ever seen. More importantly, in an increasingly neoliberal Washington, DC, the time for employing robust welfare state solutions to the problem of Cuban refugees in Miami had passed, particularly for a population that appeared to bring a whole slate of new problems and none of the old foreign policy opportunities. Without the same set of economic advantages, the Marielitos would find it more difficult to integrate into South Florida's economy.

Federal policymakers did not replicate the refugee policies of the 1960s, but those policies still shaped the reactions to the Mariel boatlift. The Cuban American community, faced with an image problem without the institutionalized support of the federal government, expended its own political capital in responding to the crisis and seeking to prevent future dangers to their community and its standing in South Florida and in the United States. This chapter recounts the events of the Mariel boatlift and its effects on Cuban Americans. Conditions in Cuba led to a new mass migration and a new dilemma for the federal government about whether to accept a massive influx with a very different reputation than the refugees who had come before and led to the instatement of a system that fundamentally failed many of the new arrivals.

The new influx of refugees in Miami served to exacerbate old conflicts and to bring about new, which can be seen in the case of the Haitian refugees, who experienced an even harsher arrival in South Florida, and how Haitian advocates sought treatment that equaled what was given to the Marielitos. Miami's African American community, seeing another race-based disparity, once again expressed their frustration with the Cuban presence in Miami and the indifference of the federal government toward their own community. Moreover, the growing backlash against the Marielitos from white Miamians spurred the growth of an "English-only" movement in South Florida that fed on this backlash to erase previous gains in bilingualism and helped amplify the anxieties of Cuban Americans about the portrayals of the new arrivals in popular culture.

Opening the Pressure Valve: The Peruvian Embassy Crisis, the "Scum" of Cuban Society, and the Opening of Mariel

On April 1, 1980, a bus crashed through the gates of the Peruvian embassy in Havana.[10] Prompted by the Peruvian government's decision to institute a more liberal policy regarding asylum seekers, bus driver Héctor Sanyustiz and five companions had commandeered the vehicle from his place of work. As Sanyustiz made a dangerous turn toward the embassy gate, the bus came under fire from the Cuban troops assigned to embassy security. Despite the obstacles and the gunfire, the asylum seekers managed to enter the sovereign Peruvian territory of the embassy.[11] This was only the latest in a series of similar incidents. By March 1980, nearly thirty Cubans had crashed vehicles against the gates of the embassies of Peru and Venezuela.[12] In the context of "the leanest years of the revolution," when housing and food shortages were severe and unemployment and underemployment were chronic, these embassy incidents were often acts of desperation.[13]

This incident was different: someone died. Pedro Ortíz Cabrera, a twenty-seven-year-old Cuban guard assigned to the Peruvian embassy, was killed during the confrontation.[14] This became a full diplomatic incident as the Cuban government demanded the return of the asylum seekers.[15] On April 4, the Cuban government removed the compound's gates, the barricades that protected them, and the Cuban security guards assigned to the embassy. By the next day, spurred by assurances from the Cuban government that they would be allowed to leave the island if they were granted visas by foreign nations, 2,000 asylum seekers had entered the grounds of the embassy.[16] By April 6, 2,000 had become 10,800.[17]

Asylum seekers refused to leave the embassy grounds for fear they would be arrested and not allowed to return. The embassy staff was completely overwhelmed. Cuban security forces provided some food for the asylum seekers, but the nearly eleven thousand people on the embassy grounds had to subsist on rations meant for twenty-five hundred. Unsanitary conditions compounded the lack of food and water and resulted in widespread suffering from dehydration, sunstroke, and gastroenteritis. The international press extensively covered the events at the Peruvian embassy, embarrassing Castro's government. In response, the Cuban government went on the offensive against the asylum seekers.[18]

Cuba's state newspaper, *Granma*, referred to the asylum seekers as "delinquents, social deviants, vagrants, and parasites."[19] A new term came into use when discussing the refugees on the embassy grounds: the asylum seekers were *escoria* (society's scum).[20] Those seeking to leave were from class backgrounds that the revolution had sought to help, but government officials explained that even in a socialist society there existed underdeveloped groups of "lumpen proletariat" who undermined the revolution and sought to leave Cuba for purely economic reasons.[21] The Cuban government's propaganda push even included claims that there had been a reduction in crime of 55% since the start of the embassy crisis. The state further contrasted the asylum seekers to Ortíz Cabrera, the guard killed in the incident, whom it held up as a symbol of the loyal Cuban citizenry. He came to represent loyal Cubans who stood in opposition to the escoria, who were so eager to desert the revolution.[22]

The Cuban government agreed to an arrangement whereby thirty-five hundred asylum seekers would go to the United States, another thirty-five hundred would go to eight other nations, and the rest would temporarily await resettlement to other countries in Costa Rica.[23] The flights to Costa Rica, which started on April 16, drew attention from the international press. The interviews with those Cubans arriving in Costa Rica painted them as ordinary men and women seeking to leave a repressive regime. This stood in direct opposition to the Cuban government's description of them as the dregs of society. Castro accused the governments of the United States and Peru of using the Costa Rican way station for propaganda purposes against his regime.[24] Castro unilaterally halted the airlift and declared that all flights carrying the refugees would have to go directly to the countries in which they were to settle.[25] This prompted the Costa Rican government to offer asylum to all the Cubans at the Peruvian embassy and to appeal to the Cuban government to allow the flights to resume.[26]

Castro changed tactics once again. The Cuban government bypassed foreign governments by informing Cubans living abroad that they could use boats to pick up those wanting to exit the country through the port of Mariel, on the outskirts of Havana.[27] Cuban Americans seized on this opportunity. By April 21, *Granma* announced that fifty lobster boats had left Florida to begin the transport of those Cubans seeking to leave, with the first two already having arrived at Mariel. *Granma*'s editorial announced that the state was not opposed to the boats taking away those who wanted to leave.[28]

The first two boats returned to Key West with some forty refugees, which prompted a State Department official to call the effort "unlawful and unhelpful."[29] Officials rightly were concerned about the fact that the number of

Cuban Americans heading to Mariel was growing significantly. Within four days, Mariel harbor was "a floating city of more than 1300 boats." On their arrival, immigration officials boarded vessels seeking identification and lists of relatives that they sought to bring back to the United States. Cuban authorities also forced each boat to take on additional passengers, while also selling them fuel and supplies.[30] The Cuban American community's enthusiasm for the boatlift resulted in 6,333 new Cuban arrivals in the United States between April 21 and April 30.[31]

Individuals and families who had not been a part of the embassy crisis soon joined the exodus. Heads of household applied for permission to leave the country in secret and kept that decision quiet for fear of their neighbors visiting violence against them, as there was no guarantee of an exit. Government forces took families to a staging area in Havana, where they would often wait for days. The would-be refugees needed to remain attentive to the instructions and calls of the Cuban authorities as those who were contacted but did not report in were simply left behind. Years later, Cuban American fashion designer Juan Carlos Piñera recounted how his parents took to sleeping in shifts to avoid the possibility of being left behind while the whole family slumbered.[32]

The mother of eight-year-old Lissette Mendez chose to leave the island when the opportunity came. Her father had been devoted to the revolution, but upon his death, her mother had decided to leave the country. She and her mother tried to keep this decision a secret, but when it came time to leave their home, secrecy was no longer an option. Officials arrived and publicly informed them that it was time to leave. At that moment, all of Mendez's neighbors gathered to yell and throw garbage at both mother and daughter.[33] This type of public rejection could easily escalate into violence and led to other traumatic experiences. Volunteers who worked with incoming refugees reported that many arrived injured by government-encouraged repudiation.[34] On the way to Mariel families would also have their valuables taken and would sometimes be subjected to strip searches.[35]

Those leaving Cuba as part of the boatlift were forced to sign documents confessing to social deviancy and crimes against the state. This created a false record of crimes committed by the migrants, one that fit the Cuban government's portrayal of the *escoria*. To reinforce this narrative, the Cuban government added convicted criminals to the general population of the boatlift. The Mariel entrants with Cuban criminal records numbered around twenty-six thousand. Only about two thousand of them had committed serious felonies.

Many others were jailed under lesser crimes ascribed to them by Cuba's *ley de peligrosidad* (law of dangerousness).[36] An oral history project undertaken among the new arrivals revealed that the crimes they had been convicted of varied greatly. Some were convicted of purchasing food or clothing on the black market, others for selling goods without permission, and still others had been political prisoners or had been imprisoned for offenses like vagrancy or fighting. With sentences ranging from thirty-one days to forty years, the *ley de peligrosidad* was particularly useful for incarcerating "practically anybody for any simple misdemeanor in which the person might be considered a public menace."[37]

The conditions in Cuban prisons made the possibility of release even more precious for these prisoners. Former prisoners described dirty, overcrowded facilities where 125 prisoners might be crammed into a space designed for 25 people. Stories of prisoners sleeping on the floor, not receiving sufficient nutrition, and being abused by their captors were common among the refugees.[38] Some prisoners actively sought the chance to participate in the boatlift, even at the risk of their own lives. A group of thirteen inmates at Sandino Prison began a hunger strike to be allowed to leave. After nineteen days without food, the strikers received a visit from the superintendent, who allowed them to join the boatlift.[39]

In addition to prison inmates, the Cuban government wanted to rid itself of LGBTQ communities in what historian Julio Capó Jr. calls "a clear episode of the Castro regime's 'institutionally promoted homophobia.'" During a speech at Havana's José Martí Revolution Square on May 1, 1980, Castro furthered his narrative of the Mariel exiles as the *lumpen* of Cuban society and specifically referred to homosexuals as part of that category, making reference to "limp wrists."[40] Homosexuality had technically been decriminalized in 1979, but the *ley de peligrosidad* left gay Cubans vulnerable if they defied the "norms of socialist morality," leading to arrests based on perceived effeminacy and on congregation with other homosexuals.[41] Gay Cubans were encouraged to leave the country. Some were even threatened with the addition of years to their sentence should they resist joining the boatlift.[42]

Some boatlift refugees suffered from a variety of conditions including mental illnesses, chronic illnesses, and mental and physical disabilities. Around fifteen hundred refugees had a mental health problem or an intellectual disability, including five hundred who were committed to mental institutions and another five hundred whom authorities placed in halfway houses in the United States. While exact numbers are not available, estimates put

Figure 10. The shrimp trawler *Lady Virgo*, overloaded with Cuban refugees, as it arrived in Key West, Florida, from Mariel during the boatlift in 1980. Photograph by Dale McDonald. Courtesy of the State Library and Archives of Florida.

the number of refugees with chronic medical problems including substance abuse, tuberculosis, or cardiovascular disease at sixteen hundred.[43]

These various groups converged on Mariel harbor and found themselves distributed among the waiting boats. Boat captains and the Cuban Americans who hired them often waited for several days while immigration officials went over the list of the family members whom they wanted to bring back to the United States. One captain had a confrontation with immigration officials when he asked for a list of the Cuban citizens he could bring aboard and received a list of three hundred—rather than the expected twenty-five—names.[44] Such scenes were common (see Figure 10). Caridad Morales rented a twenty-five-foot boat to sail down to Cuba to bring four relatives back to Florida, but their small vessel was forced to take on an additional eighteen passengers.[45] Larger vessels were also filled to dangerous levels during the boatlift. One ship, the *Hill David*, had a capacity of 150 passengers yet Cuban officials loaded on 350 refugees.[46] The overcrowding served to compound the danger as many of the rented boats were barely capable of making it to Cuba, much less return overloaded with refugees. Many could not finish the crossing and the Coast Guard had to tow them to shore.

For most of the refugees, the boatlift represented the hope for a new life. Others were forced to participate. Regardless, the trials and tribulations that accompanied the journey to Mariel and the subsequent sea voyage took their toll on most of the migrants. Once they reached the United States, the new refugees would face all the same challenges their predecessors had encountered but without the comprehensive system of aid or the positive reception of the U.S. government or the American people in general. For the Cubans who participated in the boatlift, the label of *Marielitos* would not only indicate the circumstances by which they arrived in the United States, it also created a stigma that would follow them for years to come.

A Different Type of Welcome: The Federal Government, Cuban Americans, and Mariel's Image Problem

Despite new legislation meant to streamline the admittance processes for refugees, the Mariel boatlift presented a major policy challenge to the Carter administration. Earlier in the year, the president had signed the Refugee Act of 1980 into law. The new law redefined "refugee" as a victim of "persecution, or a well-founded fear of persecution on account of race, religion, nationality, membership in a particular social group, or political opinion," without linking the persecution to a particular geographical region or political ideology.[47] It also authorized the admission of fifty thousand refugees a year who could, after one year, gain permanent resident status. In case of a large-scale emergency, this number could be adjusted through congressional consultation and approval.[48] Despite being designed for a situation in which the United States would be the country of first asylum for large numbers of refugees, the legislative structures of the Refugee Act of 1980 could only serve as far as they were put into use by the Carter administration.

On May 3, President Carter told the League of Women Voters in Philadelphia that the Cuban refugees would be welcomed with "an open heart and open arms."[49] The White House's National Security team was less effusive. They were concerned by the numbers of refugees, but also because this set a dangerous precedent. The optics of another country expelling its citizens only to have the United States receive them troubled officials. White House aide Robert Pastor worried that allowing the Cuban government–mandated boatlift in direct violation of U.S. immigration statutes would serve as an invitation to other countries to replicate Castro's strategy.[50]

Because of these concerns and in an attempt to further foreign policy aims, the administration sought to reframe the welcome extended by President Carter to the Cuban refugees "*in the context of an orderly flow.*" As such, it sought to reduce the boat flotilla by convincing the Cuban American community of the dangers of the unorganized boatlift and of the government's intention to regularize the flow of refugees. This proved ineffectual, however. The flow continued, and federal officials estimated that by mid-May, approximately between fifty thousand and fifty-five thousand Cubans had arrived in the United States as part of the boatlift. This was not likely to change given that national security officials assumed the boatlift would continue as long as Cuban Americans believed they could return with their friends and family or until an alternative system was put in its place.[51]

The federal government was growing concerned about the increasing evidence of "undesirables" in the boatlift, including "hardened criminals, the mentally ill, the retarded and persons who are diseased." Some Cuban Americans shared this concern because of the growing backlash among other communities in the United States.[52] Deputy Secretary of State Warren Christopher invited several Cuban American organizations to Washington to gain their help in stopping the boatlift. The head of the Cuban Affairs Desk at the State Department, Myles Frechette, later recalled that the meeting was a disaster, as each group was pushing its own agenda.[53] Without clearly defined leadership, the Cuban American organizations succumbed to in-fighting along well-established fault lines and were unable to stem the tide of the boatlift. Carter, however, was facing reelection at the end of the year and risked the ire of the Cuban American community should he engage in more restrictive action.

Equally problematic for Carter's political prospects were the accusations that the administration's handling of the boatlift was encouraging unauthorized immigration. By mid-May, veteran *New York Times* reporter James Reston accused the U.S. government of having lost control of its immigration policy.[54] Reston held that the Cuban refugee influx was simply a particularly dramatic example demonstrating that the United States was unable to protect its borders or enforce laws against illegal immigration at a time of high inflation and unemployment.[55] While previous forms of unauthorized immigration by other Latin American groups, who made contributions to the U.S. economy, were generally ignored, the Mariel crisis could not simply be overlooked. To Reston, Mariel posed a fundamental question as to whether the federal government had any sort of policy to deal with the problems of immigration into the United States. While he conceded that the human tragedy of the event was obvious, he pointed that out that Castro had a policy: he was "exporting his failures." Neither the White House nor Congress could say the same. The boatlift represented an image problem at a time in which diplomatic tensions between the United States and the Soviet Union were on the rise. Because the United States had not been defending its borders and enforcing its immigration laws, "this latest invasion of the Cubans in the weekend boats has not only hurt but even mocked the authority of the White House."[56]

The public image of the refugees made life more difficult for the new arrivals and compounded the political problems of the Carter administration. Where previous waves of Cuban refugees received a warm welcome from the national media, which was often driven by the work of the public relations officials of the Cuban Refugee Program, the Marielitos received a very different reception. Early on, media outlets like the *Chicago Tribune* encouraged the arrival of the refugees, embracing the types of narratives that older exiles had encountered during the 1960s. "So give us your bums, Fidel," wrote the *Tribune's* editor in late April, "send them throughout the hemisphere and the world. They certainly make better exports than your revolution."[57] Editorials in newspapers throughout the United States, including the *Wall Street Journal* and the *Washington Post*, urged the federal government to provide the refugees with humanitarian assistance.[58] This trend did not last, however.

On May 11, 1980, the *New York Times* ran an article on the boatlift entitled "Retarded People and Criminals Are Included in Cuban Exodus." Reporter Edward Schumacher claimed that Cuban soldiers were loading refugees onto vessels in Mariel harbor "in a major effort, discussed openly by Cuban officials, to rid the country of criminals, mentally retarded people, delinquents and others the Government calls 'scum' by sending them to the United States." Schumacher described a group of four "apparently retarded" people huddling on a ship called the *Valley Chief.* One young man was asked if he came from prison or a mental institution and responded by mumbling "*embajada*" (embassy), but he was unable to produce the safe-conduct pass provided to and tenaciously held on to by Peruvian embassy asylum seekers.[59]

On the pier, Cuban authorities instructed a group of prisoners and ex-convicts to state that they came from the embassy so they could avoid detention in the United States. Thirty-year-old Pedro Palmeri told Schumacher that he had served six years for the theft of a government-owned vehicle. After being arrested again for fighting with a police officer, he was pressured to join the boatlift. "I knew they would make it hard for me if I didn't go," he explained, adding, "It was an easy choice to make anyway. This whole country is a prison." Schumacher acknowledged that some refugees had been imprisoned for political crimes. Some Cuban Americans defended the convicted Marielitos either as victims of the Castro regime or as having been driven to crime by conditions in Cuba. Food rationing by the government, they argued, had forced many of the convicts to steal to feed themselves and their families. Not all Cuban Americans were as forgiving, as they feared there would be political and social repercussions in the United States. The article also quoted Antonio Aguacio, a New Jersey longshoreman, who told Schumacher that the U.S. government should "screen out the misfits and send them back."[60]

Engaged Cuban Americans took it on themselves to combat this stereotype. When Olga Vives, of Mt. Prospect, IL, read a piece in *U.S. News & World Report* about the impact of the boatlift on an ailing American economy, she needed to respond. Vives wrote a letter to the publication's editor and argued that the United States had a moral obligation to come to the aid of the Mariel refugees. She recounted how her own family had arrived in the United States in 1961, "penniless and destitute, emotionally shattered over the loss of our country," and how they had gotten a chance to rebuild their lives. Why could the United States not give the same welcome to these new refugees from Cuba? The Mariel Cubans, she argued, were fleeing oppression; they were simply trying to survive. "Has the nation gotten smaller," Vives asked, "or have the hearts of the American people become less accommodating?"[61] Although the media had portrayed them negatively, the Marielitos were fleeing the same oppression as she had. She could not understand how the American public could turn on them now. Mariel, however, was different. There was no open-arms reception for this wave of refugees. In fact, federal authorities altered the refugee status that Cubans had long received.

The mass of Mariel arrivals, along with thousands of Haitian refugees, drove federal authorities to make a decision related to the status of these refugees that would have long-term consequences. In order to gain greater leeway in terms for the refugees' legal rights, the Carter administration announced on June 20, 1980, that it would not consider these new arrivals refugees as had previous waves of Cuban arrivals. Instead, they would parole Cubans who had entered the United States between April 21 and June 19 and were in INS proceedings as of June 19 and all Haitians in INS proceedings as of that date for a renewed six-month period as "Cuban/Haitian Entrants (status pending)." By claiming that these populations were "entrants" rather than refugees, the federal government could make the claim that they had not actually "entered"

U.S. territory and that the federal government could then simply "exclude" them from the country, rather than "deport" them.[62] This decision would have decades of consequences as excludable detainees and their advocates fought this legal denomination and resultant indefinite detention.[63] Even those whom the federal government deemed as worthy of entry into the country, however, still had to deal with a much harsher reception, the trauma of seeking refuge in another country, and an uncertain economic future. Moreover, unlike in the 1960s, there would be no robust aid program for this group.

Falling Through the Cracks: Mass Processing, Family Reunions, and the Perils Faced by Vulnerable Marielitos

The sudden appearance of thousands of refugees on American soil in a matter of days presented an immediate challenge and proceeded at a rate that dwarfed any previous period of Cuban migration. The original Cuban refugee crisis was a slow-moving humanitarian disaster, a chronic problem managed by welfare state structures acting on behalf of the interests of the national security state. The response to Mariel was immediate, but as multiple, competing layers of federal bureaucracy sought to respond to the crisis and the policymakers navigated the dangers posed by the boatlift to their political prospects, the single-mindedness and purpose of the response in the early 1960s was absent from that of the Carter administration. Critics and observers equated this aimlessness with confusion and a lack of leadership. "President Jimmy Carter was totally unprepared for it," Myles Frechette remarked on the twenty-fifth anniversary of the boatlift.[64]

From the early days of the Mariel migration, various federal agencies worked on fulfilling the basic needs of the refugees, with a particular focus on entry processing and housing. In late April, the Federal Emergency Management Agency (FEMA) unveiled plans to open a processing center for the Cuban entrants.[65] FEMA also took over operations at the facility in Key West that had been receiving the Mariel entrants since the start of the refugee flow and the HEW operation at the county fairgrounds in Tamiami Park, west of Miami proper. It also designated Eglin Air Force Base, in the Florida panhandle, as a processing center for up to 5,000 refugees and prepared to close the Tamiami operation in favor of a new facility at the shuttered Opa-Locka Naval Air Station, long proposed as a destination for Cuban immigrants by Dade County citizens and officials.[66]

In some ways, the problems and their responses were very similar to events two decades before, but now on a scale so large that the federal response could only handle immediate necessities instead of longer-term outcomes aimed at regime change in Cuba. The need for military bases and large-scale processing centers came from familiar problems related to Cuban refugee arrivals. By early May, housing had already become a significant problem in Miami. Miami's HEW coordinator reported that most available housing was in use and that he had heard stories about entrants living in converted dog kennels and other ersatz structures. The problem, he went on, would only get worse as the refugee flow was expected to continue.[67] Hospitalization costs and medical supplies for the refugees also had to be dealt with as officials needed to provide medical aid to incoming emergency cases and people afflicted by tuberculosis and mental health issues.[68] Officials were forced to first contend with the most basic needs of the refugees before they could even consider the effects that the influx would have on Miami.

The federal government's ability to meet the needs of the refugees had also changed in the two decades since the original refugee crisis. The Cuban Refugee Program had ceased to exist. Some among the Cuban American community wanted the CRP refunded and restarted to deal with the Mariel entrants, particularly as the populations of the processing centers swelled. Members of the Junta Patriotica Cubana argued that a reinstated CRP would be cheaper for the federal government in the long run than the response they had witnessed thus far. Drawing parallels between the boatlift and the arrival of the earlier waves of refugees in the early 1960s, the Junta declared that "only a special program of exception such as the previously used Cuban Refugee Program, can do the job."[69] If it had worked two decades before, surely it could work again.

The United States of 1980 was not the same as the United States of 1961. Re-creating a federal agency with the expenditure levels of the original CRP, multiplied by the numbers of the Mariel boatlift was a nonstarter given the decimation of budgets for programs aimed at helping vulnerable populations. The influx of Cuban refugees threatened an already weakened social safety net. When the Department of Agriculture decided in early May that boatlift refugees would be eligible for food stamps if they registered for work, officials warned that the program's funding might dry up for Cubans and non-Cubans alike by June due to the additional strain.[70] The Cuban Refugee Program had been a foreign policy initiative publicly framed in terms of, and developed within the context of, a more robust welfare state. That state still existed, but its priorities had shifted to different sectors of society and in combination with a weak economy, it resulted in a response to the refugee flow that was far more in line with traditional avenues of refugee management. Instead of an open-door policy with a voluntary registration element for those refugees seeking aid, the 1980 response was characterized by universal registration and the opening of new processing centers and refugee-holding facilities in Miami's Orange Bowl and military bases such as Fort Chaffee, AR, and Fort Indiantown Gap, PA.[71]

While the federal government was able to provide basic amenities and health services to the Marielitos, serious problems arose from this massive effort. Attempts to transport, process, house, and treat such significant numbers of people sometimes led to health hazards, accidents, and violence. There was a significant outbreak of diarrhea and vomiting in the Orange Bowl holding center that authorities suspected might have resulted either from food contamination at the Key West facility or from a "change in the water system."[72] Two refugees suffering from leprosy were scheduled to be transferred from Key West to a hospital in Louisiana to be treated, but instead were mistakenly sent elsewhere and had to be tracked down by federal authorities who ultimately found them at the Opa-Locka facility.[73]

Because the immigration system had long sought to exclude people with a disability, which did not fit with the narrative of previous influxes, refugees who suffered from mental illness or intellectual disabilities were particularly vulnerable during the boatlift and in its aftermath. HEW officials found that the needs of those refugees who needed long-term institutionalization were not being met. They were being "passed back and forth between holding areas and the local psychiatric clinics and hospitals." This posed logistical problems for refugee transportation, but it also posed a danger of their medical care being neglected.[74] This system of part-time care led to at least one refugee injury. On May 17, three refugees were transported to a Miami clinic to be treated for mental health issues.[75] That evening, the three were standing outside the clinic awaiting evaluation when one of them began brandishing a knife and a police officer shot him.[76] The report did not list the patient's motivations or medical history, but the fact that he managed to obtain a knife at a federal holding facility, a hospital, or in transit indicates that concerns over refugees "falling through the cracks" were well founded.

Despite these difficulties and the increasingly negative image of the Marielitos in the national media, there were some people both inside and outside Miami, Cuban and non-Cuban alike, who welcomed the refugees and sought to lend them and the federal government a hand. New York City mayor Edward Koch offered FEMA between three hundred and four hundred city apartments for Marielitos, which were sponsored by the city's Cuban community.[77] Voluntary agencies like the Church World Service (CWS) once again provided their services in the resettlement of Cuban refugees. They helped match refugees with offers of sponsorship, even in the case of "problematic" or "undesirable" individuals. CWS served as the intermediary by which gay and gay-friendly organizations like the Metropolitan Community Church could identify sponsors and work toward resettling gay Cubans who did not yet have sponsors.[78] The federal government also received the help of another veteran of the Cuban refugee effort of the 1960s. Monsignor Bryan Walsh and Miami's Catholic Charities aided immigration authorities in ensuring the well-being of unaccompanied minors among the Marielitos. Walsh helped provide bilingual social workers to manage the young refugees.[79] Officials even suggested that Walsh could establish a South Florida facility for the foster home placement of unaccompanied minors.[80]

Cuban Americans held out hope of reuniting with friends and family, and some found themselves unexpectedly encountering loved ones they not seen in decades. Pablo Camacho had migrated to the United States at age twelve, twenty years before the boatlift, leaving behind the grandmother who helped raise him and other family members. By 1980, Camacho was a police officer in Little Havana, and his history made him a natural candidate for an assignment dealing with the Mariel refugees at the Orange Bowl. He was tasked with keeping the refugees from spilling over the chain-link fence once they spotted long-lost relatives. In that capacity, he witnessed firsthand the emotional intensity of those moments of reunion. "I saw six-foot tall men crying over finding relatives," Camacho told a *Miami Herald* reporter. "Some were bleeding from the hands from trying to reach over the fence."[81] What was for the refugees and their relatives an emotional, even sublime, moment soon became a matter of routine for officers like Camacho, who could appreciate the emotion of the moment but who had a responsibility to maintain order and prevent injuries.

Camacho had boarded a bus to give arriving refuges the same statement of welcome he had given to dozens of other groups when an old woman stood up and burst into tears. Clara Camacho Valmana had not seen her grandson Pablo in the twenty years since she had sent him to the United States. In the intervening years, she had seen her husband, her son, her daughter-in-law, her grandsons, and other relatives leave the island. She had kept up with her family's lives from afar and had even learned of her husband's death from a radio announcement on Miami's WQBA. Pablo Camacho had given his grandmother's name to friends in the Cuban American community in hopes that his grandmother and his aunt, his last relatives still on the island, might find a way to join the rest of the family in Miami. Despite Camacho's hopes, he did not know that Clara had managed to make her way to Miami aboard a ship called the *Georgia Cracker*. She had lost Pablo's telephone number when she was searched at Mariel. Unsure of how to find her grandson, Clara was unexpectedly and tearfully reunited with Pablo when he welcomed her bus to the holding center, causing jubilation among the passengers.[82]

The hope for family reunification as well as the chance to embarrass Castro's government drove an outpouring of generosity and aid from many Miami-based Cuban Americans. Spanish-language radio stations in the area broadcast appeals for aid that resulted in substantial donations of food, clothing, and funds. Many Cuban doctors provided free medical care to the refugees. The Cuban owner of the Everglades Hotel, Juvenal Pina, temporarily allotted 350 rooms in his hotel to house 450 refugees and charged them severely reduced rates or nothing at all.[83] A telethon on Spanish-language television raised $2 million for the Marielitos.[84] While there were some divisions within the community on how to best respond to the boatlift and the presence in the city of the new refugees, Miami's Cubans provided them with significant private aid in an effort to supplement a federal response that seemed anemic compared to that of decades past.

City of Discontent: Haitian Asylum Seekers, African Americans, and the Backlash to the Cuban Presence in Miami

While the welcome the Marielitos received was bleak in comparison with previous waves of Cuban refugees, the federal government afforded them far better treatment than that given to Haitian refugees arriving in South Florida at the same time. During the 1970s, fifty-five thousand Haitians had legally entered the United States while escaping the repressive government of Jean-Claude "Baby Doc" Duvalier. In addition to authorized migrants, some thirty thousand other Haitians attempted to enter the United States without following regular immigration procedures (see Figure 11). These asylum seekers posed a problem for the U.S. government because, unlike the Cubans, they

Figure 11. The U.S. Coast Guard cutter *Cape Strait* towing a boat it intercepted while patrolling during the Mariel boatlift. The boat carried more than fifty refugees from Haiti. Photograph by Dale McDonald. Courtesy of the State Library and Archives of Florida.

were fleeing a friendly government. As such, less than one hundred Haitians were granted asylum in the United States throughout the 1970s.[85] This difference did not go unnoticed in Dade County. "If Duvalier were a Communist," one county official stated, "the Haitians wouldn't have any problems."[86] Although the numbers of Haitians arriving on the American coasts were not on par with the mass of Cubans arriving as part of the Mariel boatlift, they still needed assistance. This led the federal government to establish the Haitian Processing Center in Miami in March 1980.[87] These refugee influxes were linked in the federal bureaucracy with the establishment of the Cuban-Haitian Task Force as the coordinating entity for dealing with the refugees.

A coalition of advocates, including religious groups and some Democratic politicians, had been attempting to get better treatment for Haitian refugees for years before the boatlift. For them, Mariel illustrated the hypocrisy of American refugee policy.[88] The poorer treatment of Haitian refugees in relation to refugees from Cuba did not start in 1980 or even in the 1970s. In 1963, a boatload of Haitians seeking refuge from persecution and violence in their home country came to the United States, only to be denied asylum and deported.[89] The treatment of Haitian refugees, as historian Carl Lindskoog has shown, is intricately tied to the development of the massive immigration detention regime by the U.S. government. The arrival of Haitian refugees in the last three decades of the twentieth century drove the federal government to reinstate immigration detention in 1981, first as a measure against the Haitians and then applied broadly as part of the immigration regime.[90] During the Mariel boatlift, however, this treatment had yet to become a broader policy. Instead, even though they shared an "entrant" status, the differences in the treatment between the Cuban and Haitian refugees were pronounced.

In order to deny many Haitians full entrance into the United States, federal authorities adhered to the entrant category and a hesitance for requesting political asylum on the part of the Haitian refugees that mirrored the hesitance of some of the Cubans who arrived in the early 1960s. Unlike the Mariel refugees, when questioned, most Haitians denied that they were fleeing political repression by the Duvalier government. There was a widespread belief among the refugees that if they sought political asylum and were deported back to Haiti they would be imprisoned or killed. Because of these assertions and because the federal government was hesitant to provide asylum to people fleeing an allied state, immigration officials deemed the Haitians economic migrants rather than political asylum seekers. Haitian refugees were thus ineligible for work permits, government aid, and other benefits. Compounding this lack of benefits was the fact that the established Haitian community in Miami was less than a tenth the size and less affluent than the city's Cuban community. "Haitians can only envy the political and economic influence of the Cubans, who have been generally credited with reviving Miami's economy," declared the *Wall Street Journal*.[91]

Haitian advocates and leaders often showed frustration, mistrust, and anger when dealing with the federal government, particularly the Cuban-Haitian Task Force. Task Force members were greeted with distrust when they met with Rulx Jean Barte, the director of the Haitian American Community Association of Dade County (HACAD). The association provided primary health care, assistance with employment, translation, emergency aid, education and referral services to the Haitian community. The organization had to cut back on some of its programs due to lack of funding. Jean Barte was "highly suspicious of the intentions of the Cuban Haitian Task Force and of the 'real' purpose or rationale for attempting to establish or reestablish communication with the Haitian community." The task force had a history with the Haitian community that fueled Jean Barte's suspicions; it only contacted Haitian agencies when it had a problem it could not solve. Jean Barte pointed out the lack of Haitian staff within the task force at the decision-making level. He charged that there was a racist and discriminatory attitude that kept Haitians from being included in the management of the crisis and kept all the high-ranking positions within the task force staffed by Americans or Cubans. He wanted to see Haitians receive fair treatment equal to that of the Cuban population, but he placed little trust or faith in the task force. Officials described Jean Barte as "very tough and direct," and they suggested that with "concrete assistance rather than promises," the task force might persuade him of the sincerity of its concern for Haitian refugees. "He will be watching what we do rather than what we say," it stated.[92]

Many African Americans in South Florida and elsewhere saw uneven treatment and often agreed with the assessment of many Haitian refugees that racial motivations drove these inequalities. The city's African Americans were no strangers to frustrations related to Cuban refugees and Cuban Americans, particularly in relation to city, state, and federal authorities. By the time of Mariel, the inequalities that had helped feed the discontent and the 1968 Liberty City riots had become ingrained into the city's power structures and its race relations. In 1980, the median family income for an African American family in Greater Miami was $11,356. The median income for Latinos was $14,491, and it was $16,616 for white Miamians. This led to significant disparities in the poverty rates in the city. The rate of African Americans living under the poverty level was 26.4% in 1979, compared to 14.8% for Latinos and 8.6% for whites.[93]

The influx of Cuban refugees and other groups from Latin America, combined with highway construction that had displaced a significant number of families from traditionally the African American Overtown, had also created an oversaturated housing situation in Liberty City and Brownsville. The population of these two communities had risen rapidly, from 48,024 in 1960 to 76,064 by the 1970s.[94] Discriminatory housing policies that were common throughout the nation directly affected these communities as well. In late May of 1980, Florida International University psychologist Marvin Dunn and his research assistant Andrea Loring, filed a report with federal authorities that noted the persistence of redlining in the predominantly African American areas of Miami. The office of the Florida State Insurance Commissioner had conducted an investigation that found that insurance companies assigned members of the Black community higher risk categories than whites regarding the procurement of business, home, and automobile insurance. The report described how low-income residents rarely qualified for lines of credit with banks and had to deal with individual businesses that would lend them money at much higher rates. The economic boom in the city of Miami had also accelerated the gentrification of low-income areas, where rising costs forced owners to sell and renters to move.[95]

To make matters worse, the heavy investment being received from Latin America rarely made its way into African American areas. "You can look at the skyline and see cranes everywhere except over the black community," said Miami city attorney George Knox, one of a few African American officials in the city.[96] An official in the Department of Housing and Urban Development clarified that differences like the influx of Latin American money and the presence of the increasingly strong Hispanic community in the city did not prevent a "striking similarity" to other cities in that the African American community was in last place in the economic mainstream. The only difference was that in Miami, African Americans lagged behind both the Latino and white communities. Now there were tens of thousands of newly arrived Cubans and Haitians, who were competing with African Americans for public resources. African Americans were frustrated by this new competition and by "the perceived quickness with which some Cuban refugees are able to enter the healthy economic mainstream."[97] These frustrations became particularly sharp when some local employers began requiring job applicants be bilingual at a time in which the rate of Black unemployment was three to four times that of the overall area and Black youth unemployment varied between 45% and 85% depending on the season.[98] A study conducted in the late 1970s also found that the vast majority of African Americans felt that Cubans were better treated than their own community, while "whites and Latins essentially dismiss the validity of those feelings."[99] This continued pattern of economic disenfranchisement and stagnation in the growth of political power in favor of new immigrants now seemed a permanent feature of life in Miami.

These tensions exploded after the resolution of the Arthur McDuffie case. On December 16, 1979, McDuffie, an African American insurance executive, was pursued through the streets of the Miami by over a dozen police cars following an alleged traffic violation on his motorcycle. Up to a dozen police officers viciously beat McDuffie at the end of the pursuit and left him with an open head injury that killed him four days later. The officers attempted to cover up the beating by making it seem that McDuffie had lost control and been thrown from his motorcycle, but physical evidence disproved this claim. At the trial of the five officers charged with his death, Dade County's chief medical examiner testified that McDuffie's brain damage was the most severe he had seen in the thirty-six hundred autopsies he had participated in or observed throughout his career. Two officers received immunity in exchange for their testimony, and witnesses also testified to the beating. The seven-week trial concluded on May 17, 1980, when an all-white jury exonerated the five defendants of all charges after only three hours of deliberation.[100] News of the acquittal spread fast and resulted in the start of several days of rioting that resulted in ten deaths by the end of the first night.[101]

While the McDuffie acquittals sparked the violence, the discontent that led to the uprising came from long-standing grievances. At the end of the year, the *Miami Herald* explained that the violence broke out not only because of McDuffie's death and the subsequent acquittals, but because "in the 12 years since Miami's first black riots in 1968, the fundamental causes of blacks' seething discontent had barely been addressed, much less corrected."[102] As in 1968, these fundamental causes were linked to the Cuban presence in Miami. One of the police officers acquitted by the jury was, in fact, a Cuban American. News reports indicated that some African Americans had bitterly commented that Cubans had "become so assimilated into American society that they now were joining whites in brutalizing blacks."[103] To many of Miami's African Americans, the presence of Miami's Cuban Americans and their status in the city were linked to the subordination of the Black community by whites and by the police.

Following the uprising, the *Wall Street Journal* spoke to a man who had thrown stones at white motorists. While protecting his identity, the piece noted that he was not a "typical race rioter." The man worked as a counselor for African American youth, but he still felt angry and hopeless in the face of his circumstances. "I get jibe from whites on the job, crap from Cubans, and when I come home, I get it from the police," the man explained, adding, "I'm convinced this is the only way we can get justice."[104] The 1980 uprising was, to many of Miami's African Americans, the only way to address years of frustrations. The high level of participation reflected the widespread nature of these frustrations: an estimated 26% of the population in the affected areas participated in the violence. This was much higher than the participation rates in Detroit and Newark in 1967, which ranged between 12% and 15%.[105]

After three days, fifteen people had died and nearly four hundred had been injured. Press reports estimated property damage after the disturbances at $100 million, most of which had been targeted against businesses owned by Latinos and whites.[106] The consequences for the affected communities would last far longer than three days, but so too would the political fallout for the Carter administration. African American community leaders, both locally and nationally, were extremely critical of the federal government's response to the riot, with Jesse Jackson comparing it negatively to the responses to the eruption of Mt. St. Helens and to the Mariel boatlift. But the White House was reluctant to declare the situation a disaster for fear that it would encourage other disenfranchised African American populations around the country to initiate their own rebellions to get federal aid into their communities.[107]

Carter's problems would continue as officials visited Miami in the months after the riot and reported that the situation in the city was "extremely volatile." "Although we have tried to separate the problems," stated the author of one report, "it is apparent to me that the impact of the influx of Cuban and Haitian refugees is inextricable from the plight of the indigenous Blacks largely concentrated in Liberty City and Overtown." Like the African Americans in these areas, federal officials recognized that the advantages accorded to Cuban refugees in the previous two decades and the recent influxes of refugees from Cuba and Haiti had exacerbated Black unemployment and had "engendered a high degree of bitterness." The official who filed the report recognized the problem but had no suggestions on how to resolve this divide beyond recommending that the refugee influx and the civil disturbances be regarded "as two elements of the same problem."[108]

Exiles in Their Own City: Xenophobia, Ableism, and the Growing Backlash Against the Marielitos in South Florida

Some white Miamians had disapproved of the arrival of previous waves of Cubans, but the backlash in response to the Mariel boatlift was more severe because of the sheer volume of refugees arriving in such a short time. The month of May alone saw 94,181 Cubans arriving in the United States, a total larger than any previous year of Cuban migration.[109] When the Cuban government finally closed the port of Mariel on September 25 and the last boat docked in Key West four days later, the total number of refugees from the boatlift was over 124,000.[110] While federal authorities placed 62,541 Marielitos in camps created while they awaited sponsorship offers, the majority of the other refugees streamed into Miami at an unprecedented rate. Due to the housing shortage in Miami, authorities warehoused many of the Cubans who could not get immediate sponsorship but whom they did not consider dangerous or suspicious in "tent cities" in parks and under expressways. The largest of these tent cities was under Interstate 95, to the east of Little Havana.[111]

Situated next to the Miami River, the Riverside Park Tent City had a Cuban refugee population in the hundreds, which varied based on the resettlement of residents. The population of the camp was overwhelmingly male; one report estimated that only fifty women resided there. Residents complained about mosquito infestations coming from the river and from stagnant water accumulating in the southwest corner of the camp. Others complained about the lack of sheets, soap, and towels. Refugees were provided breakfast and dinner and were given food stamps so that they might procure their own lunches. While jobs were scarce in Miami, refugees were able to place job applications with the Florida State Employment Service. Volunteer agencies and Cuban American organizations provided other services.[112] Resources only became more strained as more than three thousand refugees passed through the tent city in the month that followed, according to estimates from the city of Miami.[113] The visibility of the camps was a significant problem, as it fostered the anger of city residents against the refugees.

The *Wall Street Journal* reported that even before the refugee influx began, radio talk shows had "been abuzz with Anglos expressing anger about how quickly Miami has changed from an Anglo tourist resort to a major Latin city, where virtually no English is heard in many sections." The backlash against both Cuban and Haitian refugees was often racialized and rife with xenophobia. It was also, at times, deeply ableist. Miami resident Richard Rosichan lived near Little Haiti and claimed that his children had found a "ritually slaughtered goat" near some railroad tracks, before declaring that it was "grossly unfair that one small area of one city should bear almost the entire burden of one of the most impoverished, unhealthy and unskilled wave of immigrants ever to cross our shores." The perception of the refugees as unskilled "parasites" was not uncommon, nor was it new, but it was particularly prevalent during the boatlift. Residents were particularly concerned about the possibility of the refugees being housed near them, believing they would "bring with them tuberculosis, venereal disease and other ailments." The Mariel and Haitian influxes only exacerbated the anger of Miamians over the changes in their city. Officials were less hyperbolic but just as concerned about the effect of the refugees on the city and its resources. One of Miami's city commissioners, the Cuban-born Armando Lacasa, noted that Miami was quickly becoming "the refugee capital of the Americas."[114]

Increasingly Cuban Americans wielded power in Miami, but this was not true of all cities in the area. Officials in Miami Beach, where Cuban Americans held less power, were more vocal in their displeasure. In late July of 1980, for example, Miami Beach's mayor, Murray Meyerson, wrote a letter to President Carter asking for aid. Meyerson described an "intolerable situation" that had been created by "pouring more than 100,000 people into a community which has no housing surplus, no job surplus and limited welfare reserves." He described how hundreds of refugees had been "jammed" into substandard housing by well-meaning private charities and public agencies with only a month's rent and no promise of future resources. The refugees, he explained, had been reduced to "extremities of poverty." These extremes often drove the men among the refugees to turn to crime, noting that the crime rate in his city had risen by at least 30% over the previous ninety days. He pleaded with the president for help, explaining that "simple humanity and a proper regard" for the refugees and the welfare of the citizenry made it imperative that the president declare a state of emergency in Dade County.[115]

Miami Beach officials wanted federal authorities to see the palpable fear among the city's elderly residents and forwarded the minutes of a city commission meeting attended by several hundred elderly citizens in a letter to Congressman Claude Pepper and other federal officials. During the meeting, Nina Rosenberg, who had been a Miami Beach resident for thirty-five years, spoke of a beautiful, peaceful community that no longer existed. "It's became just one big prison," Rosenberg stated, "We are locked in in our apartments." She told the audience that a man who had threatened to cut her face had mugged her at 10 a.m. the previous week and that many of the people present had had similar experiences. Then she explained she did not have a problem with all refugees, only the criminals among them: "Now, we understand that there are refugees that are fine people. We sympathize with them. We've got to help them. We don't mind to pay taxes extra to feed them, to shelter them but there are undesirable elements that when we see them and they turn back and hit us and mug us and rape us and are ready to kill us, well this is too much and this we cannot take."

Rosenberg explained that she too had once been an immigrant, but that she had come to the United States as a teenager and had worked twelve hours a day for $5 a week. The difference, she declared to applause from the room, was that nobody had put her in a hotel and given her food and "shelter and money and everything." Despite her view that the Marielitos were not sufficiently pulling themselves up by the bootstraps, she reiterated that there were good people among the refugees. The problem was that residents were being mugged for drug money, and the neighborhood synagogue, barber shop, and stores had all been vandalized. Now it was the residents of Miami Beach who would be exiled from their homes, but they had no place to go.[116]

A report released in 1987 estimated that the number of Mariel entrants who committed crimes after arriving in the United States was around twenty-eight hundred.[117] Advocates for the Marielitos argued that the crimes committed by the refugees were a natural consequence of their entry situation. Miami was in shock over the arrival of tens of thousands of refugees who did not speak English and did not have jobs, with many also lacking family support. "Any city you did that to would have a problem of people turning to crime to survive," Rafael Peñalver, who provided legal representation for many of these entrants, reasoned years later. While Miami Beach city officials emphasized the more heinous crimes committed as part of the crime rate increase in South Florida, some refugees committed crimes for their survival or that of their family. While petty larceny was one of the crimes that increased significantly, some of the offenses were drug related. By 1980, Miami was a major point of transit for the drug trade into the United States. An influx of penniless, jobless refugees provided a pool of potential employees for Miami's drug runners. The refugees often worked as mules and couriers for the drug trade. They would be offered as little as one hundred or two hundred dollars to transport a package from one part of the city to another. Those caught by police found themselves facing drug-trafficking charges and helped drive up the crime rate.[118]

The newest wave of refugees drove a wave of xenophobic fears of cultural displacement, disease, crime, and economic loss that drove polarization between a significant part of Miami's non-Hispanic whites and the city's immigrant populations, both new and established. This helped the fortunes of an inchoate English-only movement in South Florida. While similar movements would arise in other areas of the United States in later years, the historic bilingual ordinance of 1973 had become the target of the opponents of bilingualism in Dade County. In 1980, an organization calling itself Citizens of Dade United introduced an ordinance prohibiting "the expenditure of any county funds for the purpose of utilizing any language other than English or any culture other than that of the United States."[119] The new ordinance would not repeal the 1973 bilingual ordinance, but it would remove any county funds for bilingual county services. A woman named Emmy Shafer, a Holocaust survivor who had come to the United States after the Second World War at age sixteen, led the drive for signatures to put this ordinance on the ballot. Shafer longed for Miami to be "the way it used to be." The Miami in her memory was friendly and safe, a place where Americans did not feel as though they were in a foreign country.[120]

Eduardo Padrón, chairman of the Spanish American League Against Discrimination, verbalized the shock felt by the Cuban American community. "They have seen themselves as great contributors, and all the statistics show that," Padrón said; "All of a sudden that feeling of not being wanted, not being appreciated, hurts." Cuban Americans and other Spanish speakers were not without allies. Despite the divisions between Miami's Cuban American and African American communities, Black leaders staunchly opposed the ordinance. The Greater Miami chapter of the NAACP passed a resolution noting that the ordinance implied that the only culture the county would fund was white culture. Many in Miami's business community came out against the proposal. The Greater Miami Chamber of Commerce spent seventy-five thousand dollars campaigning against the proposed ordinance. Despite this resistance, there was significant support for Citizens of Dade United. A public opinion poll conducted in the months before the election showed that 62% of the voters polled approved of the proposal and that the heaviest support came from Jewish voters and senior citizens, who favored the proposal by 4–1.[121]

The day before the vote, the *Miami Herald* declared that the city was sick. The disease that had left Miami "disoriented, in agony, and in danger of destroying itself," had been born of fire and water. "The fire of Liberty City and the water of Mariel have left Miami faltering, uncertain and divided, at the most crucial point in its history." The only solution was for all Miamians to come together and prevent the city's collapse with joint action. There was a danger that a city that had once assimilated six hundred thousand Hispanics and became an economic powerhouse as a result would now let its frustrations turn "Hispanic" and especially "Cuban" into dirty words. While the editorial did not make specific mention of the ballot proposal, it made it clear that Miami's Cuban community was fearful of backlash and rejection driven by the boatlift.[122]

The ballot proposal passed and became a new countywide ordinance. Critics found the vote polarizing. "It was a racist vote," said Monsignor Walsh. Other opponents hoped the alliance made between the Hispanic community and the African American community might be "the beginning of a majority black-Latin coalition that could become a power in the local government." The same election saw the first Cuban American elected to countywide office when Paul Cejas won a seat on the school board with African American support.[123] The election had proved to be a major victory for the English-only movement. This encouraged the return of Citizens of Dade United, which, in 1988, pushed an English-only amendment to Florida's state constitution. That statewide measure passed by 84%.[124]

The animosity aimed at the Cuban American community and at Hispanics in general did not dissipate as the boatlift ended, even though as time went on, the outward signs of the refugee influx began to dissipate. The tent city disappeared and the Marielitos became less identifiable from other Cubans or other Latin American immigrants in the city. The increasing presence of other groups in the city, however, only exacerbated the anger that many non-Hispanic whites felt. Some found that very label problematic. One irate *Herald* reader was offended by the newspaper's use of the term "non-Latin white." Mary Ellen Higgin wrote the newspaper to declare the term a sign of "reverse discrimination." It was the most offensive term she could think of for "Americans" and an insult that would only add to the fires of polarization. "How can you expect this county to ever be together," Higgin asked, "when you insult the people who were born here, and who built this city?"[125] Another reader argued that "the real refugees" were not those who had fled politically oppressive regimes, but rather those South Florida residents leaving to seek a better life elsewhere in the United States. Those who felt that the good life they had once known would never return, decreed Fred Moffet, were "the real refugees of South Florida."[126]

The feeling that the recent migratory influxes had made South Florida's "Americans" refugees and that foreigners had taken their city from them became a common one in the early 1980s. Bumper stickers reading "WILL THE LAST AMERICAN TO LEAVE MIAMI PLEASE BRING THE FLAG" were a common sight. They became so prevalent, in fact, that the *Herald*'s executive editor, John McMullan, once again entered the fray with a piece about the anger of many Miamians toward those who adorned their vehicles with those stickers. McMullan had had enough of "homegrown American bigots" who thought themselves to have some exclusive franchise over the United States or any of its cities. "Spare me any more dim-witted Anglos who can't speak acceptable English themselves complaining because signs that may save their lives are also written in Spanish," McMullan wrote. Even as he took others to task over overt discrimination, he also admitted that newspaper editors could speak out more often but did not. Until communication could bridge the gap between the polarized groups in the city, McMullan indicated he wanted a replacement bumper sticker, one that read: "WILL THE LAST BIGOTS PLEASE LEAVE."

Mcmullan also explained in his comment that the "saddest local story of a globally sad week" was the formation of a Cuban American group in Miami that felt it had to "campaign to correct the Cuban refugees' image."[127]

Mariel on the Silver Screen: Cuban American Image Activism and the Controversy over the Filming of *Scarface*

Mcmullan was referring to the creation of a committee of prominent Cubans calling their organization Facts About Cuban Exiles (FACE). FACE members worried about the impact a negative conception of Cubans had. Media representation had been central to making *Marielito* a dirty word. For many Cuban Americans this had become offensive, "an affront to their pride." These prominent Cubans were proud of their individual achievements, and they were proud of Dade County's majority Cuban Hispanic community, which had a combined annual income of $6.5 billion. It was an impressive achievement and they sought to defend it. "I'll be damned if I let anybody spoil it," said banker Carlos Arboleya.[128]

Arboleya and his fellow FACE committee members were not alone in defending their community in the face of unfavorable portrayals in the media. Many had fought against what they saw as a negative portrayal when the producers attempted to bring the filming of Brian De Palma's *Scarface* remake to Miami. The film, starring Al Pacino as Tony Montana, told the story of the violent rise of a Mariel refugee from common criminal to international drug trafficker and of his equally violent downfall. The film's content elicited strong negative reactions from the city's Cuban community. Even as producer Martin Bregman threatened to move the film's production elsewhere, Miami city commissioner Demetrio Pérez Jr. prepared a resolution to deny the production the permits necessary to film on city property and on city streets. Bregman was puzzled by the reaction from the Cuban community. He was not making a film about Cubans in Miami, but rather a movie about a single gangster. "The movie has more crooked Jews than crooked Cubans," the producer stated. Further, he suggested that the movie would not give Miami or Dade County a bad image. After all, it already had that image.[129]

Pérez framed his objection in terms of the possible danger to the city's public relations in a letter to the *Herald*'s editor; others were more direct in their defense of the Cuban American community itself.[130] *Herald* staff writer Guillermo Martinez argued against the filming because it could only further perpetrate a prevalent, and most often mistaken, stereotype about Marielitos. Martinez recounted how after taking pictures of a crime scene where a man had murdered eight people and fled on a bicycle before being killed himself, a photographer exclaimed that the killer had to be a Marielito because "Who else would be crazy enough to kill eight people in cold blood and then try to escape on a bicycle?" When authorities later identified the murderer, they determined that he was not a Marielito—he was not even Latino—but the stereotype about the Mariel refugees made more than one person conclude that the killer had to be one. The stereotype was so prevalent that the protagonist of the *Scarface* remake could hardly have belonged to any other group. Hollywood was both reacting to the stereotype and helping to perpetuate it. Miami's economy did not need the money that the production would bring if it damaged the image of Miami's Cuban community. What the Cuban community needed was an organization of Cubans "similar to the Anti-Defamation League of B'nai B'rith—who will act in a responsible and nonpolitical manner to make sure that Cubans are not gratuitously insulted or slandered."[131]

Cubans Americans and their allies took to writing letters to the *Herald* to express their displeasure with the filming of *Scarface* because of the harm it would bring to the community's image. James Kassir wrote that the movie would only "hurt the image of hard-working Cuban-Americans."[132] Another reader attacked the *Herald* editorial board's choice of justifying the making of the film on economic reasons, stating the offending the sensibilities of any ethnic group was un-American, regardless of the profit or justification.[133] Ana F. Crucet declared that she and her fellow Cuban Americans would not "stand by and let Hollywood propaganda make us the object of ostracism and stereotyping as criminals by other ethnic groups."[134] Edgardo O. Meneses addressed "the Anglos who want to sell the image of their city for a measly $10 million" and reminded them that tourism in Miami and Miami Beach had already suffered significantly in the previous two years. Further, he asked why Hollywood did not make movies about Cuban freedom fighters instead of Cuban gangsters.[135]

Letters either against or in support of the production of *Scarface* became a fixture of the *Herald's* letters page during August and September of 1982. They were, in fact, so prevalent that they became the subject of parody. Fort Lauderdale resident Stu Schneider wrote the *Herald's* editor a letter in mid-September in which he described himself as being "shocked, appalled, and disgusted" about plans to shoot the film *Jaws III* in Key West. "Not all sharks are man-eaters, just a minority," wrote Schneider, "but, as usual, Hollywood has decided to focus on a few bad apples that ruin the whole batch." He went on to suggest that unless filmmakers intended to treat sharks fairly, they should not be allowed to film in South Florida. "Some things are more important than money," he concluded; "What's next, *Attack of the Giant Oysters?*"[136]

Where many in Miami were offended by the possibility of the movie being shot in their city, neighboring Miami Beach rushed the passage of a resolution to welcome the filming of *Scarface* to their city.[137] Filmmakers shot only two scenes of the film in South Florida, both of them in Miami Beach. The movie was filmed mostly in Los Angeles with Pacino in the lead and former ¿*Que pasa USA?* star Steven Bauer as his lieutenant, Manny Ribera. While those opposed to the film's shooting in Miami ultimately won the day, they were unable to change the story's content or characterizations. The arguments over the image of Mariel, and the Cuban American community in general, would flare up again a few months later when *Reader's Digest* published "From Cuba with Hate" in December of that year.

During the boatlift and in the years immediately after, Miami's Cubans became keenly aware that, as the *Wall Street Journal* pointed out in 1980, political gains had not followed the Cubans' economic success. Prior to the boatlift, only 26% of Hispanics were registered to vote in Miami.[138] This had produced vulnerabilities that left them with limited influence in local and national politics and which their adversaries identified and exploited. When Emmy Shafer drove the repeal of the bilingual amendment in 1980, she claimed that the Cubans got their own way in everything because local politicians were for sale and they quickly forgot that "the English people are the ones that vote."[139] In the aftermath of the boatlift, the referendum that eliminated official bilingualism in Dade County, and years of bad publicity, many Cubans were calling for change and organization to achieve the political and social clout to match the community's standing in South Florida. Mariel set the stage for the next phase of Cuban American political activism and for a decade in which politicians and lobbyists would project the local power that the community had accrued nationally and internationally. South Florida's Cuban Americans would see the significant power of their community to influence larger trends and events, but they would also face the limits of that power.

CHAPTER 6

"A Crisis in Clout": The Maturation of Cuban American Politics, the Cuban Lobby, and the Limits of Influence

The sudden arrival of a National Guard helicopter, flying low and loud, got the attention of the men inside the federal detention facility at Oakdale, LA, on Sunday November 29, 1987. For eight days, nearly one thousand Cuban detainees had controlled the facility and held hostages. Throughout the crisis, over five hundred Bureau of Prisons (BOP) and FBI agents had guarded the perimeter of the detention center.[1] The detainees, the hostages, and the federal agents waited as the U.S. government negotiated with detainee leaders and third parties. The helicopter disrupted both the tension and the boredom with its arrival. The pilot guided the aircraft in a grand entrance, flying over the facility and finally landing in full view of the detainees just outside the fence. Then Miami's auxiliary Catholic bishop, Agustín Román, stepped off the helicopter to end the hostage crisis.[2]

Román's presence was crucial to ending the standoff that had started the night of November 21, when news that deportations were imminent following a new immigration agreement between Washington and Havana had reached the detainees.[3] A group of 250 Cuban detainees brandishing homemade weapons had confronted Oakdale staff with a cry of *"¡Somos los abandonados!"* (We are the abandoned ones!) and had taken twenty-eight hostages.[4] The stakes grew even higher the following Monday when a second group of Cuban detainees took control of the federal penitentiary in Atlanta, GA.[5] A peaceful resolution in Oakdale would be a good first step to ending the Atlanta siege as well. The detainees did not trust Attorney General Edwin Meese and had wanted Román to intercede on their behalf, even putting up a sign on the detention center that read, "We want the Bishop."[6] After eight days of waiting, the bishop had finally arrived.

Román and his partner in the negotiations, Cuban American lawyer Rafael Peñalver, climbed onto a waiting jeep. As the vehicle made slow loops around the facility with Román standing in the back in full regalia, three detainees on the inside of the perimeter fence began to follow the jeep. Three men soon became a crowd. Once he had a sufficient audience, Román took to a stage prepared for him by federal authorities. "This is a moment of peace," he told the detainees.[7] He called on the prisoners to join him in prayer, to come to the negotiating table, and to free the hostages. Years later, Peñalver would describe the effects of Román's words as miraculous. Based on the bishop's rhetoric of peace and his assurances of the terms he and Peñalver had gotten for the detainees, the rioters laid down their arms in the detention courtyard and set about releasing their hostages.[8]

The hostage crises at Oakdale and Atlanta came almost thirty years after the triumph of the Cuban Revolution, but they remained firmly rooted in the interplay between the Cuban government, the U.S. government, and the Cuban American community. The policy choices of the 1960s were just as significant to the lived experiences of Cubans and Cuban Americans on both sides of the prison walls as the choices of the period after the Mariel boatlift. The detainees had entered the country using the long-standing open-door policy established by the Eisenhower administration and had found themselves in indefinite detention because of the ongoing conflicts between Washington and Havana. Those Cuban Americans who advocated for the detainees saw the conflict in terms of the human rights violation of indefinite detention, but they also feared it would be compounded by deportation to a regime to which they were fundamentally opposed. Their standing in South Florida, much like that of Cuban American elites whose position on the detainees varied, was rooted in the migratory and assistance policies of the early exile. The choices made by policymakers and law enforcement in the 1980s necessitated a response, but the position from which Cuban Americans reacted was made possible by the evolution of South Florida as set into motion almost three decades before. Even after the collapse of the Soviet Union, some things remained the same in Miami. "In a small corner of the Western Hemisphere," read a *Miami Herald* story from October of 1992, "the Cold War endures."[9] The dynamics of the Cold War in the city were not the same as they had been in 1959, but the city's time as the open gateway into the United States did not truly end until 1995 with the resolution of the Cuban rafter crisis and the adoption of the wet foot, dry foot policy.

This chapter charts the shifts in Cuban American politics after the Mariel boatlift, the indefinite detention of Marielitos in American prisons, and the changes to federal Cuban refugee policy brought about by the end of the Cold War. Essential to these changes was the creation of a powerful political lobby, the Cuban American National Foundation (CANF), by wealthy Cuban Americans in the aftermath of Mariel. CANF embraced the politics of the Ronald Reagan era to amplify Cuban American influence and achieved its greatest success through the creation of Radio Martí and its sister television station, TV Martí. CANF also embraced the privatization and neoliberal policy objectives of the Reagan and George H. W. Bush administrations and created a private sector initiative that used the Cuban American community's own resources to provide opportunities for arriving refugees.

Out of this growing political influence, several members of the community attained political successes at the local and national levels in the 1980s. The stories of Miami's first Cuban American mayor and the first Cuban American U.S. representative illustrate the growing influence of the community in Dade County, but also the specific contours of its politics and its relations to broader political structures. In the process, electoral politics changed in Dade County, and these changes fundamentally altered Miami's place in American politics.

This consolidation of power did not end the challenges that the Cuban American community still had to face and which tested their unity and showed the limits of their growing power. The problem of the Marielitos who languished in American prisons and immigration detention facilities because they were deemed excludable but could not be deported to Cuba caused consternation for both Cuban Americans and human rights advocates. As the detention of these individuals continued over the years, tensions and the threat of violence grew. These tensions led to the uprisings in Oakdale and Atlanta, causing activists both within and outside the Cuban American community to advocate for the detainees during the crisis and during its long aftermath and also in response to the continued indefinite detention of the Marielitos.

As the Cold War drew to a close, CANF and its chairman, Jorge Mas Canosa, would continue to build on the organization's reach and find that their influence had limits. While Mas Canosa engaged in fights with his critics in the community and outside of it, the foundation's political power was tested by a new migratory crisis and a new president scarred by memories of Mariel and concerned about his party's prospects in the face of growing nativist sentiment. Ultimately, the rafter crisis fundamentally changed the patterns of Cuban migration established after the revolution and, despite CANF's lobbying, led to the establishment of the wet foot, dry foot policy, which illustrated one limit of the community's political influence.

Courting Power: The Cuban American Lobby, the Reagan White House, and Miami's Influence in the Late Cold War

In 1981, while still reeling from Mariel and the "English Only" vote in Dade County, a group of wealthy Cuban Americans, many of whom had been in Brigade 2506, came together to establish the Cuban American National Foundation (CANF).[10] CANF would describe itself as "an independent, non-profit institution providing information on the economic, political and social welfare of the Cuban people, both on the island and in exile," and working in support of a free and democratic Cuba.[11] Years later, Jorge Mas Canosa described the early days of the organization and his view of the Cuban American community in 1981. He saw his community as economically robust but lacking in political power and sophistication. Cuban Americans were stuck in a rut. The community always put forth the "same faces, same language, same thing about we talking in Spanish all the time, listening to the same radio stations, being perceived as a bunch of terrorists, right wingers, incapable of taking care of ourselves." As long as the perception of Cuban Americans as paranoid fanatics who saw communists around every corner persisted, the public at large would simply conclude that Castro and the Cuban Americans deserved each other.[12]

Cuban Americans needed political power to change this perception, but Mas Canosa believed that this scared off those who could project a new image. "Politics" was a dirty word to the "best" Cubans; those who had proven themselves in business. Successful businessmen, he thought, would bring significant problem-solving skills and a pragmatic approach to politics. Mas Canosa thought this class of Cuban American would bring some maturity to what was a "very green, very inexperienced approach to Cuba and Cuban politics."[13]

Mas Canosa and the founders of CANF were directly building on the economic power of the Cuban American community to build a political structure. The "best" Cubans had grown their wealth in an environment made fertile by the policies established two decades earlier. Now, the wealthiest among them could use that economic power to have a political voice within the oligarchical structure that directed CANF. To be a CANF trustee, Cuban Americans needed to contribute at least five thousand dollars a year to the foundation. A higher tier of directors required an annual payment of ten thousand dollars a year.[14] Mas Canosa later claimed that he contributed an average of fifty thousand dollars a year to the foundation.[15] This placed the management of the organization in the hands of the most affluent Cuban Americans, as only those who qualified for directorship could vote on foundation matters. Among these wealthy Cubans, the directorship was exclusively male until 1990, at which time only three of its sixty-six directors were women.[16]

To "take the fight out of Calle Ocho and Miami Stadium and into the center of power," CANF established its principal base in Washington, DC. No longer should Cuban American political organizations concentrate on clandestine raids on Cuba. Instead, they should now focus on influencing public opinion and governments.[17] Mas Canosa also believed that the creation of CANF had provided a safer outlet for the energies and frustrations of the Cuban American community than the violence being perpetrated by Cuban Americans on other members of their community. He viewed CANF as an instrument by which the energies of his community could be channeled more positively: "We made an effort to show [the Cuban American community] that there were other civilized ways to struggle for the democratization of Cuba, like creating Radio Marti, lobbying in Washington, doing an international effort to delegitimize Castro for his violation of human rights. And I think when you look back into history, during the last 15 years of assistance [sic] of the Cuban-American national foundation, the bombings stopped and the killings also came to a halt."[18]

The late 1970s and the early 1980s were a time of significant violence by Cuban American groups. Despite Mas Canosa's claims, the violence did not suddenly end with the creation of the Cuban American National Foundation. Bombings in Miami continued until at least 1983.[19] Mas Canosa's assertion that CANF's creation brought about a new outlet for the energies of some anti-Castro Cuban Americans was correct. However, some people questioned whether the foundation was truly the natural outgrowth of a widespread sense of frustration with the available avenues of anti-Castro action. As CANF gained influence, the foundation's critics argued that they had co-opted these frustrations and had shaped them to fit their vision of Cuba's future through wealth and careful messaging.

CANF modeled its political action committee, the Free Cuba PAC, after the American Israel Public Affairs Committee.[20] Mas Canosa copied the structure and tactics of what he considered the most successful foreign policy lobbying group in existence.[21] CANF's directors contributed to politicians who supported the organization's stance on Cuba. Mas Canosa claimed that the foundation did not make political contributions and that CANF did not "get involved in any type of partisan politics."[22] This was technically correct. CANF did not make donations directly. Instead, the Free Cuba PAC made the donations. Between 1983 and 1988, the Free Cuba PAC contributed more than $385,000 to candidates and sitting congressional representatives, both Democratic and Republican.[23] State and federal officials from Florida including Ileana Ros-Lehtinen, Lincoln Díaz-Balart, Senator Connie Mack, and Governor Lawton Chiles received aid from the Free Cuba PAC. The foundation's support extended beyond Florida and Florida's delegation to Congress to friendly politicians like New Jersey Representatives Bob Menendez and Robert Torricelli and Senator Ernest Hollings of South Carolina. These politicians then provided support and political influence for the foundation.

For candidates in tight races who supported CANF's Cuba policies, the foundation could become a significant ally. A candidate in the 1988 election for U.S. Senate in Connecticut passed CANF's test regarding this "most important consideration." Incumbent Lowell Weicker Jr. failed CANF's Cuba litmus test. The Free Cuba PAC instead supported Weicker's opponent, Joe Lieberman, who went on to win by a margin of less than 1%.[24] Lieberman would continue to court CANF's support throughout his career, and by 2000, CANF executive director Joe Garcia stated that the foundation had "no questions where Joe Lieberman stands."[25]

The foundation's potential as a lobby, the ambition of its individual members, and the enduring divides within the Cuban American community ensured that the organization would be rife with internal conflict from the start. The foundation's board originally named Frank Calzón as CANF's first executive director. Calzón had lobbying experience, having served as director of On Human Rights, a group that publicized human rights violations in Cuba, and had lobbied Congress against Castro's government. Mas Canosa and Calzón reportedly clashed over differing visions of the focus of the foundation's energies and resources. While Calzón wanted to continue mounting pressure on Washington to affect Cuba policy, Mas Canosa became increasingly embroiled in intracommunal disputes in Miami and broadened the foundation's foreign policy focus to include other issues less directly related to

Cuba. Calzón resigned. José Antonio Font replaced him, but he also resigned, protesting Mas Canosa's "dictatorial style."[26]

Despite the infighting, the Cuban American National Foundation and Mas Canosa developed a significant following among Cuban Americans, collecting contributions from more than fifty thousand members. Most of the donations made by ordinary Cuban Americans were modest. For as little as ten dollars, Cuban Americans could feel that they were contributing to Castro's ouster. Many of his supporters regarded Mas Canosa as "the most powerful and influential leader to emerge in over thirty years of exile," with some in Little Havana referred to him as "Señor Presidente."[27] Mas Canosa's reputation—his legend as a powerful figure both in exile and in American politics—grew significantly. In a profile on Mas Canosa in *Esquire* magazine, writer Gaeton Fonzi suggested that providing the simplest description of CANF's leader, that he was the most powerful Cuban exile in America, was like saying Michael Jordan was the best basketball player in Chicago.[28]

Ronald Reagan's election in 1980 helped foster the rise of both CANF and Mas Canosa. Some scholars have suggested that CANF was, in essence, the creation of Republicans who saw a need for a powerful conservative lobby in Washington and who had been keeping an eye on the Cuban community since 1980.[29] As political scientist María de los Angeles Torres has shown, CANF's supposed political neutrality, particularly during the first decade of its existence, did not exist in practice. The goals and projects for which it lobbied closely resembled the priorities of the Reagan administration. She notes, for example, that CANF became an instrument by which the Contras in Nicaragua could receive public support. "The way to Havana begins in Managua," Mas Canosa repeatedly stated during the 1980s. In return for the support of CANF and other Cuban American organizations, the Reagan administration embraced a harsher stance toward Cuba. This included a 1982 restriction of travel to Cuba under new regulations prohibiting the transfer of U.S. currency to the island. While the policy made exceptions for academics, professionals, and Cuban Americans with families still on the island, the adoption of these regulations established the first travel restrictions during peacetime in American history.[30]

Mas Canosa portrayed CANF's relationship with the Reagan White House differently: he believed they had kept the president focused on opposing Castro. In an interview in 1993, he stated that if not for the foundation, the Reagan administration would have moved toward the normalization of relations with Cuba as the Carter administration had. The United States and

Cuba would have had full economic and diplomatic relations by the early 1990s and Cuba under Castro would be enjoying some relative prosperity. He believed that the closeness between CANF and the Reagan White House was a testimony to its own successful tactics, not to a subservience to the president's agenda. After all, what other organization could boast to have had the president of the United States at one of their banquets a mere two years after its inception? "We didn't realize how powerful we could be," said Mas Canosa of Cuban Americans.[31]

CANF's goals coincided with Reagan's conservative politics and hawkish Cold War stance, but the foundation's focus on Cuba made it so their aims did not always overlap completely. When an ecstatic crowd greeted Reagan in Little Havana in 1983, Mas Canosa gave him a warm introduction. After endorsing Reagan's aims in Central America, Mas Canosa went further and urged the president to abolish any existing agreement with the Soviet Union, stating that the United States would not invade Cuba unless Soviet nuclear missiles were present on the island. Whether Mas Canosa truly believed this was a viable strategy or whether the president would even respond, did not stop him playing to the crowd. Reagan, in turn, did not address this recommendation but rather capitalized on the fervor created by his presence and Mas Canosa's introduction to denounce the "Soviet-Cuban-Nicaraguan axis" that threatened the hemisphere with a "new colonialism."[32] Both men benefited from shared interests and audiences even as they sometimes diverged on specific policies.

Broadcasting from Marathon Key: Mas Canosa, Cuban American Politics, and Radio and TV Martí

One of the earliest shared ventures of CANF and the Reagan administration was the creation of Radio Martí. Named after Cuban Patriot José Martí, this federally funded radio station was intended to serve as a prodemocracy, anti-Castro voice to be transmitted directly into the island as counterprogramming to the Cuban government's "information monopoly." Senator Paula Hawkins of Florida introduced CANF's proposal as a bill in the U.S. Senate. Critics did not see the point. Cuban audiences already had access to the Voice of America Radio and, more significantly, to Miami radio stations and their anti-Castro perspectives. Senator Christopher Dodd of Connecticut called the idea "baloney." The bill also faced opposition from the State Department's

U.S. Interests Section in Havana, which had made an agreement regarding the release of political prisoners and immigration procedures in the aftermath of the Mariel boatlift. Section Chief Wayne Smith was concerned that Castro would cancel the recent agreement if President Reagan signed the Radio Martí bill into law.[33] Smith was right. When Radio Martí started operations in 1985, Castro cancelled the immigration accord that his government had arrived at with the United States in 1984.[34] Smith resigned his post.[35] President Reagan appointed Jorge Mas Canosa to the board of directors of the station.[36]

On Cuban Independence Day May 20, 1985, Radio Martí issued its first broadcast from a facility in Marathon Key, Florida.[37] Along with news programs, Radio Martí also broadcast entertainment programming that included salsa, rock 'n' roll, and a radio soap opera. It also sought to influence minds in Cuba by taking a different rhetorical approach than Cuban American radio stations did. Where Miami's radio stations called Fidel Castro "the tyrant" and referred to Nicaragua's government as the "Sandino-Communist government," Radio Martí adhered to the Voice of America's rules regarding perceptions of fairness and impartiality. Thus, when reporters spoke of Nicaragua's Daniel Ortega, they referred to him as "the head of the Nicaraguan government."[38] While members of Miami's broadcasting community were uncomfortable with the new station's "middle ground" and the tone it took in its reporting, they were still supportive of the work that Radio Martí was doing. "When Radio Marti says that Cubans die in Angola, adjectives are not essential," said WRHC president Salvador Lew; "Truth defeats all Communist governments."[39] CANF and its allies also portrayed the creation of the station as a great success for Cuban Americans in the United States, particularly as a symbol of greater political maturity and a growing appeal to politicians of different political leanings in the United States. "By being able to relate to conservatives as well as liberals, we have substantially changed our image," Mas Canosa told the *Miami Herald*.[40] The station received high marks from both conservative and mainstream media outlets including the *Washington Times*, the *New York Times*, and the *Washington Post*.[41]

Within five years of the station's founding, however, Mas Canosa was embroiled in a public scandal over the perceived introduction of Cuban American politics into Radio Martí's operations. By 1989, Mas Canosa and CANF pushed for the establishment of a television station counterpart to Radio Martí, to be called TV Martí. Despite the success of Radio Martí, critics suggested that the television broadcast signal would be of inferior quality and easily jammed by Castro's government. Others warned that the Cuban government would see it as a sign of aggression. Finally, there were those who suggested that it was wasteful to spend taxpayer dollars broadcasting American sitcoms dubbed in Spanish into Cuba.[42] Some, like Radio Martí director Ernesto Betancourt, argued that TV Martí might bring about retaliations against the radio station and that the intended funds should be funneled into the already existing and successful enterprise.[43]

Mas Canosa did not take kindly to Betancourt's criticisms. On March 6, 1990, on the eve of a set of test television broadcasts to Cuba, Betancourt wrote a ten-page memorandum to his superiors at the U.S. Information Agency (USIA). He described "a series of bizarre incidents" that made him believe that Mas Canosa, who was also chair of the presidential advisory board for Radio and TV Martí, was engineering his removal from the station. Betancourt claimed that Mas Canosa had complained to the foundation's directors that they had "lost control" of Radio Martí. CANF had then pressured the station to increase coverage of their organization in their broadcasts. Within two days of Betancourt sending his memorandum, USIA transferred him out of Radio Martí's directorship. While some described Betancourt's style as autocratic and he had had several disputes with station staff, he was also credited with having kept the station independent and free of exile politics. "I believe Mr. Betancourt was very intelligent in how he handled these kinds of things," said former CANF executive director Frank Calzón, adding, "Until now Radio Marti has been operated as an independent station."[44] After his allegations leaked to the press, Betancourt was ordered to clear his office and was placed on administrative leave. Staffers at Radio Martí reported that Betancourt's superiors charged him with "waging war for three days against the USIA."[45] Mas Canosa took to the Herald's opinion page to declare victory, accusing Betancourt of a failed power grab.[46]

Media outlets were less effusive about the removal of Betancourt from Radio Martí's leadership and Mas Canosa's role in the affair. The same day the Herald ran Mas Canosa's piece, the newspaper's editorial board admonished that, regardless of what had happened between CANF, USIA, and Betancourt, it was more important than ever that the federal government salvage the integrity of Radio Martí. The board saw a serious conflict between the foundation's role as a lobbying group and the station's legal and moral mandate to be "scrupulously objective." They charged that CANF had recently "taken on the coloration of a future political party in a post-Castro Cuba." Mas Canosa was ambitious, and the editorial claimed that his desire to become president of Cuba was a matter of public record. As such, the ties between Mas Canosa and USIA needed to be severed. To have a federal agency serving Mas Canosa's political future was unacceptable in principle, and it was damaging to the one thing Radio Martí could not afford to lose: its credibility.[47] The *Washington Post* declared that this sort of backroom politics could not come at a worse time. The *Post* was disturbed by what it saw as "minimal denials of political influence" by the Voice of America and USIA. TV Martí's legality was already coming under question, and for the new station to start operating just as its radio counterpart was in the midst of a political scandal was inappropriate.[48]

Mas Canosa admitted that he was interested in being the first democratically elected president of a post-Castro Cuba, but he objected to claims that his work with CANF sprung from this desire.[49] Mas Canosa argued that the charge that he was acting out of an ambition to be president tainted the struggle for the democratization of Cuba that he had been involved in since the age of fifteen. He testified in an unrelated deposition that he worked with CANF because he believed in democratic values.[50] His critics, however, did not believe his motivations to be so noble. His detractors called him names such as "Señor Mas y Mas" and "the Godfather."[51]

The Initiative: CANF, the White House's Push for Neoliberal Policy, and Refugees in Third Countries

Another joint venture between the Cuban American National Foundation and the Reagan White House demonstrated the confluence of the ideological push for privatization and push for immigration restriction of American conservatives and the desire to further CANF's Cuba agenda. The attacks by the Reagan White House on the social safety net also extended to the funding for arriving refugees. While the welcome the Marielitos had received in 1980 was paltry in comparison to the funding and opportunities provided to the first waves of arrivals, it had still been extremely costly. Likewise, the memory of Mariel and its volume of refugees had played a significant role in the push for immigration restriction, the passing of the 1986 Immigration Reform and Control Act, and the increased militarization of the U.S.-Mexico border.[52] CANF was eager to bring Cuban refugees residing in third countries to the United States, but to do so it would need to make the terms palatable to the Reagan administration.

The confluence of these concerns resulted in the CANF Private Sector Initiative Program. The program, established by presidential determination through the Department of State, the Office of the U.S. Coordinator for Refugee Affairs, and the Immigration and Naturalization Service (INS), was a new model for the private resettlement of refugees in the United States. The federal government facilitated the bureaucratic aspects of the resettlement of the refugees while CANF fundraised and took care of the expenses. The foundation found stateside sponsors, ensured employment and medical insurance for the refugees so they would not become public charges, and worked to ensure that arriving refugees would "become productive members of communities."[53] Where once the Cuban Refugee Program was tasked with ensuring that refugees could find a "useful and self-supporting role," this role now fell to the Cuban American community through CANF.[54] Private sources would provide for "all reasonable costs" for the refugees' admission.[55]

The Cuban American National Foundation Private Sector Initiative aided those the *Miami News* called "first of the forgotten," those refugees who had spent years waiting to come to the United States.[56] Between 1988 and 1991, the PSI aided in the resettlement of 7,585 Cuban refugees from over twenty countries to the United States. The PSI allowed the Reagan and Bush administrations to point to orderly and small refugee arrivals that differentiated them from the lack of control of the Carter White House over the country's borders. They did so while avoiding between thirty-five and fifty million dollars in associated costs "by encouraging private groups to share in the overall fiscal responsibility of a worldwide humanitarian U.S. refugee policy."[57]

The Cuban American National Foundation's Private Sector Initiative (PSI) did more than signal the neoliberal shift in American politics, it is also representative of the difference between the federal government's vision of the Cuban refugee community in the 1960s and their relationship with Cuban American groups in the 1980s. Policymakers in the 1960s had seen potential assets in the refugees and had economically empowered them to fit their aims in Latin America. By the 1980s, wealthy Cuban Americans had created a powerful political lobby whose outlook fit the strident anticommunism of the Reagan administration. Previous foreign policy choices helped empower CANF to shape foreign policy and it would continue to push for new legislation to weaken Castro's government. For Reagan-era policymakers, however, CANF was not the envisioned basis of a post-Castro Cuba. It was a political pressure group that could drum up support for anticommunism at home by recruiting Cuban Americans and putting pressure on legislators to adopt strict stances on Cuba. Refugee admissions on a small scale could serve as a concession to the Cuban American lobby, particularly if they took care of the expenses. Rather than a robust response in the Kennedy mold, the CANF

PSI showed how federal priorities had shifted by adopting a model of which Tracy Voorhees would have approved.

CANF's power and influence, built on the policy decisions of the past, was contingent upon its ability to influence policymakers. As the Cold War began to wind down, CANF's aims would overlap less and less neatly with the priorities of the Bush and Clinton administrations. Even as events began to call the foundation's power into question, other Cuban Americans were making inroads into political power by running for office at the local, state, and federal levels.

Los Políticos: Cuban American Successes in Electoral Politics

"Because of my father and what happened to him, politics had affected my life a great deal," said Xavier Suarez, the first Cuban-born mayor of Miami.[58] Suarez was eleven years old at the time of the Bay of Pigs Invasion, when the Cuban government placed his family under house arrest under suspicion of counter-revolutionary sympathies. Cuban authorities allowed them to move to the United States in July of 1961 and they settled in a suburb of Washington where Suarez's father, Manuel found work as an engineer to support his fourteen children.[59] Suarez grew up in the mid-Atlantic, was educated at Villanova University and at Harvard Law School, and came to Miami in 1975 as an outsider who had barely spoken Spanish in years.[60] His lack of political connections and anti-Castro bona fides made him an unlikely candidate to become the first Cuban-born politician to gain citywide office. To do so, Suarez needed to strike a balance between appealing to a broader audience than previous politically engaged Cuban Americans and embracing his position as part of a transnational political landscape in which local officials needed to comment on or become embroiled in international policy.

Between 1979 and 1983, Suarez conducted two unsuccessful campaigns for city commissioner and a one for mayor. In that last campaign, he challenged incumbent mayor Maurice Ferré. Ferré, a Puerto Rican businessman of Cuban descent, had won five two-year terms as mayor, and in the 1983 campaign he used Suarez's Cuban identity as a wedge issue with voters. Ferré ran a series of radio ads aimed at Miami's black community which played on the divisions between Miami's Cubans and other ethnic groups. A Suarez victory would bring about a "Cuban takeover of Miami." While Suarez cried foul at Ferré for playing ethnic politics, his own campaigners were caught with printed Spanish language cards that read "Cubans vote Cuban." Suarez lost the 1983 election. He obtained 73% of the Hispanic vote and 47% of the non-Latin white vote, but Ferré overtook him by carrying 96% of the black vote.[61] Ferré's tactics against Suarez had borne fruit against the young Cuban upstart.

In November of 1985, Suarez once again faced Ferré in a crowded mayoral election and employed an electoral strategy that centered on a runoff election. He stepped back and allowed Cuban American banker Raul Masvidal to weaken Ferré's position with African American voters by criticizing his firing of City Manager Howard Gary, pushing the incumbent Mayor to third place. Suarez had prepared for a runoff. Masvidal had not.[62] Suarez spent the week between the general election and the runoff attacking Masvidal for lacking a substantial policy platform and for his ties to "special interests." Suarez easily defeated Masvidal by obtaining significant support from Miami's Latino population and most of the votes cast by whites. In the first round, Suarez finished fourth among non-Hispanic whites, but in the televised debate prior to the runoff he made strong appeals to the white community, and he obtained the endorsement of the white groups that had supported Mayor Ferré. Suarez also broadened his base among African American voters by obtaining many of the votes that had gone to Ferré and to Marvin Dunn.[63]

While Suarez promised to knock down the "dividing walls" that plagued community relations in the city, he sought to reinforce his anticommunist credentials.[64] This was useful in securing appealing to segments of the Cuban American community but could also appeal to potential new constituencies. During the campaign leading up to the runoff, City Commissioner Joe Carollo accused Suarez of having socialist leanings and of being "friendly with a Castro agent."[65] Suarez quickly embraced a stringent, sometimes inflammatory anticommunism in his public appearances as mayor. The year after his election, Suarez was present at the site of dueling rallies related to American aid to Nicaragua's Contra rebels. After a pro-Contra crowd, composed mostly of Cuban Americans, turned on their counterparts, riot police removed two hundred anti-Contra demonstrators from the area. Rather than defusing tensions, Suarez railed against the "Marxist groups" in the anti-Contra rally and inflamed the situation by declaring that they "unfortunately" had the right to assemble as well.[66] This spoke not only to anticommunist Cuban Americans but also to the growing community of Nicaraguans in the greater Miami area that started growing in the late 1970s and was becoming an established presence throughout the 1980s.[67]

In 1990, Nelson Mandela visited Miami to give a speech in opposition to apartheid and some Cuban Americans groups protested the visit because of past statements of solidarity with Fidel Castro by the South African freedom fighter. Suarez, along with five other Cuban American mayors of area cities, signed a declaration criticizing Mandela for not denouncing the Cuban government's human rights violations.[68] Suarez and the Metro-Dade Commission refused to honor Mandela during his visit because he would not retract his statements. In response, several African American organizations planned to boycott Miami as a convention destination unless Suarez issued an apology. Suarez refused.[69] The economic boycott of Miami by African Americans throughout the nation started on July 17 and lasted for 151 days. It cost the city an estimated $12 million in tourist and convention revenue. Suarez made a speech to try to end the boycott, but he did not apologize. He explained that he regretted the backlash that had resulted from Mandela's snubbing. One supporter of the boycott judged Suarez's statement a "non-apology" and declared that a true apology was still necessary to reconcile racial tensions in Dade County, but he suspected that it would not be politically expedient for Suarez to apologize since the majority of his constituents were Cuban.[70] What this commentator failed to note was that Suarez's success as a local politician necessitated stances on foreign policy matters because in Miami the divisions between the local and the global were particularly thin.

While Suarez and others were succeeding in local politics, Cuban Americans also attained electoral successes that projected them to state and federal offices. In 1982, a Cuban American private school owner, Ileana Ros, sought and won a seat in the Florida House of Representatives representing a district in western Dade County that was increasingly Hispanic and Republican in the Florida House of Representatives. While in Tallahassee, Ros met and married Dexter Lehtinen. In 1986, Ros-Lehtinen and her husband ran joint campaigns for state senate and joined a conservative coalition that unseated liberal Democrat Ken Jenne from the senate presidency and backed conservative Democrat John Vogt. By helping unseat Jenne, Lehtinen and Ros-Lehtinen obtained significant committee chairmanships and access to the Senate's leadership. Using this access, Lehtinen obtained Governor Bob Martínez's endorsement for the open seat of U.S. attorney for the Southern District of Florida.[71]

In May of 1989, long-serving Democratic congressman Claude Pepper died suddenly in his sleep. In a special election to fill Pepper's seat, Ros-Lehtinen campaigned to overcome the significant Democratic majority in Pepper's district. Her opponent, Democrat Gerald F. Richman, campaigned with a slogan that played on the concerns of local non-Cubans who worried about the increased power of the Cuban community. "This," he said of Pepper's congressional vacancy, "is an American seat." Ros-Lehtinen canceled all debates, called Richman's campaign racist, and stated she would not dignify it. Richman could not overcome "a giant, unified Hispanic electorate determined to send one of their own to Congress," particularly a Hispanic candidate who benefited from fundraising visits by President George W. Bush and his vice president, Dan Quayle. Ros-Lehtinen beat Richman 53%–47%, and after having become the first Cuban woman in both chambers of the Florida Legislature, she achieved three further milestones, becoming the first Cuban American, first Republican, and first woman in Congress from Dade County. On the night of her victory, Celia Cruz, the Cuban queen of salsa, entertained the crowd of supporters waiting for the triumphant candidate. Cruz joyfully exclaimed that the people had spoken and "everyone" had chosen Ros-Lehtinen. As she exited the stage, however, Cruz triumphantly shouted, "The Cubans won!"[72]

Many expected that when Ros-Lehtinen arrived on Capitol Hill, she would vote along Republican Party lines. After her election, the *Miami Herald* described Ros-Lehtinen as "a conservative party loyalist."[73] Ros-Lehtinen fell in line with most Republican positions in Congress, but she broke ranks with a group of Republicans who attacked a bill to pay $1.25 billion in compensation to sixty-two thousand Japanese Americans interned during World War II because of its impact on the budget. Ros-Lehtinen had one thought: "What if it happened to the Cubans?"[74] Ros-Lehtinen sought to balance staunch support for the Republican Party with a record for voting based on her experiences as a Cuban American. The growth in political power of Cuban Americans in South Florida allowed politicians to embrace the experiences of their community as a successful electoral strategy and as a driving force for their decisions once in office.

Re-Aligning Dade: The Cuban Vote and the Shifting Political Winds in South Florida

Political developments in the 1980s and into the 1990s helped solidify the perception tying the Cuban American community to the Republican Party. Another Cuban American Republican, Lincoln Díaz-Balart, joined Ileana Ros-Lehtinen in Congress. While the Cuban American National Foundation claimed not have an interest in partisan politics and made strategic alliances with individual lawmakers from both major parties, their connections to the Republican Party ran deep. This was the view of the Republican National Committee, which informed the Bush White House that CANF was an influential group that was "very interested in the Republican Party."[75] Reagan's single-minded anticommunism fostered this interest, which presented an ideologically convenient and politically expedient alliance for the foundation.

Other factors contributed to the strong public association of the Cuban American electorate with the GOP. The community's rocky history with the Democratic Party had set the stage for this public association. Reagan's open antagonism of international communism made him seem strong where previous Democratic administrations had seemed weak. Even as Reagan faced the most significant public setback of his presidency, the Iran-Contra scandal, many Cuban Americans doubled down on their support of the president. One sixty-four-year-old exile fashioned and distributed flyers reading, "Support Reagan against Betrayal." He told reporters that it hurt him to see the Democrats and the media denigrate "the best president this country has ever had." Amid the scandal, thousands of Cuban Americans and Nicaraguan exiles flocked to the Dade County auditorium to listen to White House communications director Pat Buchanan defend the president and other Iran-Contra figures. Supporters held signs that read, "We follow you Reagan," "We love freedom, we fight Communism," and "100 percent with Reagan." Buchanan blamed Reagan's political opponents for fanning the flames of the scandal, but he told an excited crowd that Miami's Cuban American community had "always been in the vanguard of the Reagan revolution."[76]

A Cuban American banker, Carlos Salmán, assumed the presidency of the Republican Party in Dade County in pursuit of three initial goals: to keep the party united, to grow the party's ranks in the area and increase Cuban American participation in elections, and to obtain the necessary funds to keep the Party's county offices open. Salmán was particularly proud of the rapid growth of the GOP in Dade County. While he felt that he had played a part in increasing registrations, Salmán credited "a little old man named Ronald Reagan" who had boosted the Republican Party's popularity. He explained that attempts by Democrats to oppose Reagan had not dampened the enthusiasm of Cuban American voters. Salmán had reason to be confident about the Cuban support for the Republican Party. July of 1988 saw 905 voter registrations by Cuban Americans: 703 registered as Republicans, 102 registered as Democrats, and 72 registered as independents. Of the 172,753

Latino registered voters in the county, 117,169 were registered Republicans and 41,085 were registered Democrats.[77]

These new demographics were changing the electoral landscape in Dade County. Some veteran politicians, like Dante Fascell, were able to weather these changes because of their long association with Cuban Americans. In the 1984 campaign, Jorge Mas Canosa wrote a letter supporting Fascell's candidacy, noting that he had opposed Castro for two and a half decades. Mas Canosa encouraged his fellow Cubans to support Fascell so he could continue to fight for a Cuba free of Castro and of communism.[78] The Free Cuba PAC also spent thousands of dollars to place newspaper ads on behalf of Fascell in the *Miami Herald* and *Diaro las Americas* on the eve of the 1990 election.[79] While Fascell had the support of several key Cuban Americans, the Florida Democratic Party was concerned about the Cuban American community's perception of the Party at large. The State Party Chairman, Charles A. Whitehead, wrote a letter to Democratic office holders outlining a program to change the perception by many Cuban Americans that they did not represent their interests.[80]

The increased presence of the Cuban American community as part of the Dade County electorate and a strong identification with the Republican Party were fundamentally altering what had been a solid Democratic stronghold. While these changes brought challenges to the Democratic Party in Dade County and in Florida, they did not take the party out of contention entirely. The support of the Cuban American lobby and increasingly powerful Cuban American electorate could be obtained by selectively embracing policy positions. The power of the lobby, the electorate, and of Cuban American politicians had limits. A series of events in the waning years of the Cold War showed that maintaining influence in the American political system and serving the Cuban American constituency simultaneously was not always possible.

Not Technically in This Country: The Politics of Indefinite Detention

One of the more complex issues that faced both the Cuban American lobby and the larger community was that of Cuban detainees in indefinite detention. In the years between the Mariel boatlift and the uprisings by the detainees in Atlanta and Oakdale in 1987, a complex legal struggle began over the fate of Mariel "entrants" deemed excludable by immigration authorities.[81] The INS normally repatriated excludable aliens to their home countries, but the Cuban

government's refusal to accept these deportees meant that this was not possible in the case of Mariel refugees. This, combined with the federal government's refusal to release these deportable refugees from detention, meant that
thousands of refugees spent months or years detained after serving sentences
for crimes committed in the United States or without ever having been convicted. As time went on and the situation ossified without an end in sight,
the detainees and their advocates grew increasingly frustrated. Some Cuban
Americans advocated for these detainees from the start. Others feared being
associated with them as they had been with the general impression of criminality of the boatlift.

Marielitos started arriving in the Atlanta Federal Penitentiary (AFP) in
1980. In March of that year, the Bureau of Prisons, the U.S. Public Health
Service, and the INS had entered into an agreement that allowed the INS
to use BOP facilities to "screen, process, and detain aliens who are in the
United States illegally."[82] Those arriving at AFP were entering a seventy-eight-
year-old building designed for 1,500 inmates and that already held more than
2,000.[83] It had also been condemned the previous year.[84] In March 1981, federal authorities decided it would be more practical, economically and admin-
istratively, to detain all Cubans with criminal records in one location. This
caused the Cuban population of the AFP to go from 772 detainees to 1,765
within one month. By August, that number had grown again to 1,844. Immigration judges began conducting hearings to determine which of the detainees were excludable and should be deported back to Cuba, determining that
1,200 detainees should not be released. As the Cuban government refused
repatriations, federal authorities first considered the question of whether they
would hold these detainees indefinitely.[85]

Federal authorities also considered Atlanta as a location in which Cubans
without previous convictions could be warehoused. Soon after the end of the
boatlift, some in the U.S. government suggested that eight hundred to one
thousand "hostile and anti-social Cubans" with no criminal history should
also be transferred to the Atlanta Federal Penitentiary. The BOP objected to
this placement on legal grounds, noting that there was "questionable, if any,
legal authority to hold those with anti-social personalities in a federal prison,
co-mingled with those who have been convicted."[86]

Even as the federal government made determinations about the first
group of detainees, their numbers grew as Marielitos were convicted of
crimes in the United States. Some detainees were violent offenders, but many
others were convicted of nonviolent offenses including working as drug

mules for the city's thriving drug trade. Of the estimated 2,800 Marielitos convicted of crimes in the United States, around 80% had committed relatively minor crimes with sentences of up to four years.[87] The thousands of arrests that stemmed from an economy of desperation overwhelmed the legal system. Most of the Cuban defendants had no knowledge of the American legal system and had no resources with which to secure legal representation. The sheer number of arrests also overwhelmed the public defender system in South Florida. The State Attorney for Dade County, Janet Reno, offered these offenders plea bargains with reduced sentences for their crimes. For defendants facing stiff penalties related to drug trafficking, the prospect of serving shortened sentences of one, two, or three years was far more attractive. The defendants were not advised, however, that on completion of their sentences, INS would immediately detain them for having violated the terms of their status as parolees.[88] Instead of being released, the detainees were transferred to maximum-security facilities.[89]

Not all the detainees had been convicted of a crime: some had no criminal history but had been determined to be dangerous by federal authorities. This meant that some Cubans were indefinitely detained despite having never been charged with a crime. These detainees, frustrated and angry at their situation, would often be written up for disciplinary infractions that reinforced the narrative of their detention. One detainee was arrested in June 1982 but was not prosecuted. Despite this, the arrest was enough for INS to revoke his parole and put him in indefinite detention.[90] Another detainee wrote the Atlanta Legal Aid Society for help in 1986 and claimed that while he had never been in legal trouble in Cuba, INS officers had unfairly targeted him while at a refugee camp in Wisconsin. Someone had apparently told an INS officer that Roberto Méndez Suárez had been a killer in Cuba and, given that he could neither speak nor read English at the time, he did not understand that the officers were having him sign an admission of guilt. He had attempted to clear up the issue multiple times and he had passed the General Educational Development (GED) test while in Atlanta, but over the years of detention he had also had some disciplinary problems, leaving him still detained years later.[91]

When the federal government labeled a Cuban detainee as an excludable alien without a means of deportation to their country of origin, immigration authorities adhered to the idea that the detainee was in a legal limbo. The federal government argued that violation of their parole made it so the detainees were, legally speaking, no longer in the country and no longer entitled to constitutional rights in the period in which they waited repatriation. Repatriation was a simple concept, but not easily executed. The Cuban government did not want to see any of the Marielitos returned. In the years after the boatlift, several rounds of negotiations led to potential agreements regarding the return of the detainees. A 1984 agreement resulted in a list of prisoners that the Cuban government would accept if repatriated. As an advocate for the detainees pointed out, however, the list of those detainees to be deported did not include violent offenders, which the Cuban government did not want to receive. Instead, it was the nonviolent offenders who would be sent back to the country from which they had fled. "We were deporting those who least deserved to be deported," Rafael Peñalver later recalled. The agreement would not be implemented as expected because the launch of Radio Martí caused the Cuban government to withdraw from the accord and it once again made the detainees' stay in federal facilities indefinite.[92]

The combination of continued detention, the threat of deportation, and the harsh conditions of detention led to discontent and acts of rebellion by the detainees. On October 14, 1984, fifty detainees assembled in peaceful protest at the Atlanta Penitentiary's recreation field holding bedsheets that read the word "*libertad*," freedom. Prison guards equipped with riot gear responded in force and put over 1500 Cuban detainees into 24-hour lockdown without running water. This led to detainees breaking plexiglass and setting small fires. On November 1, a second, larger disturbance led to more fires and breaking of windows and prison authorities responded by deploying tear gas and placing the Mariel detainees into twenty-three-hour-a-day lockdown. One cellblock remained on lockdown until September of the following year, and three others until the disturbances in November of 1987.[93] At the time of the 1984 disturbances, the Atlanta Penitentiary's population was at 156% of the facility rating. In 1986, to alleviate conditions, the Bureau of Prisons and the INS redesignated the Federal Alien Detention Center in Oakdale, LA, as a center for Cuban detainees and began to transfer some of the population to this facility.[94]

The fear of deportation remained for detainees, and it was driven both by testimony of those who had returned to Cuba and rumors that spread through the populations. One Marielito, Manuel García-Díaz, had joined the boatlift voluntarily and had experienced repudiation, but by October of 1980 he had grown homesick and along with five others he purchased a small vessel and returned to Cuba. Upon arrival, the Cuban government arrested, interrogated, and subjected García-Díaz and his companions to sleep deprivation and other forms of physical and psychological torture. They were called traitors and put on trial. In April of 1981, Cuban security forces gave them back the clothes they had worn when they returned from the United States and took them to their vessel. A lieutenant colonel then told them that they were no longer Cubans and that they were being sent back to the United States. Furthermore, if they ever returned, they would be shot.[95] Relatives in Cuba helped spread these narratives when they wrote to detained family members. In 1985, for example, one detainee's grandmother sent him a letter telling him to fight his potential deportation tooth and nail, as she had learned that the Cuban government had executed a group of repatriated Marielitos only six days after their return to the island.[96] The fear felt by detainees and their families about the consequences of repatriation drove them to seek out any aid they could get.

The detainees did have allies fighting for them, though they faced several uphill battles in trying to secure detainee releases. The plight of the detainees attracted the attention in Atlanta upon the arrival of Cubans at the penitentiary in 1980. The Atlanta Legal Aid Society first became involved in representing Mariel detainees that year. Legal Aid Society personnel and volunteer private lawyers sought to litigate the legality of the detentions and the conditions under which the Cubans were held in Atlanta. They had also served as a point of contact for detainees' families and a resource for individual parole hearings, even lobbying the Atlanta Bar Association to establish a pro bono project to provide counsel to hundreds of detainees.[97] The Eleventh Circuit Court of Appeals complicated these efforts through its consistent position that the Mariel Cubans had no due process rights at all.[98]

The problem was, in part, one of visibility; advocates for the detainees needed to make the problem known and to overcome the messaging put forth by the INS. In a July 1987 segment of *Nightline with Ted Koppel*, a representative from the INS defended indefinite detention as a way to protect American citizens by preventing the release of violent individuals. Dale Schwartz, the president of the American Immigration Lawyers Association, countered that not all the detainees were violent. He had surveyed the list of crimes of the detainees and claimed to have found individuals found guilty of offenses like driving without a license or like stealing a loaf of bread or a quart of milk due to hunger. "They are not dangerous criminals," Schwartz admonished, "and we ought to be doing something to separate those people from those who are more serious."[99]

The plight of the detainees also caught the attention of a first-term congressman representing Atlanta who took to the floor of the U.S. House of Representatives to speak on their behalf. Just days after fellow civil rights movement veterans Hosea Williams and Dick Gregory had been arrested while picketing for the release of the Atlanta detainees, John Lewis launched into an impassioned defense of the detained Marielitos and excoriated the courts for their inaction.[100] He accused the courts of adhering to a legal fiction that the Marielitos were not in the United States, yet hundreds of them were in his district under terrible conditions. The detainees, he explained, were particularly vulnerable to harm in indefinite detention. There had been twenty murders and suicides in that population in the previous six years, along with more than 150 serious suicide attempts and 4,000 episodes of self-mutilation. Congress could not ignore fifteen hundred men detained in his district because of their status and not as a punishment to any crime. On the two hundredth anniversary of the U.S. Constitution, lawmakers needed to demand "that elemental concepts of justice, decency, and human dignity prevail." To fail in this regard would put the United States in line with oppressive regimes around the world. "Mr. Speaker, we do not maintain gulags in this country," Lewis charged; "We are not the Soviet Union or South Africa."[101]

Miami's Catholic Church also advocated for the detainees, charging that immigration authorities had placed many of those detained in Atlanta due to errors during the screening process for the Marielitos. They decried the fact that the attorney general of the United States had testified before Congress in July of 1981 and had "failed to differentiate among those being held in the Atlanta Federal Penitentiary when he described them all as criminals." Church volunteers had identified some four hundred of the detainees as mentally ill or intellectually challenged. These detainees would remain wards of the U.S. government for the rest of their lives unless the Cuban government could be persuaded to accept their return. After the removal of these four hundred detainees, church workers estimated that some six hundred of the remaining detainees would pose a threat to the community if released. The remaining eight hundred were "young men who are not guilty of anything that would merit long term imprisonment in the United States." To delay their release meant delaying the incorporation of these men into society. "We cannot be indifferent to a serious violation of basic human rights which, though it had its origins in the actions of the government of Cuba, has too long been perpetuated by our own government," concluded a statement issued by Edward

McCarthy, the archbishop of Miami, Auxiliary Bishop Agustín Román, and Monsignor Bryan O. Walsh.[102]

Bishop Román consistently advocated for the detainees and developed a good working relationship with lawyer Rafael Peñalver. Prior to this work, however, Peñalver was unaware of the problem of indefinite detention, despite being engaged in Cuban American and Florida politics. In this way, he was like many other Cuban Americans. He came to learn about the detainees during his stint as chairman of the Florida Commission of Hispanic Affairs. The commission, which was created by the Florida State Legislature in 1978, met in a different city in the state each month to hold public hearings where Hispanic residents could voice complaints, which the commission would then forward to the governor's office. When the families of detainees held at the prison in Tallahassee petitioned the commission for a meeting in that city, the group reluctantly agreed. They believed that the families were associated with the violent offenders Castro had included in the boatlift. At the meeting, Peñalver was stunned to hear about detainees who had served their sentences yet were still incarcerated. Their families directed Peñalver to speak to Bishop Román, who, in turn, verified the situation.[103]

Román and Peñalver campaigned on behalf of the detainees, arguing that indefinite detention was a violation both of the U.S. Constitution and of basic human rights. Román asked Peñalver to write a legal brief concerning the problem of indefinite detention, and in late 1986, he drafted pastoral letter on behalf of Román and the two other Cuban-born bishops, Eduardo Boza-Masvidal and Enrique San Pedro. The bishops were unable to change the policies of the federal government, but their advocacy helped strengthen Román's identity as an advocate for the detainees.[104]

In the year before the rebellions in Atlanta and Oakdale, the detainees, their families, and their advocates were growing increasingly frustrated with the lack of progress. Attempts to get the detainees released through the courts appeared stalled after the U.S. Supreme Court declined to hear the case of the Marielitos in a 7–2 decision.[105] While the INS had proposed a new plan for hearings related to their possible release, Lewis and others criticized the plan as insufficient. There were still fifteen hundred detainees in Atlanta alone, and the recent stabbing death of one detainee in early July of 1987 led Representative Lewis to warn that it was a portent of things to come. "These inmates are forgotten people," Lewis said in a statement, "and unless something is done to release the Cubans who are not a threat to society, then we could see more violence."[106] Within months, he was proven right.

Crisis and Stagnation: The Oakdale and
Atlanta Uprisings and Their Aftermath

The spark that ignited the violence in Atlanta and Oakdale was a rare break-through in negotiations between Washington and Havana. In November of 1987, the U.S. government announced it had reached a new immigration pact with Cuba that could result in the arrival of between 23,000 and 25,000 Cuban immigrants to American shores each year. Part of the accord included continued talks for the deportation of 3,700 former prisoners detained by the INS and 3,500 Cubans serving prison sentences.[107] The accords included a reinstatement of parts of the discarded 1984 agreement, specifically the list of detainees that the Cuban government was willing to accept if repatriated. Upon learning that extraditions to Cuba were imminent, the Cuban detainees at the Federal Detention Center in Oakdale rioted and took hostages. Three days later, the detainees at the Federal Penitentiary in Atlanta followed suit.[108]

As tensions rose between the hostage takers and federal authorities, various groups and individuals tried to step in and negotiate between the parties. The families of Cuban detainees waiting outside the federal penitentiary grew ever more fearful as they heard over a police frequency that the members of the uprising had declared they would rather die than return to Cuba. When rumors spread that the police might take the penitentiary by force, the families of the detainees turned to John Lewis. Lewis asked law enforcement officials to be allowed to enter the penitentiary in order to negotiate an end to the standoff but was told that would be too dangerous.[109] Federal authorities attempted to conduct negotiations themselves, but they were unable to come to terms with the detainees.

Cuban American leaders grew increasingly anxious as the standoffs dragged on, exclaiming that their potential as negotiators was being ignored. Speaking at a press conference held by Facts About Cuban Exiles, banker Carlos Arboleya complained that top officials in the Reagan administration were all but ignoring the eager Cuban Americans who wanted to help end the hostage situations. Jorge Mas Canosa stated that he was in touch with Attorney General Edwin Meese, but he criticized the federal government's handling of the crisis and their hesitancy to allow for judicial reviews on a case-by-case basis as the detainees were demanding. Others were concerned about the impact on their community. Antonio Varona, the head of the Junta Patriotica Cubana, warned that supporting the rioters was dangerous because of "public American opinion, which could fall upon all of us."[110]

Even as prominent Cuban Americans were growing increasingly impatient, the Reagan administration had already reached out to Bishop Román and Peñalver. The federal government was eager to end the crisis, not just because of the potential for violence and loss of life, but also because of an impending state visit by Soviet premier Mikhail Gorbachev.[111] The day after the Oakdale riot, the detainees had requested that Román be the one to negotiate on their behalf, so the bishop was essential to the process. Román had Peñalver negotiate terms with the Justice Department before they would go anywhere near either facility. The bishop was ready to travel to Atlanta the Monday after the riots, but the trip was postponed when the Justice Department refused to provide written guarantees that the detainees would receive individual reviews before the courts. The detainees and their advocates wanted to ensure that each man would get a hearing to determine if they would remain in the country instead of being deported as a group. As phone negotiations between Peñalver and the Justice Department continued, the refusal to allow for the requested review system kept Román from becoming involved. "I cannot trick the prisoners—or anyone," said the bishop.[112]

There was a deep sense of mistrust among the detainees even as the Justice Department offered a "full, fair, and equitable review" of each individual's eligibility. After years of attempts at establishing a review process, the Justice Department's promises rang hollow to many of the leaders of the uprising. They were particularly distrustful Attorney General Meese and wanted a "no deportation" clause added to any potential agreement. Because the Justice Department insisted on an "indefinite moratorium" instead, negotiations had stalled.[113]

Peñalver and Román, along with Carlos Arboleya, traveled to Washington, DC, to negotiate with Attorney General Meese. Peñalver sought to secure a specific process of individual review, to differentiate between violent and nonviolent offenders, and to stop the practice of indefinite detention. Meese, using the legal fiction Lewis had ridiculed earlier in the year, explained that the detainees were not, legally speaking, in the country. He used the metaphor of a chain-link fence being erected around the country and he told the bishop to imagine that the detainees were on the other side; they had not entered the country and therefore had no rights. "If they are not in the country," Román asked Meese, "then how have they taken over two of your largest federal penitentiaries?" The pair's entrenched advocacy of the detainees enraged Meese, who asked how a man of the cloth could allow his lawyer to blackmail the federal government. Román denied there was any blackmail happening but insisted that he would not allow himself or Peñalver to be used. "What you are suggesting," he told Meese, "is to use the Church and use an attorney to solve the problem that you yourselves created."[114]

The meeting in Washington did not yield an agreement between the federal government and Román, but Román and Peñalver continued to negotiate with a team that traveled down to Miami. The federal government agreed to broad terms and flew the bishop and his lawyer to England Air Force base in Alexandria, LA, to sort out the details of what they could offer the detainees. After a long negotiation, Román and Peñalver made their dramatic entrance at Oakdale, resolving the situation.[115] When they traveled to Atlanta, they were met with greater skepticism from the detainees. The Atlanta detainees declared that the Oakdale pact was unacceptable as a solution to their situation.[116] But the bishop managed to negotiate terms with the Atlanta detainees as well, ending what the *Miami Herald* called "the longest prison uprising in American history" shortly after 1 a.m. on December 4, 1987. The crisis that once threatened to end only in bloodshed ended instead in a crowd of detainees crowding the roof of the penitentiary's hospital, celebrating with music and dancing as Bishop Román entered the building (see Figure 12).[117]

Once the hostages were released and the federal government took control of both facilities once again, the long process of individual review of each case began. The Department of Justice dispersed the Atlanta and Oakdale detainees to facilities around the country. Peñalver created an organization named Due Process, Inc., which had teams of volunteer lawyers and law students who traveled to the facilities now holding the detainees.[118] The Atlanta Legal Aid Society continued the work they had begun years before. By August of 1988, hundreds of detainees had been released and hundreds of others had been approved for release and were awaiting sponsorship or space in halfway houses.[119] In December of that year, however, INS deported the first five post-review detainees to Cuba.[120] By the winter of 1990, over 2,500 detainees had been released, but 148 had been sent back to Cuba.[121]

As time went on, the detainees who remained incarcerated or new detainees who had finished their sentences after the 1987 uprisings grew increasingly frustrated. A significant reason for the frustration was the inconsistent nature of the reviews that were secured in the 1987 agreements. Two immigration officials who had received a single day's training and had no experience as parole officers conducted the hearings, and representatives for the detainees complained that their files were often kept from them.[122] In some cases, the INS officials denied the detainees the representation of the volunteers who

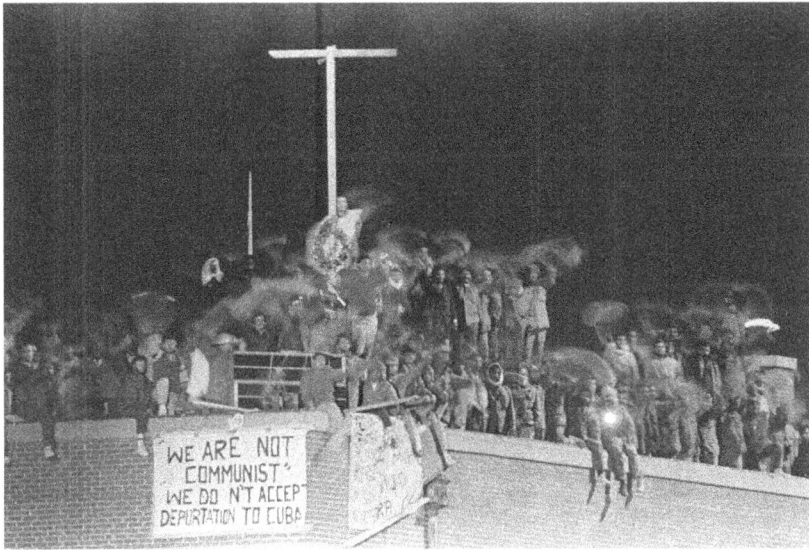

WE ARE NOT
COMMUNIST
WE DO N'T ACCEP
DEPORTATION TO CUBA

Figure 12. Cuban detainees atop the Atlanta Federal Penitentiary's hospital dormitory celebrate the end of the hostage crisis and standoff with federal authorities in December 1987, after an agreement for the individual review of cases was negotiated with the U.S. government by Bishop Agustín Román and attorney Rafael Peñalver. Courtesy of Getty Images.

had traveled specifically for their hearings.[123] The continued problems with the review process led Ángel Núñez Hernández, one of the leaders of the detainee uprising at the Oakdale facility who was paroled for his role in negotiating the end of the siege, to warn of the potential for further violence. "At this time," he told a reporter a year after the uprisings, "the Cubans could be more organized and could become more dangerous again."[124] While the dispersal of Cuban detainees to facilities throughout the country prevented mass uprisings of the size of those in Atlanta and Oakdale, disturbances continued in the years that followed.

Not every instance of protest against continued detention was violent, but one was sufficiently high profile that it helped secure the appointment and confirmation of an ambitious attorney to a cabinet-level position. In July of 1989, 110 Cuban detainees attempted a failed hunger strike at the Webb County Jail in Laredo, TX, to protest their continued detention and the conditions at the facility.[125] In the summer of 1990, smaller disturbances, mostly focused on property damage but with a few injuries, occurred in at the U.S. Penitentiary in Lewisburg, PA, and the Avoyelles Parish Jail in Marksville,

LA.[126] The most significant explosion of discontent took place the following year at the Talladega Federal Correctional Institution in Talladega, AL. On August 21, 1991, 121 detainees seized a cellblock and ten hostages the night before 32 of them were scheduled to be deported to Cuba.[127] Unlike the Oakdale and Atlanta sieges, the Talladega uprising did not end with a negotiation. Instead, the acting U.S. attorney general, William Barr, ordered a predawn raid that ended the standoff and secured the hostages. This action earned Barr accolades from Senate Republicans, and according to a Senate Judiciary Committee staffer, it served to convince many of them that he was worthy of confirmation for the post, which he received in November of that year.[128]

Who remained in detention years after the uprisings in Atlanta and Oakdale? Some, of course, had been convicted of crimes, sometimes serious ones. However, years after the accords that ended the sieges, there were still detainees in custody who had been convicted of nothing or who seemed to be held because of a bad attitude. The Atlanta Legal Aid Society represented one such person, a man named Florentino González who had arrived during the boatlift and by 1990 had spent ten years in detention. Once in the United States, González had never experienced life outside confinement, having come to the attention of authorities while in the Fort Chaffee camp in Arkansas for being "hostile, uncooperative, and violent" and was later classified by prison officials as "obnoxious, hostile, and uncooperative." While in Fort Chaffee, he had received a forty-day sentence for his attack on another refugee, a man who González claimed had attempted to sexually assault his brother. In the ten years that followed, González had received disciplinary actions for possibly being involved in a fight, not wanting to work in the prison, and refusing to turn down his radio. González, mostly, seemed to remain in indefinite detention because he was angry and unpleasant to immigration and prison officials, who were certain that he had to have far more incidents that those listed in his file, because he was "just so bad that they didn't bother to write up incident reports on him."[129]

Another detainee, a woman name Agraspina Manso Gueverra, was detained for eleven years despite never having been charged with a crime. Manso Gueverra and her brother had participated willingly in the boatlift, and she had found a sponsor when she was sent to live with a family in Arkansas. The family, however, complained that she had a difficult personality and withdrew their sponsorship. When the last refugee camp closed, INS put Manso Gueverra in prison. She was paroled in 1984 and released to a halfway house in Los Angeles, but she left the house without authorization with a man who had been accused of stealing a car. While she was never charged with a crime, she was sent back to prison, where she remained until she was released from detention in September of 1991.[130] The stories of the Cuban detainees being released from American prisons or languishing there still reflected the stories of detainees held prior to the 1987 uprisings, a fact well understood by their advocates. By the summer of 1991, the Atlanta Legal Aid Society was ending the day-to-day operations of their project to assist the detainees. In a final report to the Edna McConnell Clark Foundation, one of their main financial backers, the Legal Aid Society reported that they had undertaken 1,730 repatriation and parole review panels. Between their work and that or associated projects, of the 3,800 Cuban detainees in American prisons at the time of the 1987 uprisings, close to 3,000 were ultimately approved for release. In that time, 426 detainees had been deported to Cuba and 200 more stood to be deported. Even as the day-to-day work wound down, however, hundreds of detainees approved for release were still in prison because they had no sponsorship. Despite the releases and the deportations, there were still other detainees that remained in indefinite detention, pending litigation. "Ironically," the Legal Aid Society reported, "this puts us pretty much where we were prior to the uprisings in late 1987; there are large numbers of detainees who remain in indefinite detention in our nation's prisons."[131]

After over a decade of advocacy, the uprisings, the deportation of hundreds of detainees, and the release of thousands of others, the issue of indefinite detention of Mariel refugees was far from settled. It would not be resolved until 2005, when the U.S. Supreme Court issued a 7–2 ruling indicating that indefinite detention for Mariel refugees violated statutes that barred indefinite detention for stateless immigrants who had been lawfully admitted to the United States but made excludable by crimes committed after arrival. At the time, the ruling was expected to affect as many as a thousand detainees still being held in American prisons.[132]

The Limits of Influence: Cuban Americans "Coming of Age," CANF's Political Battles, and the Rafter Crisis

The bloodless end of the 1987 standoffs was a relief to many Cuban Americans, and for some it signaled the potential power of a unified Cuban community. "Now we all feel proud when we see a *marielito* waving a Cuban flag from the roof of the Atlanta prison," said a Cuban American who had worked for the detainees.[133] Others suggested that this temporary union showed the Cuban American community's new maturity. In an opinion piece in the *Miami Herald*, Guillermo Martinez wrote that the resolution showed that the community had come of age. Martinez was particularly complimentary of men like Rafael Peñalver and Carlos Arboleya, who had supported Román's effort to resolve the crisis. And he emphasized that Arboleya's group FACE had gone beyond its original mission of improving the Cuban American community's image and had "played a crucial role in helping to prevent that image from deteriorating."[134]

As with other incidents in Cuban American politics, while the community was largely united in public, there were still significant cleavages away from the public eye. According to Peñalver, the members of Facts About Cuban Exiles wanted the federal government to make an agreement with Román for the bishop to end the standoffs. Others, however, exerted pressure for a resolution that would also serve their interests. While Román and Peñalver negotiated with the federal government over the details of individual review, federal authorities brought pressure on the Cuban American community. Influential Cuban Americans, in turn, brought pressure on Román and Peñalver to give the federal government the swift end to the crisis it wanted.[135] Given the recalcitrance of the bishop and the attorney, the federal government attempted to bring in other Cuban American negotiators, including Jorge Mas Canosa and Xavier Suarez. Before Román brought an end to the Oakdale crisis, the FBI attempted to conclude the Atlanta standoff by teaming an FBI negotiator with two former political prisoners and Mas Canosa to negotiate with the prisoners. The detainees refused the deal even after fifteen high-profile Cubans including Suarez, Ileana Ros-Lehtinen, Lincoln Díaz-Balart, Antonio de Varona, and Huber Matos attempted to visit the detainees to convince them to release the hostages.[136] While all parties wanted to conclude the hostage situations before any fatalities occurred, some members of the Cuban American community were far more interested in pleasing the federal government than in assuring the rights of the detainees. Peñalver recalls that the detainees understood this well, leading to their distrust of the Cuban American National Foundation. "They wanted to impress the American government that they were able to deliver," he says of CANF, "and by impressing the American government that they were able to deliver, they lost their constituency."[137]

Peñalver was far from the only critic of Jorge Mas Canosa and CANF. The foundation and its chairman were criticized from within the Cuban American community and from without. Mas Canosa contended that his critics outside the community wanted to create an image of Cuban Americans as "haters."[138] Weeks before the uprisings in Atlanta and Oakdale, Mas Canosa had leveled such a charge at a frequent antagonist of the Cuban American community: the *Miami Herald*. Mas Canosa took out a full page ad in the *Herald* in which he accused the paper of being "aggressive in its ignorance" of Cuban Americans and of refusing to understand that the community saw the struggle against totalitarianism as a "personal, ever-present struggle."[139] Other Cuban American figures sided with CANF, but softened their tone, suggesting that the *Herald's* lack of sensitivity was not a conspiracy, but a lack of understanding of the Cuban American community and its importance to the city.[140] The *Herald* attempted to once again engage Dade's Hispanic community by rebranding its Spanish edition, *El Herald*, as *El Nuevo Herald* in November of 1987. Staff changes and a greater editorial independence for *El Nuevo Herald* did not satisfy Mas Canosa, however.

The CANF chairman's conflicts with Miami's largest newspaper continued as the global Cold War wound down and circumstances suggested the Cuban government would soon collapse. Many in Miami's Cuban American community were convinced that the dissolution of the Soviet Union meant that Fidel Castro's days were numbered. In May of 1992, Jorge Mas Canosa predicted that Castro would fall within a year or two.[141] With Castro's international support system disintegrating, CANF and its allies sought to strengthen economic restrictions on Cuba, hastening the end of Cuba's revolutionary regime. A new bill, the Cuban Democracy Act of 1992, was introduced by New Jersey Congressman Robert Torricelli. A piece in *Esquire* magazine suggested that the "usually liberal congressman" had found himself in need of courting the conservative Cuban American communities in the northern part of his state and had suddenly gotten the notion to tighten the twenty-nine-year-old U.S. embargo against Cuba. The bill was meant to restrict trade with Cuba by the subsidiaries of American corporations based abroad, to prevent American firms from obtaining tax deductions for expenses related to subsidiary trade with Cuba, and to restrict foreign ships traveling to Cuba for trade from stopping at U.S. ports. Gaeton Fonzi, the author of the piece, was less than complimentary toward the Torricelli bill, calling it "a near reduction ad absurdum of the United States' historic big-stick-no-carrot policy toward Cuba." The Department of State was another strong opponent of the bill, calling it "self-destructive" and noting that the ban on subsidiary trade would provoke the allies of the United States. In due course, the British and Canadian governments issued strong objections and the European Economic Community formally stated that it would not accept an extraterritorial extension of U.S. jurisdiction and that the bill went against international law.[142]

During the discussion of the Torricelli bill, Jorge Mas Canosa once again picked a fight with the *Miami Herald*. In January of 1992, the *Herald* ran an editorial opposing the bill. It admitted that Robert Torricelli had built a reputation as a leader on Latin American issues, but it also reminded readers that President George H. W. Bush had vetoed similar legislation in 1990 because it would harm relations with trading partners like Canada. The newspaper called for Congress to defeat the Torricelli bill. "Making the embargo airtight will not promote democracy or liberty in Cuba, but it could promote chaos and catastrophic violence," the editorial cautioned. The editorial board warned that such a tightening could "conceivably worsen the Cuban people's deteriorating living conditions while offering Mr. Castro rhetorical ammunition for harsher repressive measures and for his denunciations of U.S. 'conspiracies' against his regime." The most sensible policy that Washington could adopt toward Cuba was to leave things as they were. To exert additional pressure on the Cuban government ran the risk of making the United States' Cuba policy completely ineffective.[143]

Mas Canosa denounced the *Herald* for "manipulating information like *Granma*." The CANF chairman took to Cuban radio to denounce the newspaper and its leadership. He claimed that the *Herald* had conducted a continuous and systematic campaign against Cuban Americans, and he called on the newspaper's leadership to resign.[144] The same day the *Herald* published the editorial against the Torricelli bill, *El Nuevo Herald* published a column by assistant city editor Andrés Reynaldo criticizing Cuban American leaders who espoused violence against the Castro regime but expected others to carry out that violence. Reynaldo singled out Armando Pérez-Roura, general manager and commentator for Radio Mambi, who was leading a petition drive asking President Bush to grant the exile community the right to use force against Castro's Cuba. Mas Canosa took this as a combined assault on both the Cuban American community's allies and the community itself. "Just like *The Miami Herald* attacks Congressman Robert Torricelli, a friend of the Cubans, it also attacks Cubans and institutions like Armando Pérez-Roura," Mas Canosa charged. The *Herald* called the attacks on itself and its sister publication "sad and painful and unfair." Writers Alfonso Chardy and Cynthia Corzo reiterated that the newspapers had treated news about Cuba and Cuban Americans with respect, integrity, and sensitivity. They acknowledged that the *Herald* was not perfect, but stated that when they had made mistakes, they had been willing to correct them. While the newspaper had sought diverse perspectives in its news columns, it had given regular coverage to human rights violations and the situation on the island. "On the editorial pages of *The Herald*," they went on, "where our own opinion appears, our position in support of a free Cuba has been unequivocal."[145]

Mas Canosa was not impressed. He enlisted the aid of the right-leaning Inter-American Press Association, which published a negative report on the *Herald*'s practices. Mas Canosa and his allies then purchased advertising space on the side of buses that read, "I don't believe in *The Herald* / Yo no creo en *El Herald*."[146] Mas Canosa acknowledged these actions but denied having been part of the larger campaign against the *Herald* and its staff that accompanied them. Incensed members of the community organized letter writing campaigns to advertisers. The newspaper's vending machines were smeared with feces and staffers received death threats. During this campaign, the *Herald*'s publisher David Lawrence began to fear he would be the victim of a bombing and began using a remote-control device to start his car each morning.[147] In March, Lawrence published a piece entitled "No, Mr. Mas, Intimidation Won't Work," declaring that the *Herald* would not surrender to Mas Canosa's bullying. The newspaper would welcome and convey Mas Canosa's opinion, but never his opinion alone. "All the billboards in the Americas, all the national TV that he can buy, all the analysts whom he can strong-arm, all the huffing and bluster, still won't give him control of this newspaper. Ever." Lawrence wrote.[148]

The Torricelli bill remained a point of contention throughout 1992 as the country headed into a presidential election. President George Bush, following the suggestions of the State Department, initially opposed the Torricelli bill. In April, Arkansas governor Bill Clinton visited Miami and announced that he was backing the proposed legislation. On that day, Clinton received more than $275,000 in campaign contributions from Hispanic donors. The following month, on Cuban Independence Day, Clinton returned to Miami and four Cuban American businessmen presented him with a hundred thousand dollars. In response to Clinton's endorsement of the bill, President Bush stated that he would use an executive order to implement a new policy prohibiting vessels that engaged in trade with Cuban from coming into U.S. ports. The State Department remained quiet, but one official admitted off the record that the department was "bending over on this and taking it." With the stated and implicit support of the two leading presidential candidates, the bill easily passed both the Senate and the House.[149]

"It's a bad day in Havana," gushed Robert Torricelli after the passage of the Cuban Democracy Act in the House and the Senate. The *Herald*, however, called attention to the fact that "for some, the significance of the Cuban Democracy Act ... was its testament to the ability and clout of the Cuban American National Foundation."[150] The Cold War had ended with the fall of the Soviet Union, but CANF had significant influence over American politics still. The Free Cuba PAC had donated more than $1 million to congressional candidates in the previous decade and lawmakers understood that any vote against an anti-Castro policy carried with it the potential danger of being labeled as soft on communism. At that moment, the political capital of Mas Canosa and CANF was reaching a high-water mark. Even a previous critic of Mas Canosa's, Wayne Smith, had to admit that the courtship of Bill Clinton had been "a masterful job."[151] The foundation's relationship with Clinton would yield them a smooth transition from being associated with the Republican Party to a significant relationship with the Democratic contender. This was not without its controversy among many Cuban Americans. Republican loyalists in the community claimed that meetings between Mas Canosa and Governor Clinton showed "a lack of principle, a lack of loyalty, a negative image," and that the CANF chairman wanted "to be with God and with the devil." The foundation, however, chose continued influence over ideological purity or party association. "Your statements on Cuba have demonstrated to us here in Miami, as well as to the entire Cuban-American community throughout the United States," read a foundation statement following a meeting between the candidate and Mas Canosa, "that we need not fear a Bill Clinton administration."[152]

While George Bush still won the state of Florida, he did so by a much smaller margin than when he faced Michael Dukakis in 1988. Clinton managed to make inroads into the Cuban American community in 1992 and in 1996, when he gained as much as 40% of its vote.[153] Mas Canosa's relationship with Clinton allowed the Cuban American National Foundation to have continued access after the Republican Party lost the White House. Some critics of the CANF chairman saw this relationship as detrimental to Clinton and to American policy. One contentious magazine profile labeled the president Mas Canosa's "indulgent patron" and suggested that as a candidate, Clinton had entered in a "Faustian deal" to win the state of Florida.[154] The goals of the CANF and like-minded Cuban Americans seemed within reach. Clinton had embraced a harsher stance against Castro's Cuba. The Torricelli bill became law. The Soviet Union had collapsed, causing the end of subsidies to the island and the disappearance of Cuba's Eastern European trading partners. The period between 1991 and 1996, which was euphemistically called the *período especial* by Castro's government, saw a precipitous economic decline in Cuba. This massive economic downturn had its seeds in the period leading up to the fall of the Soviet Union, where the premiership of Mikhail Gorbachev led to a period in which trade with and aid to Cuba remained stagnant and price subsidies declined. The Cuban government also instituted policies during the late 1980s that were meant to roll back market reforms that been instituted in the 1970s and early 1980s. This left the Cuban economy in a particularly weak position as external aid and trade with Eastern Europe collapsed and the Toricelli bill was enacted. In the first three years of this period, Cuba's gross domestic product (GDP) declined by 35%. The daily lives of many Cubans were soon shaped by increasing precarity, hunger, and disease.[155]

This sharp economic decline exacerbated an immigration trend that began in the mid-1980s.[156] Starting in 1985, desperate Cubans began attempting the dangerous crossing of the Florida Straits in *balsas*, makeshift rafts constructed of tires and other materials available to them. The crossing was an incredibly dangerous endeavor during which the would-be refugees risked drowning, starvation, dehydration, or shark attacks. Between 1985 and 1993, some six thousand *balseros* reached the United States on these makeshift vessels. The situation became all the more dire in the summer of 1994 as the Cuban economy further declined and Castro once again used this migration impulse as a pressure release valve on Cuban society. Castro ordered the Cuban Coast Guard not to stop any rafters found attempting to exit the island's territorial waters. The new permissiveness of Castro's government drove thirty-four thousand rafters to leave Cuba's shores that summer.[157]

The Clinton administration was particularly concerned about these developments. Clinton remembered the political damage that the Mariel boatlift had done to Jimmy Carter and the problems that it had caused him as governor of Arkansas. Clinton's attorney general, Janet Reno, had also had significant experience with the crime surge in South Florida following the boatlift. Reno saw the rafters as a wave of illegal aliens trying to enter the United States. In response, the U.S. Coast Guard blocked the progress of the rafters at sea and redirected them to the American naval base at Guantanamo Bay.[158] When he publicly announced that the rafters would be sent to Guantanamo in an August press conference, Clinton called the Cuban government's actions "a

cold-blooded attempt to maintain the Castro grip on Cuba, and to divert attention from his failed communist policies." He accused Castro of attempting to
export to the United States the political and economic crises he had created
in Cuba in defiance of a larger movement toward democracy in the Americas.
"The Cuban government will not succeed in any attempt to dictate American
immigration policy," Clinton warned, "the United States will do everything
within its power to ensure that Cuban lives are saved and that current outflow
of refugees is stopped."[159]
     When asked whether the embargo and the increased economic burden on
the island caused the new influx, the president remained true to his previous
commitment to imposing restrictions on Cuba. Clinton told reporters that he
supported the embargo and the Cuban Democracy Act and did not believe the
United States should change its policies. When asked why a policy of isolation
toward Cuba had been adopted while he dealt with authoritarian regimes in
China and North Korea on a regular basis, Clinton gave a vague answer about
circumstances being different in those cases. The president made it clear, however, that the Cuban Adjustment Act was still the law of the land and that any
Cubans who reached American shores would be detained for review and be
treated in accordance with immigration law, including the act. When asked if
intercepting the rafters and sending them to Guantanamo Bay was immoral,
Clinton stated that it was his belief that "the American people and that the
Cuban American people and the people of Florida— ... the people of the
entire United States—do not want to see another Mariel boatlift."[160]
     Clinton's reaction to the rafter crisis also came in in the context of a
broader anti-immigrant sentiment becoming more prevalent in the United
States. The month before Clinton's press conference, activists under the heading of the "Save Our State" initiative had managed to get Proposition 187 on
the California state ballot for the 1994 election. The proposition intended to
block undocumented immigrants from accessing social services and benefits
like nonemergency healthcare and education.[161] The politics of 187 only grew
more contentious as the campaign went on and Republican governor Pete
Wilson embraced the proposition as part of his bid for reelection, bringing
increased attention to questions of immigration restriction on a national level.
     For Cuban Americans, however, the rafter crisis was still largely colored
by their memories of Mariel. *La voz de la calle* (The voice of the street), a
Cuban American newspaper, ran a headline in late August which read, "Massive Exodus Continues; the Second Mariel Has Begun."[162] The *Miami Herald* described how, as Clinton's policy toward the rafters evolved, the initial

reaction of ambivalence or perplexity on the part of the Cuban American community grew into anguish and discord. The former chairman of the state Democratic Party, Alfredo Durán, described a situation of "extreme confusion" in the community. The images of the rafters standing behind barbed wire in Guantanamo or at the Krome detention center in Miami evoked another ghost of Mariel: indefinite detention. This time, however, indefinite detention was to be the fate of all Cuban refugees, not only those suspected of or convicted of crimes. "It has changed status and privileges Cubans had for past 34 years," Durán told the newspaper.[163]

The feeling that the ground had suddenly shifted beneath their feet was widespread throughout the Cuban American community. Historian Félix Masud-Piloto began to revise his 1988 history of the Cuban diaspora in the United States, *With Open Arms: Cuban Migration to the United States*. When he published a new edition in 1996, Masud-Piloto added a new chapter on the rafter crisis and changed the title of the book to *From Welcomed Exiles to Illegal Immigrants: Cuban Migration to the U.S., 1959–1995*. Masud-Piloto felt that this new title more accurately reflected "the evolution of and contradictions of U.S. policy."[164] American policy toward the rafters changed longstanding realities for Cuban exiles, but it also changed so rapidly that the shock forced many outside the community to adopt new positions. On August 20, 1994, the *Herald* urged support for the Clinton-Reno policy, despite the pain that indefinite detention caused. It explained that the detention of the rafters hurt exiles, but it would also hurt Castro and might even topple him.[165] Less than a week later, the *Herald* denounced what it called "a dizzying, unfair change." The newspaper reiterated that indefinite detention was necessary, but the new policy changes that would deny them the right to apply for political asylum would be "unfair and unwise" and it would undercut support for American policy.[166]

The Cuban American lobby needed to negotiate a complicated political landscape in dealing with the rafter crisis. Some journalists portrayed the lobby's influence as absolute. Ann Louise Bardach reported that at an August 19 meeting at the White House, Jorge Mas Canosa attempted to dictate U.S. Cuba policy to President Clinton. According to Bardach, Clinton had left his own birthday party to meet with Mas Canosa, Florida governor Lawton Chiles, and other Miami Cuban Americans. There, Mas Canosa "thumped and slapped the table as he spoke, demanding the president punish Fidel Castro for the refugee crisis."[167] The situation became even more difficult, however, as the crisis dragged on into 1995 and the Clinton administration made another policy change that solidified a new status for the Cuban American and refugee communities. In early May, Janet Reno announced that most of the Cuban refugees detained in Guantanamo would be allowed to come to the United States. Any new refugees found at sea, however, would be sent back to Cuba.[168] The *Herald* regarded the altered policy as difficult, but opined that it adopted "the 'least worst' of a set of options containing *no* wholly satisfying choices." While no one relished the idea of returning Cuban rafters to the island on American vessels, the new agreement between the Cuban and U.S. governments expanded the number of legal visas to leave Cuba. It was important, the *Herald* warned, that the federal government fully observe its pledge to heed rafters who claim reason for political asylum.[169]

Some greeted the news of this policy announcement with delight. Two groups in the state of Florida, the Save Our State Committee and Floridians for Immigration Control, had been preparing to present voters with measures cutting off aid to undocumented immigrants in the state. Modeled after Proposition 187, the measures would propose constitutional amendments in the 1996 statewide ballot. The Clinton administration's decision to allow Cubans detained in Guantanamo to enter the United States would be "fuel to the fire," explained the supporters of these ballot measures in a tone described as "almost gleeful." Clinton's policy decision, said sociologist Lisandro Pérez, was a balancing act that offended both those who were against the arrival of the Cuban rafters as well as the "Cubans offended by the notion of a deal with Fidel Castro."[170] This was particularly true of the Cuban American National Foundation and its allies, who immediately took to Cuban radio to denounce the deal. The foundation pledged to lobby the U.S. Congress to subtract all funds spent to interdict the Cuban rafters from the military services budget. More problematic was CANF's announcement that it would withdraw as a voluntary sponsor of Cuban immigrants. "By this gesture, the CANF puts its narrower political agenda above the broader and infinitely more important imperative to help these Cubans—these human beings—to being life anew in the United States," admonished the *Herald*.[171]

The problem for CANF and other groups, the newspaper would report some days later, was "a crisis in clout." The foundation had bitterly broken its ties to the Clinton administration over the issue of repatriation. This was not without consequences. "After years of wielding effective veto power over U.S. policies toward Cuba," reported Christopher Marquis for the *Herald*, "the conservative Cuban-American lobby suddenly finds itself in a radically altered landscape that is much less sympathetic to its agenda." Even as

CANF and other Cuban Americans denounced the Clinton administration, they found less than ideal support from the Republican Party. Fiscal hawks in the House Budget Committee were calling for the elimination of government funding to Radio and TV Martí for the fiscal year to follow. Following the election of 1994 and the so-called "Republican Revolution," the desire for budget cuts and the anti-immigrant sentiment in Congress left CANF standing on unstable ground. Some, including State Department officials, predicted that there would be a shift in the Cuban community. The time was "ripe for a Democratic Mas Canosa." The change in Cuban immigration policy, however, had left Cuban American Democrats feeling "neutered" and too stunned or dismayed to step into the void.[172]

Marquis and other observers were heralding the decline of the Cuban American National Foundation and similar groups too hastily, but they were correctly identifying the frustration felt by the Cuban American lobby regarding the limits of their power. For decades, the Cuban American community had built on the federal largesse granted to the early waves of refugees and on its drive and background to grow its economic and political power in South Florida. The Cuban American community came of age as it solidified its place in Miami. In doing so, it came to wield the clout necessary to influence American foreign policy. The community sought to have a voice in determining its own destiny. The most effective lobbying organization in the Cuban community, the Cuban American National Foundation, was formed to exercise this power and to protect the image of the Cuban American community. In order to retain this influence, the foundation and other groups often sought to aid the federal government in attaining its goals at the expense of what some of its constituency saw as the community's best interest. As the balsero crisis threatened another Mariel, however, the political juggernaut of the Cuban American lobby encountered the immovable object of American politics and discovered the limits of its power: it was power preserved and retained, but also a power with restrictions. In 1995, the Cold War came to an end in Miami. The Cuban American community had not given up the desire to fight, but the federal government, which had by turns been its patron and its tool yet had never shared the same devotion to a post-Castro Cuba, had moved on.

"We'll Be Back in Cuba in Six Months"

Dairon Elisondo Rojas and his partner arrived at the southwestern border of the United States in August of 2019 after a journey that took
over a month. When they approached the U.S. immigration authorities, they received a very different welcome from that which characterized the
experiences of hundreds of thousands of Cubans after 1959. "We arrived, presented ourselves and they sent us right back to Mexico," Elisondo Rojas told the
New York Times in December of that year. Elisondo Rojas, a Cuban physician,
was prevented entry into the United States by policy changes enacted by two
different presidential administrations. In 2017 Barack Obama's presidential
administration had ended the wet foot, dry foot policy that had been in place
since the Clinton administration, making Cubans who arrived in the United
States subject to the same immigration policies as asylum seekers from other
nations. In early 2019, Donald Trump's Department of Homeland security
had enacted the "Migrant Protection Protocols," more commonly known as
the "Remain in Mexico" policy, which stranded asylum seekers in Mexico and
only allowed them to enter the United States for court appearances. When the
Times found Elisondo Rojas in migrant camp in Matamoros, Mexico, he was
working for a medical clinic run by an organization called Global Response
Management. Global Response Management paid him thirty dollars a day to
use his expertise as a critical care physician. The clinic cared for the twenty-
five hundred migrants in the camp along with another one thousand migrants
who lived elsewhere in Matamoros. While he kept working as a doctor, Rojas
hoped to win his asylum case without legal representation, to learn English,
and to practice medicine in the United States. If Rojas lost his case, however,
the executive director of Global Response Management had plans to send him
to other parts of the world to continue working as a physician. His training
made him a highly valued employee to the organization.[1]

Had Dr. Elisondo Rojas arrived in the United States in the 1960s, the federal government would have considered him a valuable potential asset, brought him into the country, and provided opportunities to learn English and obtain certification to practice medicine in the United States through the Cuban Refugee Program. His experience in critical care would have been widely sought after in American hospitals, and he might have been an attractive candidate for the Alliance for Progress programs. His disillusionment with the Cuban government and his experience working as a physician in Venezuela would have made him a valuable communicator in seeking domestic support for the Cold War. In 2019, decades removed from the end of the Cold War, Rojas was a valuable asset to medical relief organizations, but the federal government made him the subject of the same harsh, exclusionary policies that characterized broader American immigration policy.

In Miami during those same decades, the specter of the Cold War still hung in the air. Since the institution of the wet foot dry foot policy, struggles continued over Cuban migration and U.S.-Cuba policy. Because of the long-term changes created by policy decisions in the 1960s, what had once been an urgent hope and desire for a group that saw itself as temporarily exiled from their home had become a political stance to be defined within another South Florida constituency. The oft-heard statement from the early days of the exile, "We'll be back in Cuba in six months," had long since become a bitter reminder of the dashed hopes of the early refugee waves.[2] By the mid-1990s, many Cuban Americans cared deeply about Cuba and Cuban migration, but any sense of transience had gone. A survey of Cuban-born Miamians conducted in late 1995 found that most respondents preferred to call themselves Cuban Americans rather than exiles. Fulfilling the prediction that Daniel San Román had made more than two decades earlier, only 17% of those who responded to the survey said they would permanently return to Cuba after the potential fall of Fidel Castro's regime. "Although their hearts and memories are in Cuba, their bank accounts, children and grandchildren are here," explained one of the men who oversaw the survey of Cuban Americans.[3] Groups within the community would continue to exert pressure on policymakers, but they did so with the understanding that a return to an idealized Cuba that had long since disappeared, if it ever existed, was no longer in the cards.

The shift in Cuban immigration policy by the Clinton administration led to an increased adoption of confrontational measures by the Cuban American groups. The implementation of the new policy led to a week of traffic

blockades across Miami in protest of the policy.[4] When these protests failed
to change the policy, Cuban American groups like Hermanos al Rescate
(Brothers to the rescue) redoubled their efforts to find Cuban rafters at sea
before the U.S. Coast Guard could intercept them. They pushed the enve-
lope further by organizing "protest flights" into Cuban airspace. The Cuban
government responded by shooting down two of the group's planes. Faced
with international outrage, the Cuban government claimed it had begged the
U.S. government to end the group's flights, only to have the plea ignored.[5]

Relations between the Cuban American community and the Clinton
administration came to their nadir over the handling of the Elián González
affair. González was a five-year-old Cuban child who was rescued at sea after
the boat he, his mother, and eight others were using to attempt to cross to
Florida sank. The boy was found by fishermen on Thanksgiving Day 1999,
delivered to American authorities, and then released into the custody of his
great-uncle Lázaro González in Miami. Soon, the boy's father, who was back
in Cuba, sought the return of the child with the support of his government.[6]
The Cuban American National Foundation, meanwhile, circulated an image
of the boy with a heading that read, "Another Child Victim of Fidel Castro."[7]
After federal authorities ordered Lázaro González to turn over Elián, Cuban
Americans closed ranks around the family's home, with one retired school-
teacher declaring, "This is a battle between good and evil, and right now
America is evil."[8] Historian Lillian Guerra has argued that the González affair
brought to the fore questions of the Cuban community's place in the United
States. "For these exiles and U.S.-born Cubans," Guerra writes, "what was
at stake during the Elián saga was not simply the future of Cuba, but more
importantly, that of the United States."[9] That future was called into question
when, after a prolonged standoff, an armed federal strike team raided the
González home in the early hours of the morning of April 22, 2000, and the
child was subsequently returned to Cuba and his father, causing outrage
among Cuban Americans.[10]

As many people in Miami sought to heal the wounds left by the Elián
González affair, many people also sought to obtain retribution for the actions
of the Clinton administration.[11] Going into the election of 2000, Clinton's
vice president, Al Gore, was trailing by almost twenty points in the state of
Florida. Gore attempted to distance himself from Clinton and Reno's actions,
but many saw this as pandering.[12] While the vice president carried the heav-
ily Cuban American Dade County on Election Day, the inroads Clinton had
made into the Cuban American community were almost entirely reversed

in 2000. In a contested state where the vote differential came down to a few hundred ballots, the Cuban American community cast a quarter of a million more votes for George W. Bush than they did for Gore.[13] "Who can dispute that the Cuban vote elected President Bush?" asked Miami City Commissioner Tomás Regalado.[14]

Even as Regalado claimed that the Cuban American community had fulfilled the predictions of political scientists and swayed a national election, Miami continued to evolve as other groups grew in size and prominence. This was part of a longer trend whereby the city and its Spanish speaking groups had diversified. In 1970, 90% of the city's Hispanic community had been of Cuban origin; by 1990 that number had decreased to 58%. One of the fastest growing groups, as the city entered the twenty-first century, was the Venezuelan population, which numbered 61,000 by 2017. Colombians constituted about 6.6% of the county's foreign-born population by that year, and Central Americans constituted 13.8%. Meanwhile, 83,000 Haitians resided in Miami-Dade County and another 80,000 in Broward County. There were also significant growing populations from the Dominican Republic, Spain, Brazil, and South Asian countries. "Miami has never been more diverse," declared the *Miami Herald* in 2019, "with more foreign-born residents than ever."[15]

Alongside these new residents, in the period between 2010 and 2017, Miami's Cuban-born population also grew significantly, by about 21% or 120,000 people, which was a reflection of the larger changes to the relationship between Havana and Washington and of a larger immigration trend that helped drive policy changes.[16] In December of 2014, after eighteen months of secret talks involving the Vatican, the Obama administration moved for the restoration of full diplomatic relations with Cuba and ordered a new embassy opened in Havana. "We will end an outdated approach that for decades has failed to advance our interests, and instead we will begin to normalize relations between our two countries," Obama declared in a nationally televised statement from the White House. The move drew rebukes from Cuban Americans and Republican lawmakers, in particular from Marco Rubio, an ambitious young Cuban American senator who declared the policy shift as being based on the illusion that "more commerce and access to money and goods will translate to political freedom for the Cuban people."[17] The improving relations between Washington and Havana, however, had the effect of increasing Cuban migration to the United States. In 2013, 4,890 Cubans had arrived in the United States. By 2016, the volume of arrivals from Cuba resembled some of the heavier years of migration in decades past, with 53,416 Cubans arriving in the United States without first securing a visa, often through the southern border.[18] This increase in migration and pressure from Havana led Obama to end the wet foot, dry foot policy as one of his last acts in office.

The transition from the Obama administration to the Trump administration proved a windfall for Rubio as keeping the senator and other Cuban American politicians happy became a significant part of the new president's reelection strategy. This meant that Trump gave a significant amount of power to his former political rival, the man he had denigrated on the campaign trail with the moniker "Little Marco," and great influence over U.S. foreign policy toward Cuba and Venezuela. This was worrisome for Cuban Americans who disagreed with hard-line economic and diplomatic stances and saw them as harmful to common people in Cuba, but also to State Department professionals. "We knew early on that on Latin America policy Trump wasn't taking cues from career officials," a former State Department official told *Politico* in August of 2020; "he was taking cues from harder-line Cuba folks in Miami." Political allies like Tomás Regalado credited Rubio with keeping the Trump administration from straying from a hard line on Cuba, but others were critical of Rubio's laser focus on Cuba, Venezuela, and Nicaragua. One critic, described as a conservative Latin America analyst, suggested than rather than advancing American interests abroad, Rubio was bolstering his image in his home state. "He's not making foreign policy," the analyst said; "it's Florida electoral politics."[19] Rubio used this relationship to play to hard-line elements in his state and he could point to policy changes that rolled back not only the normalization policies of the Obama administration, but also longer established policies, as when the Trump State Department suspended the vast majority of private charter flights to Cuba.[20]

The effectiveness of these policy choices in drumming up support for Trump in South Florida was put to the test in the presidential election of 2020. Despite the hopes of Democratic operatives and voters, Trump beat former vice president Joe Biden in the state by four points. Trump significantly improved his margins in Miami-Dade County, which he had lost by 30 points four years earlier, and only lost the county to Biden by seven points.[21] There was anecdotal evidence of Venezuelan Americans and others voting for Trump based on his Latin American foreign policy.[22] Other reports, however, suggested the presence of an older pattern: superior Republican outreach in South Florida and a lack of organization by the Democrats. Democratic pollster Fernando Amandi impugned both the absurdities of the Republicans calling Democrats "communists" and the lack of an effective Democratic

message in response. In the words of a disappointed senior staffer on election night, "*Socialismo, socialismo*—the campaign had no message to counter
that." Much as Dante Fascell once sounded the alarm about the GOP outor-
ganizing his party in South Florida to little response, the Biden campaign
ignored dozens of requests and warnings from their Latino-outreach team
in the three months before the election. Cuban American Chris Wills, the
campaign's Hispanic vote director for South Florida, attempted to shock
the senior members of Biden's team by sending an email on October 29 with
the subject line, "WE ARE ON TRACK TO LOSE FLORIDA." Wills hoped to course
correct months of inaction in the last few days of voting. In the end, Trump
lost the 2020 election, but exit polls showed that his fortunes in the state of
Florida were boosted by winning 55% of the Cuban American vote, 30% of
the Puerto Rican vote, and 48% of the vote in other Latino groups in Miami-
Dade County.[23]

The political legacy of the Cold War shaped local politics in Miami in
other ways that year. Hard-line conservatives continued to inject the threat
of communism into local issues. During the COVID-19 public health crisis, Miami-Dade commissioner and mayoral candidate Daniella Levine Cava
proposed legislation that would have provided paid sick days for airport security guards and others who worked for county contractors. This led another
commissioner and rival candidate, Cuban American Republican Esteban
"Steve" Bovo, to liken the policy to the actions of Marxist governments. "In
countries like Nicaragua, and Venezuela and in Cuba, these are the kind of
policies that they begin to implement," said Bovo, "people leave those countries because government begins to put their foot on everybody's throat . . .
it's ridiculous we continue to entertain these kind of policies."[24] Just a few
weeks later, another Florida politician, Senator Rick Scott took to Twitter to
appeal to hard-liners by making claims about the national Black Lives Matter
protests responding to the death of George Floyd at the hand of the Minne-
apolis Police Department. Specifically, Scott made unproven allegations that
the Venezuelan government of Nicolás Maduro was supporting violent insti-
gators at Miami-area protests. When challenged, Scott pointed to a *Diario las
Americas* news report sourced from a blog.[25]

Claims that any expansion of the social safety net or any movement
for civil rights were communist influence or infiltrated were not new, but
by 2020, there was little to separate them from Republican Party ortho-
doxy, even as some issues once considered explosive in Miami politics had
become less prevalent. Where deportation of Cubans back to their home

country once triggered debate, prison uprisings, and a years-long effort to provide representation for Cubans facing deportation, the agreement signed with Havana under the Obama administration and the targeting of migrants under the Trump administration had led to increasing numbers of deportations of Cubans from the United States. In 2017, there had been 160 arrests of Cubans by federal authorities. That number had increased to 463 the following year. In 2019, federal authorities had arrested 1,140 Cubans nationwide. Deportations of these individuals had more than doubled between 2018 and 2019. As of August 31, 2019, 39,000 Cubans in the United States were facing orders of removal for criminal convictions or immigration violations. For many people, this potentially explosive situation had become the new status quo. When ICE deported 119 Cubans, Miami immigration attorney Wilfredo Allen told the *Miami Herald* that such a number was no longer shocking. "Years ago, people would gasp at this news," he told the newspaper, "But now, there is no surprise that 120 Cubans are deported. It's normal."[26] When the advent of the COVID-19 pandemic led the Cuban government to stop accepting flights of deportees, American immigration authorities once again kept hundreds of Cuban detainees in indefinite detention. By January 2021, eight Cuban detainees, who had been held between six and eleven months by immigration authorities without release or projection of when they might be sent back to Cuba, filed a lawsuit in federal court to demand their release. Echoing previous struggles by detainees, their lawyers sought to use the same precedent that led to the 2005 Supreme Court ruling on Cuban detainees.[27]

Even events that once would have been earth-shattering now seemed a part of a longer history that no longer promised fundamental change. When Fidel Castro died, many Cuban Americans took to the streets of Little Havana to celebrate long into the night, but it was hardly the fulfilment of a dream of a post-Castro Cuba. Castro died of natural causes after having left an active role in Cuba's government years before, and his brother and successor Raul announced his death on the night of November 25, 2016. Even as people honked their horns and set off fireworks, Cuban Americans on the street debated whether this would bring about seismic change or if little would result from it as the system of government created by the revolution remained.[28] The day passed, and the normal ebb and flow of Cuban American politics and the everyday reality in Miami continued even under changes brought about by a new presidential administration. Life went on.

By the second decade of the twenty-first century, Miami's Cuban Americans lived in an environment shaped by policy choices made decades before, as well as the Cold War rhetoric that helped drive those choices, but increasingly the major changes brought to mind the experiences of a generation whose numbers have dwindled over time. Some in the crowd the night that Castro died had been among the early waves arriving from Cuba, including eighty-year-old Elisa Martin, who had left Cuba in 1962. As she watched the people with amazement, her son, a Miami-born engineer, noted that it was hard to believe Castro was dead after false rumors had spread many times throughout the years. "I have so many family members who never lived to see this day," he said. A twenty-seven-year-old named Abraham Quintero began to cry, saying, "I wish my dad was here to see this."[29] The emotional catharsis of the moment did not come with a matching shift in geopolitics and many of those who had fervently awaited Castro's death simply did not live long enough to see it.

In 2006, *Diario las Americas* columnist Uva de Aragón wrote on the exile experience and on one of the ways in which exile ended, in death. Her book, *Morir de exilio* (Death by exile) collected "pages of mourning," death notices and articles about the deaths of prominent Cubans having appeared in her newspaper between 1961 and 2005. In her introduction, de Aragón wrote about the psychic wound of exile, which was so commonly used as a punishment in antiquity, and noted that the exile dreamed of a return to their home, always looking back, not forward. Beyond that, she posited, those who viewed themselves as exiles lived in another time. "The exile also lives out of time," she explained, "because often . . . his vision of the country freezes at the moment he left, as if he wished to stop the clocks and calendars to return, even just through memory, and find intact that city, that neighborhood, that home, that he one day was forced to abandon."[30] The men and women whose stories were told in de Aragón's book, as with so many others at the time of writing and after, could never return to Cuba because even if they physically traveled to the country of their birth, it was not the country of their memory. In Miami, de Aragón went on, Cubans had, over four decades, attempted the impossible task of replicating that which they had left behind. It was that Cuba that lived inside them that was far more authentic due to its refusal to fade away, even if clouded by distance and nostalgia.[31]

There had been those who sought to re-create Cuba in Miami, but these were not the Cuban refugees. Most early arrivals would have seen such a goal both as impractical and as a betrayal of the home to which they sought to return. Cold Warriors in the U.S. government tried to build a new Cuba in Miami in the 1960s, one that they could transplant back onto the island in the future. The early waves of Cubans arriving in Miami after the revolution used their resources, abilities, focus, and a significant amount of federal aid to create new lives for themselves. In doing so, many were able to recreate the class structures they had left behind and to foster the growth of Cuban culture in the city. By the dawn of the third decade of the twenty first century, the Miami that these two groups built was neither a replica of old Cuba nor a ready-made state to transplant into a post-Castro nation. With fewer and fewer Cuban Americans left with even an idealized memory of a Cuba before the revolution and with an increasingly diverse foreign-born population, Miami was a global city with a Cold War streak in its politics that was more reflex than choice. Many Cuban Americans still actively supported Cuban migrants, and those of other nations, but for many others the sense of urgency that would once have triggered mass outrage over Cubans stuck in Mexico and deportation lists was gone. For them, the history of Cuba and the Cuban diaspora was a justification for a political position more than a singular driving force stemming from the loss of their home.

The complex politics of Cuban American Miami were no longer the politics of exile. No arrival from Cuba had ever been simply a refugee or an exile. Race, class, gender, sexual orientation, political affiliation, and many other factors had shaded the individual experiences of a shared banishment. But in a Miami that had not stopped evolving, these factors created overlapping senses of identity that were, for many Cuban Miamians, more urgent than the ever-more-distant label of "exile." This did not mean the label no longer had influence; exile remained a powerful narrative to evoke in discussing shared suffering and resiliency among Cuban Americans. While that moniker represented the past more than the present, that shared past was all around them. After all, it had helped build the only home many Cuban Americans had ever known.

ARCHIVES, COLLECTIONS, AND ORAL HISTORY SOURCES

Archives and Libraries

BUSC   Barry University Special Collections, Barry University, Miami Shores, Florida

CHC   Cuban Heritage Collection, University of Miami, Coral Gables, Florida

DUSC   Duke University Special Collections, Duke University, Durham, North Carolina

FIU   Special Collections, Florida International University, Miami, Florida

GBPL   George H. W. Bush Presidential Library, College Station, Texas

GFPL   Gerald Ford Presidential Library, Ann Arbor, Michigan

JCPL   Jimmy Carter Presidential Library, Atlanta, Georgia

JFK   John F. Kennedy Presidential Library, Boston, Massachusetts

JGK   James G. Kenan Research Center at the Atlanta History Center, Atlanta, Georgia

LBJ   Lyndon Baines Johnson Presidential Library, Austin, Texas

RUSC   Special Collections and University Archives, Rutgers University, New Brunswick, New Jersey

UMSC   Special Collections, University of Miami, Coral Gables, Florida

UMUA   University Archives, University of Miami, Coral Gables, Florida

WCPL   William Clinton Presidential Library, Little Rock, Arkansas

WLSC   Wilson Library Special Collections, University of North Carolina, Chapel Hill, North Carolina

Manuscript and Record Collections

Alpha 66 Records, CHC

Anderson, Gwen A., 1974–1977, GFPL

Baer, Don, Communications, Clinton Presidential Records, WCPL

Barnes, Karen, Files, White House Office of National Service, GBPL

Benes, Bernardo Papers, CHC

Botifoll, Luis J., Oral History Project, CHC

Brzezinksi, Zbigniew, Material: Brzezinski Office File, Staff Office Files, JCPL

216216

216216

216216

2162216

216216

Brzezinksi, Zbigniew, Material: Staff Evening Reports File, Staff Office Files, JCPL
Caribbean Sea Migration Collection, DUSC
Carter, Jimmy, Plains File, JCPL
Carter, Jimmy, White House Central File, Jimmy Carter Presidential Papers, JCPL
Cuban Detainees' Litigation Paper Records, 1981–1994—MSS 734, JGK
Cuban Living History Project, FIU
Cuban Refugee Center Records, CHC
Cutler, Lloyd, Files, JCPL
Exile Periodicals Collection, CHC
Fascell, Dante B., Congressional Papers, 1955–1993, UMSC
Ford, Gerald, President Ford Committee Records, 1975–1976, GFPL
Ford, Gerald, White House Central Files, GFPL
Fort Chaffee Collection, CHC
Hartman, Robert T., Files 1974–1977, GFPL
Johnson, Lyndon B., Enrolled Legislation, President, 1963–1969, Papers of Lyndon
    Baines Johnson, LBJ
Johnson, Lyndon B., Legislation, White House Central Files, President, 1963–1969,
    Papers of Lyndon Baines Johnson, LBJ
Johnson, Lyndon B., National Security File, President, 1963–1969, Papers of Lyndon
    Baines Johnson, LBJ
Johnson, Lyndon B., Records of the National Commission on the Causes and Preven-
    tion of Violence, Papers of Lyndon Baines Johnson, LBJ
Kennedy, John F., National Security Files, Presidential Papers, Papers of John F. Ken-
    nedy, JFK
Kilberg, Counsel to the President Bobbie Greene, 1974–1977, GFPL
King, Mary—Donated Historical Material, JCPL
Miró Cardona, José, Papers, CHC
New Republic–Jorge Mas Canosa Collection, 1979–1996, FIU
Pearson Administration, Office of the President Records (Collection No. U0064),
    UMUA
Records of the Cuban-Haitian Task Force, JCPL
Santeiro, Luis, Papers, CHC
Schneider, Cabinet Secretary Paula, Subject Files, Staff Offices, Carter Presidential
    Papers, JCPL
Shoemaker, Don, Papers, 1937–1998, WLSC
Staff Material: North/South, JCPL
Tron, Barrie Tron Files, White House Office of Public Affairs, GBPL
Vertical File, CHC
Vorhees, Tracy S., Papers, RUSC
Walsh, Bryan O., Papers, BUSC

Watson, Jack, O-A, Cabinet Secretary & Intergovernmental Affairs, Staff Office, Carter Presidential Papers, JCPL

Oral History Interviews

Peñalver, Rafael. Interview by author. Digital recording. Coral Gables, Florida, March 14, 2013.

NOTES

Introduction

1. Daniel San Román, "Un rio de sangre nos separa de la coexistencia," *America libre*, October 17, 1972, Exile Periodicals Collection, Cuban Heritage Collection, University of Miami, Coral Gables, FL (hereafter CHC).

2. See Daniel San Román, "Clerigos desvergonzados y pro comunistas," *America libre*, June 25, 1971, Exile Periodicals Collection, CHC; San Román, "Cuba en peligro de ser vendida," *America libre*, November 19, 1971, Exile Periodicals Collection, CHC; and San Román, "McGovern es un demagogo o algo peor," *America libre*, June 9, 1972, Exile Periodicals Collection, CHC.

3. Daniel San Román, "Comenzó la batalla de Washington," *America libre*, May 21, 1971, Exile Periodicals Collection, CHC.

4. Daniel San Román, "Guerra, o demagogia de algunos," *America libre*, August 13, 1971, Exile Periodicals Collection, CHC.

5. Daniel San Román, "La séptima provincia de Cuba," *America libre*, August 6, 1971, Exile Periodicals Collection, CHC

6. Information gathered by the 2000 U.S. Census. According to that census, the number of Cubans that had arrived in the United States since 1959 was 828,577. See Silvia Pedraza, *Political Disaffection in Cuba's Revolution and Exodus* (New York: Cambridge University Press, 2007), 5.

7. The number of Cubans living in Miami as the postrevolutionary migration began in earnest might have been significantly lower, as many Cubans living in the city had been doing so after escaping Fulgencio Batista's regime and many had returned to Cuba after his ouster. For the mid-1950s estimate, see Melanie Shell-Weiss, *Coming to Miami: A Social History* (Gainesville: University Press of Florida, 2009), 152.

8. This number does not consider those Cuban born Miamians who had died in the six decades since the revolution or the number of Cuban Americans who live in the county. See Rob Wile, "Miami's Biggest New Wave of Immigrants Looks a Lot Like Its Previous Ones," *Miami Herald*, August 5, 2019, https://www.miamiherald.com/news/business/article232514327.html.

9. The invasion is covered within the context of Cuban exile politics in Chapter 3.

10. Figure quoted in Miguel A. De La Torre, *La Lucha for Cuba: Religion and Politics on the Streets of Miami* (Berkeley: University of California Press, 2003), 37.

11. This foreign policy intervention on American soil reflects several established patterns, but it fits as a variant of a long-standing U.S. approach toward Latin America generally and toward Cuba in particular: a policy of uplift. Historian Lars Schoultz has argued that American hostility toward any Cuban government is a symptom of Washington's "uplifting mentality," the idea that Cubans would welcome the opportunity to be guided "toward a higher and better civilization" by the United States. Further, Schoultz has shown how uplift serves as a strategy that serves both foreign policy realists and altruists, aligning with American policy aims while allowing Washington policymakers to claim their involvement as a part of a selfless mission. Based on their backgrounds, the refugees were seen as the most developed elements of Cuban society. Federal agencies portrayed this population as exceptional and by giving them the tools to further develop into a productive and economically self-sufficient group, U.S. policymakers sought to Americanize them and then reinject them into Cuban society as uplifters in a postsocialist landscape. The Cuban refugees were afforded an unprecedented welcome in accordance with this aim. See Lars Schoultz, *That Infernal Little Cuban Republic: The United States and the Cuban Revolution* (Chapel Hill: University of North Carolina Press, 2009), 557; and Schoultz, *In Their Own Best Interest: A History of the U.S. Efforts to Improve Latin Americans* (Cambridge, MA: Harvard University Press, 2018), 7.

12. This was part of an attempt by the *Miami Herald* and other South Florida institutions to call attention to the growing refugee crisis; it is detailed in Chapter 1.

13. Juanita Greene, "Refugees Trading Jewelry for Food," *Miami Herald*, November 30, 1960.

14. María Cristina García, *Havana USA: Cuban Exiles and Cuban Americans in South Florida, 1959–1994* (Berkeley: University of California Press, 1996), 4–7.

15. Ibid., 2. For examples of other scholarship, see María de los Angeles Torres, *In the Land of Mirrors: Cuban Exile Politics in the United States* (Ann Arbor: University of Michigan Press, 1999); Silvia Pedraza, *Political Disaffection in Cuba's Revolution and Exodus* (New York: Cambridge University Press, 2007); Guillermo J. Grenier and Lisandro Pérez, *The Legacy of Exile: Cubans in the United States* (Boston: Allyn and Bacon, 2003); Thomas A. Tweed, *Our Lady of the Exile: Diasporic Religion at a Cuban Catholic Shrine in Miami* (New York: Oxford University Press, 1997); and Gustavo Pérez Firmat, *Life on the Hyphen: The Cuban-American Way* (Austin: University of Texas Press, 1994).

16. For scholarship on competing conceptions of the revolution see Lillian Guerra, *Visions of Power in Cuba: Revolution, Redemption, and Resistance, 1959–1971* (Chapel Hill: University of North Carolina Press, 2012), 8–9. More recently, Guerra has expanded on these questions of historical memory, placing post-1959 Cuba in a longer continuity with a culture for radical change with the past and with American involvement. Her work also shows how Fidel Castro worked to scuttle memories of this revolutionary culture to remove the memory of other movements whose recognition might subvert his own standing and agenda. See Lillian Guerra, *Heroes, Martyrs & Political Messiahs in Revolutionary Cuba, 1946–1958* (New Haven: Yale University Press, 2018), 14–15. For the point on nostalgia and political baggage, see Michael J. Bustamante, *Cuban Memory*

Wars: Retrospective Politics in Revolution and Exile (Chapel Hill: University of North Carolina Press, 2021), 10.

17. Maddalena Marinari, Madeline Y. Hsu, and María Cristina García, "Introduction," in *A Nation of Immigrants Reconsidered: US Society in an Age of Restriction, 1924–1965*, ed. Maddalena Marinari, Madeline Y. Hsu, and María Cristina García (Urbana: University of Illinois Press, 2019), 7.

18. See Senate Committee on the Judiciary, Cuban Refugee Problems: Hearings before the Subcommittee to Investigate Problems Connected with Refugees and Escapees, 87th Cong., 1st sess., 1961, 44.

19. Alejandro Portes and Ariel C. Armony, *The Global Edge: Miami in the Twenty-First Century* (Oakland: University of California Press, 2018), 66–70.

20. Bruce J. Schulman, *From Cotton Belt to Sunbelt: Federal Policy, Economic Development, and the Transformation of the South, 1938–1980* (New York: Oxford University Press, 1991), 142.

21. Ibid., 151.

22. In a 2003 monograph, for example, Alex Stepick, Guillermo Grenier, Max Castro, and Marvin Dunn note that the United States welcomed Cuban exiles when they fled the island in the aftermath of the revolution, pointing out that the federal government "showered unparalleled benefits upon them" and that the Cuban community wielded "enormous influence over U.S. foreign policy toward Cuba." While the authors are correct in their assessment, this openness and aid is accepted as a given rather than the outcome of a specific set of policy negotiations and national security assessments. See Stepick, Grenier, Castro, and Dunn, *This Land Is Our Land: Immigrants and Power in Miami* (Berkeley: University of California Press, 2003), 8.

23. This book seeks to build on the work of Andrew Friedman, whose study of suburban Northern Virginia shows how spaces in the United States can shape and be shaped by American imperial ambitions. See Friedman, *Covert Capital: Landscapes of Denial and the Making of U.S. Empire in the Suburbs of Northern Virginia* (Berkeley: University of California Press, 2013).

24. Some historians have suggested that muscular Cold War action allowed politicians in both parties greater freedom to pursue domestic policy. Jonathan C. Brown, in his study of the impact of the Cuban revolution beyond the island, has suggested that the administrations of Dwight D. Eisenhower, John F. Kennedy, and Lyndon B. Jonson pursued a muscular form of anticommunism to pursue progressive reforms domestically. Brown argues that these administrations aimed to deflect conservative accusations of "creeping socialism" at home through their pursuit of anticommunism abroad, declaring that the 1960s were a time of "reactionary liberalism." Jonathan C. Brown, *Cuba's Revolutionary World* (Cambridge, MA: Harvard University Press, 2017), 15–16.

25. Benjamin Francis-Fallon, *The Rise of the Latino Vote: A History* (Cambridge, MA: Harvard University Press, 2019), 355.

26. Geraldo Cadava, *The Hispanic Republican: The Shaping of an American Identity, from Nixon to Trump* (New York: Ecco, 2020), xxiii.

27. In *The Cubans of Union City*, sociologist Yolanda Prieto recounts an October 1993 visit by Cuban American National Foundation chairman Jorge Más Canosa that sparked protests by local Cuban American Republicans "denouncing what they saw as the CANFs meddling with local and state concerns." Prieto's source speculates that this was done by local Republican leaders to bolster their own agendas, but it clearly denotes how dominant Miami Cuban American political operatives were in national politics and how creating a distinction from these operatives could be politically useful for other Cuban Americans. See Prieto, *The Cubans of Union City: Immigrants and Exiles in a New Jersey Community* (Philadelphia: Temple University Press, 2009), 129.

28. This has been particularly prevalent in the literature on Asian immigration to the United States. In an article on the Australian response to the national origins quotas imposed by the United States in the 1920s, David C. Atkinson calls attention to the importance of this literature. He argues that scholars have "illustrated how the changing dynamics of international politics in the Pacific both reflected and contorted American exclusion and discrimination practices before, during, and after the Second World War." Atkinson argues that the adoption of migratory policy, in this case the quota system of the 1920s, brought about indirect and unintentional consequences around the world that require further study from scholars of foreign relations. See Atkinson, "The International Consequences of American National Origins Quotas: The Australian Case," *Journal of American Studies* 50, no. 2 (May 2016): 378.

29. This reflects the case of the Cubans post-1959, as Meredith Oyen writes that these policies made the Chinese migrants "cold warriors" who influenced international relations both voluntarily and involuntarily. See Oyen, *The Diplomacy of Migration: Transnational Lives and the Making of U.S.-Chinese Relations in the Cold War* (Ithaca, NY: Cornell University Press, 2015), 9.

30. In her study of Chicago, for example, Lilia Fernández notes that the encounters between African Americans and whites only tell part of the story, calling attention to the waves of (im)migrants from Mexico and Puerto Rico whose historical imprint has largely gone unacknowledged. See Fernández, *Brown in the Windy City: Mexicans and Puerto Ricans in Postwar Chicago* (Chicago: University of Chicago Press, 2012), 4. Other scholars have also sought a more complex understanding of race in the United States, sometimes with Latinx communities outside of large population centers and sometimes considering the impact of other communities such as Japanese Americans. See Scott Kurashige, *The Shifting Grounds of Race: Black and Japanese Americans in the Making of Multiethnic Los Angeles* (Princeton, NJ: Princeton University Press, 2008); and José M. Alamillo, *Making Lemonade Out of Lemons: Mexican American Labor and Leisure in a California Town, 1880–1960* (Urbana: University of Illinois Press, 2006).

31. For an example of this approach from a different discipline, see Sarah Lynn Lopez, *The Remittance Landscape: Spaces of Migration in Rural Mexico and Urban USA* (Chicago: University of Chicago Press, 2015). An example of this type of scholarship from a historian is Julio Capó Jr.'s excellent book on Miami's queer history, which reinterprets that history in a transnational perspective. See Capó, *Welcome to*

Fairyland: Queer Miami before 1940 (Chapel Hill: University of North Carolina Press, 2017), 5–7.

32. A. K. Sandoval-Strausz, *Barrio America: How Latino Immigrants Saved the American City* (New York: Basic Books, 2019), 16, 23–24.

33. Ibid., 17.

34. Ibid., 11.

35. Llana Barber, *Latino City: Immigration and Urban Crisis in Lawrence, Massachusetts, 1945–2000* (Chapel Hill: University of North Carolina Press, 2017), 57.

36. Barber, *Latino City*, 69.

37. I have written about the importance of the Cold War to the discipline of Latino urban history and of case studies beyond Miami and the Cubans elsewhere. See Mauricio Castro, "'In the Grips of the Monster that Forced Us to Flee': How the Cold War Made Our Latino Cities," forthcoming in *Metropolatinx: Latina/os and the Future of Urban History*, ed. A.K. Sandoval-Strausz (Chicago: University of Chicago Press, 2024).

38. Schulman discusses this trend in the eighth chapter of his monograph, *From Cotton Belt to Sunbelt*.

39. Paul Ortiz, *An African American and Latinx History of the United States* (Boston: Beacon Press, 2018), 86–92.

40. Andrew Gomez, "Jim Crow and the Caribbean South: Cubans and Race in South Florida, 1885–1930s," *Journal of American Ethnic History* 36, no. 4 (Summer 2017): 25–48.

41. Chanelle N. Rose, *The Struggle for Black Freedom in Miami: Civil Rights an America's Tourist Paradise 1896–1968* (Baton Rouge: Louisiana State University Press, 2015), 164, 185.

42. Parallels can be drawn here to the limited scope of other liberalizing actions during the Cold War. Specifically, Mary L. Dudziak's concept of Cold War Civil Rights is significant. Dudziak demonstrates how the federal government's need to respond to foreign critics allowed them to challenge the racial status quo, but only to the extent to which it was useful in an international context. See Dudziak, *Cold War Civil Rights: Race and the Image of American Democracy* (Princeton, NJ: Princeton University Press, 2011), 13.

43. Devyn Spence Benson, *Antiracism in Cuba: The Unfinished Revolution* (Chapel Hill: University of North Carolina Press, 2016), 135.

44. There is a long and complicated history of Latino communities in the United States trying to distance themselves from African Americans, sometimes embracing discriminatory language. A. K. Sandoval-Strausz, for example, notes that Mexicans living in Dallas, TX, sometimes embraced violent racism against African Americans whether because of colorism ingrained from the Mexican racial context or because they sought to be understood not as people of color, but as white. See Sandoval-Strausz, *Barrio America: How Latino Immigrants Saved the American City* (New York: Basic Books, 2019), 81.

45. Marvin Dunn, *Black Miami in the Twentieth Century* (Gainesville: University Press of Florida, 1997), 317–319.

46. N. D. B. Connolly, *A World More Concrete: Real Estate and the Remaking of Jim Crow South Florida* (Chicago: University of Chicago Press, 2014), 217.

47. Miami's deviation from the norm has long been understood in the literature on the city. In 1993, sociologists Alejandro Portes and Alex Stepick began the preface to their monograph *City on the Edge: The Transformation of Miami* by declaring that the city was hardly a model for understanding other metropolitan areas. "Miami is not a microcosm of the American city," they wrote; "It never was." Portes and Stepick believed, however, that the city could provide insights into broader questions, as when they wrote that Miami's "experiment in bicultural living" could provide lessons for the United States as immigration drove the creation of a multicultural society. See Portes and Stepick, *City on the Edge: The Transformation of Miami* (Berkeley: University of California Press, 1993), xi–xii.

Chapter 1

1. Tom Lownes, "U.S. Given Details of Cuban Riot Here," *Miami Herald*, July 8, 1959.

2. John Morton and Al Finkelstein, "Cuban Consul Flees Miami Riot Charges," *Miami Herald*, July 7, 1959.

3. Al Finkelstein and Eddie Gong, "Riot Squad Quells Cuban Mix," *Miami Herald*, July 5, 1959.

4. James Buchanan, "Miami the Casablanca of Caribbean," *Miami Herald*, July 20, 1959.

5. The influence of nonstate actors is central to several studies of American diplomatic relations. Scholars have explored the influence of groups as diverse as protesters, banking networks, and groups of scientists and their influence on American foreign policy in the last two centuries Some examples include Andrew Rotter, *Hiroshima: The World's Bomb* (New York: Oxford University Press, 2008); Jay Sexton, *Debtor Diplomacy: Finance and American Foreign Relations in the Civil War Era, 1837–1873* (Oxford: Oxford University Press, 2005); and Jeremi Suri, *Power and Protest: Global Revolution and the Rise of Détente* (Cambridge, MA: Harvard University Press, 2003). Other scholars have explored the implications of American foreign policy on local areas both domestically and abroad, but less work has been done on the impact of local actors on high-level diplomatic relations. See, for example, Jeffrey A. Engel, ed, *Local Consequences of the Global Cold War* (Stanford, CA: Stanford University Press, 2007); and Kristin Hoganson, *Consumer's Imperium: The Global Production of American Domesticity, 1865–1920* (Chapel Hill: University of North Carolina Press, 2007).

6. Louis A. Pérez Jr., *On Becoming Cuban: Identity, Nationality, and Culture* (Chapel Hill: University of North Carolina Press, 1999), 432–433.

7. Julio Capó Jr., *Welcome To Fairyland: Queer Miami before 1940* (Chapel Hill: University of North Carolina Press, 2017), 240.

8. Ibid., 12.

9. Chanelle N. Rose, "Tourism and the Hispanicization of Race in Jim Crow Miami, 1945–1965," *Journal of Social History* 45, no. 3 (2012): 737–738.

10. N. D. B. Connolly, "Sunbelt Civil Rights: Urban Renewal and the Follies of Desegregation in Greater Miami," in *Sunbelt Rising: The Politics of Space, Place, and Region*, ed. Michelle Nickerson and Darren Dochuk (Philadelphia: University of Pennsylvania Press, 2011), 165.

11. N. D. B. Connolly, *A World More Concrete: Real Estate and the Remaking of Jim Crow South Florida* (Chicago: University of Chicago Press, 2014), 3.

12. Ibid., 278.

13. Raymond A. Mohl, "Miami: The Ethnic Cauldron," in *Sunbelt Cities: Politics and Growth since World War II*, ed. Richard M. Bernard and Bradley R. Rice (Austin: University of Texas Press, 1983), 62–63. In 1960 the *Herald* reported that the growth Dade's suburban areas had "rocketed to the nation's top at 158 per cent." "Metro Government: What it Costs . . . And Will Cost . . . And Why," *Miami Herald*, October 18, 1960.

14. See Connolly, "Sunbelt Civil Rights," 164–187, for a full discussion of this process.

15. "Urban Renewal Is Our Hope," *Miami Herald*, April 4, 1959.

16. Connolly, "Sunbelt Civil Rights," 171.

17. Ibid., 165.

18. Pérez Jr., *On Becoming Cuban*, 105.

19. Ibid., 115.

20. The sophistication of Havana's finance community, for example, was often held well above its counterparts in other Latin American countries and, at times, their counterparts in certain parts of the United States. Carlos Arboleya, a prominent Cuban who would eventually become vice chairman of South Florida Barnett Bank, remembers that the experience he had gained working for Citibank and the Banco Continental Cubano made him more experienced than many in Miami's established banking communities. He recalled that on finding his first banking job in Miami, the bank he was employed at "did not even know how to issue a letter of credit. I was the one who showed that bank how to issue letters of credit." Arboleya was effusive about the state of Cuba's banking industry before the revolution, stating that it was not on the same level as New York's banking enclave, but was on a corresponding level with the rest of the United States. See Carlos Arboleya, interview by Julio Estorino, August 17, 2010, Luis J. Botifoll Oral History Project, Cuban Refugee Center Records, Cuban Heritage Collection, Coral Gables, FL (hereafter CHC).

21. Pérez, *On Becoming Cuban*, 431–432.

22. Rose, "Tourism and the Hispanicization of Race in Jim Crow Miami, 1945–1965," 739.

23. Ibid., 746.

24. Chanelle N. Rose, *The Struggle for Black Freedom in Miami: Civil Rights and America's Tourist Paradise, 1896–1968* (Baton Rouge: Louisiana State University Press, 2015), 3.

25. Bryan O. Walsh, "Castro or No Castro, Miami Would Be Hispanic," 1983, Folder Castro or No Castro, Miami Would Be Hispanic, 1983, Box 39, Series III, Bryan O. Walsh Papers, Barry University, Miami, FL (hereafter Walsh Papers).

26. "Cuban Exile Group is on Parole in U.S.," *New York Times*, January 28, 1959.

27. Masferrer was seemingly right to stay in hiding as a few weeks later Miami law enforcement received intelligence that Castro agents were in South Florida to kidnap the former senator and take him back to Cuba. See George Southworth, "Most Wanted Cuban Hides in Poverty Here," *Miami Herald*, February 22, 1959; and Southworth, "Castro Agents Here to 'Get' Batista Aides?," *Miami Herald*, April 5, 1959.

28. George Southworth, "Batista's Brother Comes Here; Opens a Business in Hialeah," *Miami Herald*, March 26, 1959.

29. The fall of Batista seemed, in fact, to be part of a larger trend of decline in dictatorships in Latin America. After Batista's escape from Havana only four traditional dictators remained in the smaller countries of the Western Hemisphere: in Haiti, Dominican Republic, Nicaragua, and Paraguay. See Jonathan C. Brown, *Cuba's Revolutionary World* (Cambridge, MA: Harvard University Press, 2017), 8–9, 227–228.

30. John B. McDermott, "Should U.S. Be Haven for Dictators?," *Miami Herald*, April 5, 1959.

31. Bryan O. Walsh, "Cubans 84," 1984, Folder Cubans 84 Institute of Cuban Studies (UM), Miami, FL, August 3, 1984, Box 41, Series III, Walsh Papers.

32. Bryan O. Walsh, "Cubans in Miami—The Factual Story," 1966, Folder Cubans 1960–2000, Box 26, Series II, Walsh Papers.

33. James Buchanan, "Anti-Castro Newspaper Pops Up in Miami Area," *Miami Herald*, March 8, 1959.

34. Carl Lindskoog, *Detain and Punish: Haitian Refugees and the Rise of the World's Largest Immigration Detention System* (Gainesville: University of Florida Press, 2018), 2.

35. Arthur Johnsey, "Batistan Exiles Hit 500," *Miami Herald*, June 30, 1959.

36. Carl J. Bon Tempo, *Americans at the Gate: The United States and Refugees during the Cold War* (Princeton, NJ: Princeton University Press, 2008), 109.

37. Edward Lustgarten, letter to Dante B. Fascell, August 29, 1960, Folder 14, Box 1906, Dante B. Fascell Congressional Papers, 1955–1993, University of Miami Special Collections, University of Miami, Coral Gables, FL (hereafter DBF Papers).

38. Tracy S. Voorhees, "Report to the President of the United States on the Cuban Refugee Problem," 1961, Folder T. S. Voorhees President's Representative for Cuban Refugees—Documents—Reports—TSV Final of January 18, 1961, Box P, Tracy S. Voorhees Papers, Special Collections and University Archives, Rutgers University, New Brunswick, NJ (hereafter Voorhees Papers).

39. Ibid.

40. C. B. Sweet, letter to Norman P. Mason, December 27, 1960, Folder T. S. Voorhees President's Representative for Cuban Refugees—Documents—Misc., Box P, Voorhees Papers.

41. Nestor Morales, letter to Dante B. Fascell, July 26, 1960, Folder 14, Box 1906, DBF Papers.

42. Juanita Greene, "How Cubans Pay $100 Each to Stay in the U.S.," *Miami Herald*, August 24, 1960.

43. A.V. Bethencourt, open letter to Cuban clients, undated, Folder 14, Box 1906, DBF Papers.

44. "Got No Advance Fee, Attorney Declares," *Miami Herald*, September 1, 1960.

45. Jack L. King to Dante B. Fascell, April 28, 1960, Folder 14, Box 1906, DBF Papers.

46. Jack L. King to Dante B. Fascell, August 5, 1960, Folder 14, Box 1906, DBF Papers.

47. Dante B. Fascell to Jack L. King, August 23, 1960, Folder 14, Box 1906, DBF Papers.

48. This attitude has been seen as the definitive feature of this group. Sociologist Silvia Pedraza went so far as to label this first wave of exiles as "those who wait." See Silvia Pedraza, *Political Disaffection in Cuba's Revolution and Exodus* (New York: Cambridge University Press, 2007), 79.

49. George Southworth, "Cuban Predicts a Blood Bath," *Miami Herald*, November 2, 1960.

50. Tracy S. Voorhees, "The Cuban Refugees," 1971, Folder T. S. Voorhees President's Representative for Cuban Refugees—Essay 1, The Cuban Refugees, March 1971, Box O, Voorhees Papers.

51. Francis E. Walter to Dante B. Fascell, August 23, 1960, Folder 14, Box 1906, DBF Papers.

52. Bryan O. Walsh, report to Bishop Coleman Carroll, December 6, 1960, Folder Cubans 1960–2000, Box 26, Series II, Walsh Papers.

53. Juanita Greene and E. V. W. Jones, "Dade's Cuban Exiles Hunt for Food, Work," *Miami Herald*, October 2, 1960.

54. Walsh, "Cubans in Miami—The Factual Story," 1966, Folder Cubans 1960–2000, Box 26, Series II, Walsh Papers.

55. Ibid.

56. Walsh, "Castro or No Castro, Miami Would Be Hispanic."

57. Juanita Greene and E. V. W. Jones, "Cubans in Exile, Who Can Help?," *Miami Herald*, October 2, 1960.

58. Bryan O. Walsh, draft of speech prepared for Bishop Coleman Carroll, March 12, 1963, Folder Cubans 1960–2000, Box 26, Series II, Walsh Papers.

59. Greene and Jones, "Cubans in Exile, Who Can Help?," *Miami Herald*, October 2, 1960.

60. Greene and Jones, "Dade's Cuban Exiles Hunt for Food, Work," *Miami Herald*, October 2, 1960.

61. Ibid.

62. Greene and Jones, "Cubans in Exile, Who Can Help?," *Miami Herald*, October 2, 1960.

63. Greene and Jones, "Dade's Cuban Exiles Hunt for Food, Work," *Miami Herald*, October 2, 1960.

64. Juanita Greene, "Cuba Refugees Cover Worry with a Smile," *Miami Herald*, November 28, 1960.

65. Juanita Green, "26 Cubans Live on What 3 Earn," *Miami Herald*, November 29, 1960.

66. "Our Many-Sided Refugee Problem," Editorial, *Miami Herald*, October 13, 1960.

67. See Tracy S. Voorhees, "Cuban Refugee Assignment—Oct. 1960 to February 1961," 1961, Folder T. S. Voorhees President's Representative for Cuban Refugees—Essay 2, Cuban Refugee Assignment—Oct. 1960 to February 1961 (October 1961), Box O, Voorhees Papers.

68. The committee had several members already involved in the handling of aid to the refuges, including Bishop Carroll, Reverend Buell, and Franklin Williams.

69. Juanita Greene, "Expert in Refugees to Survey Miami," *Miami Herald*, October 4, 1960.

70. Juanita Greene, "New Group to Aid Cuban Refugees," *Miami Herald*, October 12, 1960.

71. Ira F. Willard to Dwight D. Eisenhower, October 17, 1960, Folder 14, Box 1906, DBF Papers.

72. David Kraslow, "Commission to Assist In Handling Refugees," *Miami Herald*, October 25, 1960.

73. Voorhees, "Cuban Refugee Assignment—Oct. 1960 to February 1961."

74. Bon Tempo, *Americans at the Gate*, 75–81.

75. Voorhees, "Cuban Refugee Assignment—Oct. 1960 to February 1961."

76. The Cuban Refugee Committee sent a telegram to the White House on November 5 insisting that the federal government must appoint an official with the power to deal with the situation in Miami and warning that "a serious crisis" was impending unless prompt action was taken. See Cuban Refugee Committee to Robert Merriam, November 5, 1960, Folder 1, Box 1, Series I, CHC.

77. Juanita Greene, "Refugee Expert Coming Here," *Miami Herald*, November 11, 1960.

78. Voorhees, "Cuban Refugee Assignment–Oct. 1960 to February 1961."

79. Juanita Greene, "Ike Aide in Miami to Discuss Cuban Refugee Plight," *Miami Herald*, November 17, 1960.

80. Voorhees, "Cuban Refugee Assignment—Oct. 1960 to February 1961."

81. Ibid.

82. Voorhees, "The Cuban Refugees."

83. Anita Casavantes Bradford, *The Revolution Is for the Children: The Politics of Childhood in Havana and Miami, 1959–1962* (Chapel Hill: University of North Carolina Press, 2014), 135.

84. Voorhees, "The Cuban Refugees."

85. Rick Tuttle, "U.S. Lets Cuban Refugees Stay," *Miami Herald*, November 1, 1960.

86. Nat Altshul, letter to the editor, *Miami Herald*, November 25, 1960.

87. Arthur H. Patten Jr. to Senator Spressard L. Holland, January 9, 1961, Folder T. S. Voorhees President's Representative for Cuban Refugees—Documents—Correspondence—Congressional, Box O, Voorhees Papers.

88. "Refugees Oppose a Camp in Florida," *New York Times*, January 11, 1961.

89. Voorhees, "Cuban Refugee Assignment—Oct. 1960 to February 1961."

90. Juanita Greene, "Miami Moves Ahead on Four Fronts to Relieve Plight of Cuba Refugees," *Miami Herald*, November 23, 1960.

91. Voorhees, "Cuban Refugee Assignment—Oct. 1960 to February 1961"; and Voorhees, "The Cuban Refugees."

92. Walsh, "Cubans 84."

93. Voorhees, "Cuban Refugee Assignment—Oct. 1960 to February 1961"; and Vorhees, "The Cuban Refugees."

94. Tracy S. Voorhees to Dwight D. Eisenhower, December 1, 1960, Folder T. S. Voorhees President's Representative for Cuban Refugees—Documents—Reports—TSV Confidential Report to President, December 1, 1960, Box P, Voorhees Papers.

95. Voorhees, "The Cuban Refugees."

96. Although officials in the State Department had previously accused the Castro regime of being influenced by communism, the *New York Times* noted that this assertion upon the granting of Voorhees's request was the first time in which the United States had officially accused the Cuban government of being communist controlled. See Felix Belair Jr., "President Allots $1,000,000 to Help Cuban Refugees," *New York Times*, December 3, 1960.

97. This provision was known as the known as the Dirksen-Douglas amendment. See ibid.

98. Voorhees, "The Cuban Refugees."

99. Juanita Greene, "Miami Moves Ahead on Four Fronts to Relieve Plight of Cuba Refugees," *Miami Herald*, November 23, 1960.

100. Felix Belair Jr., "President Allots $1,000,000 to Help Cuban Refugees," *New York Times*, December 3, 1960.

101. Voorhees, "The Cuban Refugees," and Tracy S. Voorhees to Kerry King, Texaco Corporation, February 27, 1961, Folder T. S. Voorhees President's Representative for Cuban Refugees—Documents—Texaco Inc, Box P, Voorhees Papers.

102. Voorhees, "The Cuban Refugees."

103. Bryan O. Walsh to Coleman Carroll, November 10, 1966, Folder Commission on Cuban Refugees 1966, Box 6, Series I, Walsh Papers.

104. Tracy S. Voorhees, "Report to the President of the United States on the Cuban Refugee Problem."

105. Ibid.

106. Ibid.

107. Ibid.

108. Voorhees also indicated that in the same time period, 112 accountants and auditors, 125 lawyers and judges, 142 professors and teachers, 81 engineers, and 166 business managers were interviewed at the center, compared to only 172 semiskilled and unskilled laborers.

109. Ibid.

Chapter 2

1. Tracy S. Voorhees to Herbert Hoover, February 14, 1961, Folder T. S. Voorhees President's Representative for Cuban Refugees—Essay 1, The Cuban Refugees, March 1971, Box O, Tracy S. Voorhees Papers, Special Collections and University Archives, Rutgers University, New Brunswick, NJ (hereafter Voorhees Papers).

2. John F. Kennedy to Tracy S. Voorhees, undated, Folder T. S. Voorhees President's Representative for Cuban Refugees—Essay 1, The Cuban Refugees, March 1971, Box O, Voorhees Papers.

3. Quoted in Voorhees in "The Cuban Refugees," 1971, Folder T. S. Voorhees President's Representative for Cuban Refugees—Essay 1, The Cuban Refugees, March 1971, Box O, Voorhees Papers.

4. Ibid.

5. Bryan O. Walsh, "Diary—Cuban Refugee Problems 1961," January 14, 1961, Box 41, Series III, Bryan O. Walsh Papers, Barry University, Miami, FL (hereafter Walsh Papers).

6. Bryan O. Walsh, "Cuban Refugee Children," *Journal of Inter-American Studies and World Affairs* 13, nos. 3–4 (July–October 1971): 387.

7. Walsh, "Cuban Refugee Children," 389.

8. María de los Angeles Torres, *The Lost Apple: Operation Pedro Pan, Cuban Children in the U.S. and the Promise of a Better Future* (Boston: Beacon Press, 2003), 63–64.

9. Walsh, "Cuban Refugee Children," 390.

10. Ibid., 379.

11. María de los Angeles Torres defines *patria postestad* as "a Roman legal concept regarding the authority to make decisions for children. In Roman law the father had almost absolute authority over his children. This later evolved into parental rights. By the early twentieth century, it was well established that this authority, including how to educate children, fell to the parents." See Torres, *The Lost Apple,* 89.

12. Anita Casavantes Bradford, *The Revolution Is for the Children: The Politics of Childhood in Havana and Miami, 1959–1962* (Chapel Hill: University of North Carolina Press, 2014), 109–111.

13. "Castro to Put Children under State Control?" *Miami Herald,* November 9, 1960.

14. Walsh, "Cuban Refugee Children," 395.

15. Ibid., 397.

16. Torres, *The Lost Apple,* 69.

17. Yvonne M. Conde, *Operation Pedro Pan: The Untold Exodus of 14,048 Cuban Children* (New York: Routledge, 1999), 47.

18. Walsh, "Cuban Refugee Children," 378.

19. "Catholic Welfare Bureau Fact Sheet," September 20, 1963, Folder Catholic Welfare Bureau Cuban Children's Program 1963, Box 5, Series I, Walsh Papers.

20. Torres, *The Lost Apple,* 75–76.

21. "Catholic Welfare Bureau Fact Sheet," September 20, 1963.

22. Estimates regarding this number vary. María de los Angeles Torres estimates that the number of children cared for by friends or relatives was closer to six thousand. See Torres, *The Lost Apple,* 148.

23. Bryan O. Walsh, "Operation Pedro Pan," March 1, 2001, Folder Cuban Children's Program 1964–2001, Box 26, Series II, Walsh Papers.

24. "Catholic Welfare Bureau Fact Sheet," September 20, 1963.

25. Walsh, "Operation Pedro Pan," March 1, 2001.

26. Torres, *The Lost Apple,* 148.

27. Conde, *Operation Pedro Pan,* 56.

28. Ibid., 74–76.

29. Ibid., 91.

30. Torres, *The Lost Apple,* 169–170.

31. Conde, *Operation Pedro Pan,* 77–79.

32. Ibid., 125–127.

33. Ibid., 98.

34. Translation of letter from Ángel Wong Alcázar to Bryan O. Walsh, August 8, 1964, Folder Cuban Children's Program 1964–2001, Box 26, Series II, Walsh Papers.

35. Wong Alcazar to Walsh, August 8, 1964.

36. Quoted in Louise W. Holborn, "The Cuban Refugee Program: Its Development and Implementation," July 31, 1965, Folder 121, Box 40, Series VI, Cuban Refugee Center Records, Cuban Heritage Collection, Coral Gables, FL (hereafter CHC).

37. Lourdes Gil, "Operation Pedro Pan," Folder Operation Pedro Pan—Title of Program 2000-01, Box 35, Series II, Walsh Papers.

38. Walsh, "Operation Pedro Pan," March 1, 2001.

39. Holborn, "The Cuban Refugee Program: Its Development and Implementation," July 31, 1965.

40. Abraham Ribicoff, "Report of Secretary Abraham A. Ribicoff on the Cuban Refugee Problem," February 2, 1961, Folder 78, Box 4, Series I, Cuban Refugee Center Records, CHC.

41. Ribicoff, "Report of Secretary Abraham A. Ribicoff on the Cuban Refugee Problem," February 2, 1961.

42. Holborn, "The Cuban Refugee Program: Its Development and Implementation," July 31, 1965.

43. Ibid.

44. Ibid.

45. Jeanne Mahaffey, "U.S. Cuban Refugee Program," February 6, 1962, Folder 71, Box 4, Series 1, Cuban Refugee Center Records, CHC.

46. Jack Oswald, "Cuban Needy Given First U.S. Checks," *Miami News,* February 27, 1961.

47. Carl J. Bon Tempo, *Americans at the Gate: The United States and Refugees during the Cold War* (Princeton, NJ: Princeton University Press, 2008), 109.

48. Silvia Pedraza, *Political Disaffection in Cuba's Revolution and Exodus* (New York: Cambridge University Press, 2007), 99.

49. Paul P. Kennedy, "U.S. Helps Train an Anti-Castro Force At Secret Guatemalan Air-Ground Base," *New York Times*, January 10, 1961.

50. Lars Schoultz, *That Infernal Little Cuban Republic: The United States and the Cuban Revolution* (Chapel Hill: University of North Carolina Press, 2009), 148.

51. Tad Szulc, "Castro Foes Map Multiple Forays with Guerillas," *New York Times*, April 10, 1961.

52. "Hombre precavido," *El avance criollo*, April 21, 1961, 13.

53. The political implications of the invasion and its effect on the relationship between the exile population and the federal government are discussed at length in Chapter 3.

54. J. Arthur Lazell to Marshal Wise, June 27, 1961, Folder 3, Box 1, Series I, Cuban Refugee Center Records, CHC.

55. "Revised Cuban Refugee Program," April 29, 1961, Folder Cuba, Subject Exiles 1961, Box 48, National Security Files, Presidential Papers, Papers of John F. Kennedy, John F. Kennedy Presidential Library, Boston, MA (hereafter JFK Library).

56. "U.S. Policy toward Cuban Exiles," May 3, 1961, Folder Cuba, Subject Exiles 1961, Box 48, National Security Files, Presidential Papers, Papers of John F. Kennedy, JFK Library.

57. This program is discussed in Chapter 3.

58. "U.S. Policy toward Cuban Exiles," May 3, 1961.

59. Senate Committee on the Judiciary, Cuban Refugee Problems: Report of the Committee on the Judiciary United States Senate Made by Its Subcommittee to Investigate Problems Connected with Refugees and Escapees Pursuant to S. Res. 50, Eighty-Seventh Congress First Session as Extended, 87th Cong, 1st sess., 1962, S. Rep. 1328, 6.

60. Robert F. Kennedy, "Testimony of Senator Robert F. Kennedy Senate Judiciary Subcommittee on Refugees and Escapees New York University Eisner and Lubin Auditorium," April 13, 1966, Folder 202, Box 27, Series II, Cuban Refugee Center Records, CHC.

61. Senate Committee on the Judiciary, Cuban Refugee Problems, 117.

62. Errol T. Ballanfonte, Interview with Tomas García Fuste, February 17, 1967, Folder 91, Box 4, Series I, Cuban Refugee Center Records, CHC.

63. "The Cuban Refugee Emergency Center: Its Programs and Operations," December 1961, Folder 168, Box 8, Series I, Cuban Refugee Center Records, CHC.

64. Cuban Refugee Center, "Public Information Activities Report, Cuban Refugee Center, Miami for Period January 1—August 20, 1962," Folder 187, Box 9, Series I, Cuban Refugee Center Records, CHC.

65. See Cuban Refugee Center, "Jaycee-a-gram," and Cuban Refugee Center, "Your 'Make Mine Freedom' Reminder," Folder 191, Box 9, Series I, Cuban Refugee Center Records, CHC.

66. "U.S. Cuban Refugee Program," Folder 71, Box 4, Series I, Cuban Refugee Center Records, CHC.

67. Don Shoemaker to John S. Knight, James L. Knight, Alvah Chapman Jr., George Beebe, and Lee Hills, January 10, 1966, Folder 73 Dade County, Subseries 3.1, Series 3, Don Shoemaker Papers 1937–1998, Southern Historical Collection, Louis Round Wilson Library Special Collections, University of North Carolina, Chapel Hill (hereafter Shoemaker Papers).

68. Bon Tempo, *Americans at the Gate*, 110.

69. Alejandro Portes and Alex Stepick, *City on the Edge: The Transformation of Miami* (Berkeley: University of California Press, 1993), 103–104.

70. Don Shoemaker to John S. Knight, James L. Knight, Alvah Chapman Jr., George Beebe, and Lee Hills, January 10, 1966, Folder 73 Dade County, Subseries 3.1, Series 3, Shoemaker Papers.

71. Bon Tempo, Americans at the Gate, 110.

72. Don Shoemaker to John S. Knight, James L. Knight, Alvah Chapman Jr., George Beebe, and Lee Hills, January 10, 1966.

73. Torres, *The Lost Apple*, 212.

74. Conde, *Operation Pedro Pan*, 180.

75. See Torres, *The Lost Apple*, 212–213.

76. U.S. Cuban Refugee Program, "New Life in Iowa Pleases Cuban Couple," *Resettlement Re-Cap*, November 1962, Folder 192, Box 9, Series I, Cuban Refugee Center Records, CHC.

77. Pedro Heng, "El miedo de abandonar Miami se volvio felicidad," Folder 186, Box 9, Series I, Cuban Refugee Center Records, CHC.

78. U.S. Cuban Refugee Program, "The Score," *Resettlement Re-Cap*, October 1962, Folder 192, Box 9, Series I, Cuban Refugee Center Records, CHC.

79. U.S. Cuban Refugee Center press release, May 7, 1963, Folder 25, Box 2, Series I, Cuban Refugee Center Records, CHC.

80. Cuban Refugee Program, "Fact Sheet," December 31, 1970, Folder 14, Box 1, Series I, Cuban Refugee Center Records, CHC.

81. One such estimate, from January 1966, estimated the rate of return to Miami at 2%. See Don Shoemaker to John S. Knight, James L. Knight, Alvah Chapman Jr., George Beebe, and Lee Hills, January 10, 1966, Folder 73 Dade County, Subseries 3.1, Series 3, Shoemaker Papers.

82. J. A. Lazell to Voluntary Agencies and State Welfare Department [presumably 1962], Folder 5, Box 1, Series I, Cuban Refugee Center Records, CHC.

83. Cuban Refugee Center, "Initial Study of Cuban Refugee Profile Dade County, Florida," September 1965, Folder 169, Box 8, Series I, Cuban Refugee Center Records, CHC.

84. Statistics from the Cuban Refugee Program, "U.S. Cuban Refugee Program," February 6, 1962, Folder 71, Box 4, Series I, Cuban Refugee Center Records, CHC.

85. Holborn, "The Cuban Refugee Program: Its Development and Implementation," July 31, 1965.

86. Miguel A. De La Torre, *La Lucha for Cuba: Religion and Politics on the Streets of Miami* (Berkeley: University of California Press, 2003), 37.

87. U.S. Cuban Refugee Center press release, May 28, 1971, Folder 35, Box 2, Series I, Cuban Refugee Center Records, CHC.

88. William R. Amlong, "How the CIA Operated in Dade," *Miami Herald*, March 9, 1975.

89. De La Torre, *La Lucha for Cuba*, 40–41.

90. Jonathan C. Brown, *Cuba's Revolutionary World* (Cambridge, MA: Harvard University Press, 2017), 167.

91. John Egerton, "Cubans in Miami: A Third Dimension in Racial and Cultural Relations," November 1969, Folder 111, Box 39, Series IV, Cuban Refugee Center Records, CHC.

92. University of Miami School of Medicine, "Interim Report of the Bilingual and Translation Sub-Section of the Postgraduate Medical Education Program," February 16, 1961, Folder 1, Box 25, Series II—Pearson Administration, Office of the President Records (Collection No. U0064), University Archives—University of Miami, Coral Gables, Florida (hereafter UM Archives).

93. University of Miami School of Medicine, "Postgraduate Medical Education for Latin American Physicians University of Havana School of Medicine in Exile University of Miami School of Medicine," February 15, 1963, Folder 1, Box 25, Series II—Pearson Administration, Office of the President Records (Collection No. U0064), UM Archives.

94. "Fleeing Cuban Doctors Here Given $60,000 in Study Aids," *Miami Hurricane*, February 10, 1961.

95. María Cristina García, *Havana USA: Cuban Exiles and Cuban Americans in South Florida, 1959–1994* (Berkeley: University of California Press, 1996), 26.

96. University of Miami School of Medicine, "Postgraduate Medical Education for Latin American Physicians University of Havana School of Medicine in Exile University of Miami School of Medicine," February 15, 1963.

97. Rafael Peñalver, "Cuban Refugee Physicians: An Interview with Rafael Penalver, M.D.," March 1963, Folder 164, Box 7, Series I, Cuban Refugee Center Records, CHC.

98. "Cuban Doctor Named to State Hospital Post," *Kansas City Kansan*, November 3, 1967, reprinted by U.S. Cuban Refugee Program, Folder 186, Box 9, Series I, Cuban Refugee Center Records, CHC.

99. Peñalver, "Cuban Refugee Physicians," March 1963.

100. Homer F. Marsh and Ralph Jones to Jay F. W. Pearson, February 9, 1961, Folder 1, Box 25, Series II—Pearson Administration, Office of the President Records (Collection No. U0064), UM Archives.

101. García, *Havana USA*, 28.

102. U.S. Cuban Refugee Program, "The Score," *Resettlement Re-Cap*, February 1963, Folder 192, Box 9, Series I, Cuban Refugee Center Records, CHC.

103. Louise W. Holborn, "The Cuban Refugee Program: Its Development and Implementation," July 31, 1965.

104. Ibid.

105. Antonio A. Micocci to Norman R. A. Alley, August 4, 1965, Folder 257, Box 13, Series I, Cuban Refugee Center Records, CHC.

106. Loans Branch, DSFA, Bureau of Higher Education to Institutions of Higher Education, March 15, 1967, Folder 257, Box 13, Series I, Cuban Refugee Center Records, CHC.

107. U.S. Cuban Refugee Center, "Are You Improving Your English?," undated, Folder 18, Box 1, Series I, Cuban Refugee Center Records, CHC.

108. U.S. Cuban Refugee Program, "Attention Manufacturers!," *Resettlement Re-Cap*, September 1962, Folder 192, Box 9, Series I, Cuban Refugee Center Records, CHC.

109. U.S. Cuban Refugee Program, "A Narrative History of 'Training for Independence,'" March 1967, Folder 76, Box 4, Series I, Cuban Refugee Center Records, CHC.

110. U.S. Cuban Refugee Program, "Training for Independence: A New Approach to the Problems of Dependency," 1967, Folder 11, Box 35, Series IV, Cuban Refugee Center Records, CHC.

111. Ibid.

112. U.S. Cuban Refugee Program, "A Narrative History of 'Training for Independence,'" March 1967.

113. U.S. Cuban Refugee Program, "Training for Independence: A New Approach to the Problems of Dependency," 1967.

114. U.S. Cuban Refugee Program, "Cuban Refugee Program Annual Report—1965," Folder 72, Box 4, Series I, Cuban Refugee Center Records, CHC.

115. U.S. Cuban Refugee Program, "Training for Independence: A New Approach to the Problems of Dependency," 1967.

116. For a more complete description of Miami's garment industry, see Melanie Shell-Weiss, *Coming to Miami: A Social History* (Gainesville: University Press of Florida, 2009), 139-143.

117. "Cuban Labor Fueling Growth of Miami's Busy Garment Industry," *New York Times*, November 19, 1967.

118. Research Institute for Cuba and the Caribbean Center for Advanced International Studies, "The Cuban Immigration 1959-1966 and Its Impact on Miami–Dade County, Florida," January 31, 1967, Folder 59.1, Box 33, Series III, Cuban Refugee Center Records, CHC.

119. Carlos Arboleya, interview by Julio Estorino, August 17, 2010, Cuban Heritage Collection Luis J. Botifoll Oral History Project, CHC.

120. De La Torre, *La Lucha for Cuba*, 38.

121. First Research Company, "The Latin Market (Dade County Florida) 1970 Report," 1970, Folder 105, Box 39, Series IV, Cuban Refugee Center Records, CHC.

122. George Volsky, "Cuban Refugees Mark '61 Invasion," *New York Times*, April 18, 1971.

123. Don Shoemaker to John S. Knight, James L. Knight, Alvah Chapman Jr., George Beebe, and Lee Hills, January 10, 1966, Folder 73 Dade County, Subseries 3.1, Series 3, Shoemaker Papers.

124. Volsky, "Cuban Refugees Mark '61 Invasion."

125. First Research Company, "The Latin Market (Dade County Florida) 1970 Report," 1970.

Chapter 3

1. "Cubans in Miami Press for Power," *New York Times*, July 29, 1972.

2. Allusions to Democratic "betrayal" and their importance to Cuban American politics are common in popular culture and discourse. In scholarship, they are best illustrated by sociologist Silvia Pedraza's discussion of the role of Democratic administrations in creating the programs that made life possible for Cuban refugees in the United States, the values of many Cuban Americans, and the rejection of the party by many in the community. Pedraza writes that "despite the frank efforts many Democratic administrations over the years have made toward Cuba, in my view the sense of betrayal at the hand of the Democratic Party is too strong to allow such party identification among many Cubans who otherwise do share many of the social democratic values espoused by the Democratic Party." See Silvia Pedraza, *Political Disaffection in Cuba's Revolution and Exodus* (New York: Cambridge University Press, 2007), 303. Other scholars have discussed the perceived political affiliation of Cuban Americans with the Republican Party in the 1980s, describing Miami, under Cuban Americans, as a "Republican bastion" by that decade and noting that Democrats had lost their hold on registered Cuban voters by that decade in part because of Reagan's anticommunism and in part because the GOP was more willing to back local Cuban American candidates. This study seeks to place the mechanics that shaped this association, not in the early 1960s or in the 1980s, but in the late 1960s and in the 1970s. See Alejandro Portes and Alex Stepick, *City on the Edge: The Transformation of Miami* (Berkeley: University of California Press, 1993), 158; and María de los Angeles Torres, *In the Land of Mirrors: Cuban Exile Politics in the United States* (Ann Arbor: University of Michigan Press, 1999), 122.

3. "U.S. Warns Cuban Exiles," *New York Times*, November 4, 1959.

4. María Cristina García, *Havana USA: Cuban Exiles and Cuban Americans in South Florida, 1959–1994* (Berkeley: University of California Press, 1996), 123–125.

5. Central Intelligence Agency, "Major Cuban Exile Organizations," document attached to John McCone to Maxwell D. Taylor, May 3, 1962, Folder Cuba, Subject Exiles 1/62–10/62, Box 48, National Security Files, Presidential Papers, Papers of John F. Kennedy, John F. Kennedy Presidential Library, Boston, MA (hereafter JFK Library).

6. Central Intelligence Agency, "Counter Revolutionary Handbook," October 10, 1962, Folder Cuba, Subject Exiles 11/62–12/62, Box 48, National Security Files, Presidential Papers, Papers of John F. Kennedy, JFK Library.

7. Pedraza, *Political Disaffection in Cuba's Revolution and Exodus*, 100.

8. Ibid., 95.

9. García, *Havana USA*, 32–34.

10. C. V. Clifton to McGeorge Bundy, December 29, 1962, Folder Cuba, Subject Exiles: Brigade 2506 7/62–4/63, Box 48, National Security Files, Presidential Papers, Papers of John F. Kennedy, JFK Library.

11. Richard N. Goodwin to John F. Kennedy, May 17, 1961, Folder Cuba, Subject Miro Cardona Material Sent to Palm Beach, Box 45A, National Security Files, Presidential Papers, Papers of John F. Kennedy, JFK Library.

12. "Text of U.S. Policy Statement Read to Dr. Miro by Mr. Hurwitch," October 31, 1961, Folder Cuba, Subject Miro Cardona Material Sent to Palm Beach, Box 45A, National Security Files, Presidential Papers, Papers of John F. Kennedy, JFK Library.

13. Senate Committee on the Judiciary, Cuban Refugee Problems: Report of the Committee on the Judiciary United States Senate Made by Its Subcommittee to Investigate Problems Connected with Refugees and Escapees Pursuant to S. Res. 50, Eighty-Seventh Congress First Session as Extended, 87th Cong, 1st sess., 1962, S. Rep. 1328, 6.

14. "Cuba," March 29, 1962, Folder Cuba, Subject Miro Cardona Material Sent to Palm Beach, Box 45A, National Security Files, Presidential Papers, Papers of John F. Kennedy, JFK Library.

15. Central Intelligence Agency, "Feelings of the Cuban Brigade against Jose Miro Cardona, Head of the Cuban Revolutionary Council (CRC)," January 5, 1963, Folder Cuba, Subjects Exiles: Brigade 2506 7/62–4/63, Box 48, National Security Files, Presidential Papers, Papers of John F. Kennedy, JFK Library.

16. Natasha Mella, letter to the editor, *Miami Herald*, April 19, 1963.

17. "Miro Irked at Policy, May Resign," *Miami Herald*, April 9, 1963.

18. José Miró Cardona to "Martha and Bebo," June 24, 1971, Folder 9, Box 30, José Miró Cardona Papers, Cuban Refugee Center Records, Cuban Heritage Collection, Coral Gables, FL (hereafter CHC).

19. "We Make Our Policy, Amigos," editorial, *Miami Herald*, April 17, 1963.

20. Office of Coordinator of Cuban Affairs, Miami to Department of State, April 13, 1964, Folder Cuba Exile Activities, Volume 1 11/63–7/65 [2 of 2=3], Box 22, Country File, National Security File, President 1963–1969, Papers of Lyndon Baines Johnson, Lyndon Baines Johnson Presidential Library, Austin, TX (hereafter LBJ Library).

21. Gordon Chase to John Crimmins, February 18, 1965, Folder Cuba Exile Activities, Volume 2, 1964–1965 [2 of 2], Box 22, Country File, National Security File, President 1963–1969, Papers of Lyndon Baines Johnson, LBJ Library.

22. Wilfred H. Rommel to Lyndon Baines Johnson, October 29, 1966, Folder PL 89-732 11/2/66 HR 15183, Box 45, Enrolled Legislation, President, 1963–1969, Papers of Lyndon Baines Johnson, LBJ Library.

23. Carl J. Bon Tempo, *Americans at the Gate: The United States and Refugees during the Cold War* (Princeton, NJ: Princeton University Press, 2008), 127.

24. William F. Ryan to Lyndon Baines Johnson, October 12, 1965, Folder LE-IM 9/21/65–12/2/65, Box 74, Legislation, White House Central Files, President, 1963–1969, Papers of Lyndon Baines Johnson, LBJ Library.

25. Bon Tempo, *Americans at the Gate*, 129.

26. Ibid., 128.

27. "Report of the Miami Task Force on Civil Disturbances in Miami, Florida during the week of August 5, 1968," Salmon Folder, Box 1, Series 60, Task Force VIII, Records of

the National Commission on the Causes and Prevention of Violence, Papers of Lyndon Baines Johnson, LBJ Library.

28. "Report of the Miami Task Force on Civil Disturbances in Miami, Florida during the week of August 5, 1968."

29. Ibid.

30. N. D. B. Connolly, *A World More Concrete: Real Estate and the Remaking of Jim Crow South Florida* (Chicago: University of Chicago Press, 2014), 220–221.

31. Milton D. Smith, "Interview with Milton D. Smith [Butterball]," Folder—Transcripts of Interviews Conducted Part II, Box 2, Series 60, Task Force VIII, Records of the National Commission on the Causes and Prevention of Violence, Papers of Lyndon Baines Johnson, LBJ Library.

32. Bruce Schulman has written on a set of policies that put "place" over "people" in the development of the Sunbelt. These policies diverted federal funds to enrich impoverished areas without aiming to uplift the poor in those areas. As a result, the benefits of this economic transformation were reaped almost exclusively by white middle- and upper-class Americans, while African Americans and poor whites were neither empowered nor destigmatized for their poverty. See Bruce J. Schulman, *From Cotton Belt to Sunbelt: Federal Policy, Economic Development, and the Transformation of the South, 1938–1980* (New York: Oxford University Press, 1991).

33. "Cuban Refugees," editorial, *Miami Times*, December 17, 1960.

34. "Refugee Problem," editorial, *Miami Times*, November 11, 1961.

35. "Cuban Refugees," editorial, *Miami Times*, November 26, 1965.

36. Senate Committee on the Judiciary, Cuban Refugee Problems, 73.

37. While these structures of segregation were sometimes less strict for Afro Cubans than for African Americans, many moved on from Miami due to South Florida's discriminatory environment. For instances of this discrimination, see Devyn Spence Benson, *Antiracism in Cuba: The Unfinished Revolution* (Chapel Hill: University of North Carolina Press, 2016), 141–146.

38. Senate Committee on the Judiciary, Cuban Refugee Problems, 77.

39. Quoted in "Negroes Face Loss of Jobs to Cubans," *Miami Times*, October 22, 1965.

40. Ricky Thomas, "Out of the Dark," *Miami Times*, April 17, 1970.

41. John Egerton, "Cubans in Miami: A Third Dimension in Racial and Cultural Relations," November 1969, Folder 111, Box 39, Series IV, Cuban Refugee Center Records, CHC.

42. Benson, *Antiracism in Cuba*, 138–139.

43. John Egerton, "Cubans in Miami: A Third Dimension in Racial and Cultural Relations," November 1969.

44. One example showing how established and widespread this talking point had become was published five years before when the newsletter of Americans for Conservative Action, published in Indianapolis, IN, indicated that anti-Castro Cubans had been warning for "quite some time" that Cuban communists were stimulating terrorism in

the civil rights struggle. See Edward R. Scheme, "They Were Right Before," *ACA Newsletter* 2, no. 4 (September 8, 1964).

45. Harry L. Tyson, letter to the editor, *Miami Herald*, December 12, 1967.

46. Effie Knowles to Dante Fascell, August 22, 1962, Topical Files—Anti-Cuban Sentiment—Miami, 1961–1962, Box 1924, Dante B. Fascell Congressional Papers, 1955–1993, University of Miami Special Collections, University of Miami, Coral Gables, FL (hereafter DBF Papers).

47. A. A. Micocci to Dante Fascell, September 24, 1962, Topical Files—Anti-Cuban Sentiment—Miami, 1961–1962, Box 1924, DBF Papers.

48. Effie Knowles to Dante Fascell, October 3, 1962, Topical Files—Anti-Cuban Sentiment—Miami, 1961–1962, Box 1924, DBF Papers.

49. Ibid.

50. Phone message discussed in Dante Fascell to Violette McCrary, August 13, 1970, Folder 14, Box 2052, DBF Papers.

51. Mrs. Samuel J. Constance to Dante Fascell, July 25, 1970, Folder 15, Box 2052, DBF Papers.

52. Fred C. Oakley to Dante Fascell, July 7, 1970, Folder 14, Box 2052, DBF Papers.

53. Lee Winfrey, "Cuban 'Invasion' of Miami, Politicos 'Roasted' in Annual Newsmen Farce," *Miami Herald*, April 26, 1963.

54. Ibid.

55. "Cuban Airlift Simply U.S. Aid to Castro," editorial, *Miami Herald*, February 11, 1970.

56. "Collins Suggests New Cuba," *Miami Herald*, March 10, 1963.

57. Ibid.

58. Humberto Medrano, "'No, Mr. Collins, There Are No Instant Nations,'" *Miami Herald*, March 20, 1963.

59. Mrs. Samuel J. Constance to Dante Fascell, July 25, 1970, Folder 15, Box 2052, DBF Papers.

60. Commission of the City of Miami, Florida, Resolution No. 40983, 2, Folder 11, Box 2067, DBF Papers.

61. The widespread cultural concerns related to adopting American citizenship will be discussed in Chapter 4. It should also be noted that, in keeping with longstanding policies, the congressional report attached to the Cuban Adjustment Act noted that the legislation "should not be taken as any indication that the United States believes that the Castro regime has any permanency." See Senate Committee on the Judiciary, Adjusting the Status of Cuban Refugees to That of Lawful Permanent Residents of the United Sates, and for Other Purposes, 89th Cong, 2nd sess., 1966, S. Rep. 1675, 5.

62. Concurrent Resolution 492, HR 492, 90th Cong., 1st sess., August 16, 1967, 2.

63. The list of Cubans invited included bankers, lawyers, doctors, media personalities, and political figures in the exile community. See "Personas invitadas a la comida privada con el Representante al Congreso de los Estados Unidos, Honorable Claude

Pepper, el Domingo 17 de Septiembre, en Miami, Florida" [presumably September 1962] Folder 22, Box 2063, DBF Papers.

64. Dante Fascell declined this invitation issued by the Washington firm of Frank R. Lee & Associates. See Frank R. Lee to Dante Fascell, September 22, 1967, Folder 22, Box 2063, DBF Papers.

65. "Cuban Exile Activities in Support of Draft Resolution 492, Introduced by Congressman Claude Pepper," undated [presumably late 1967], Folder 22, Box 2063, DBF Papers.

66. Mike Thompson for Congress Committee, "¿Por que los Cubanos-Americanos respaldan a Mike Thompson para el Congreso?," 1968, Folder 25, Box 2063, DBF Papers.

67. Elizabeth Hanunian, trans., "Why Do the Cuban-Americans Endorse Mike Thompson for Congress?," September 1968, Folder 25, Box 2063, DBF Papers.

68. Luis V. Manrara to Dante Fascell, June 10, 1966, Folder 10, Box 2180, DBF Papers.

69. Reproduction of Dante Fascell, "The 68th Anniversary of Cuban Independence: 'Independence' in Fidel Castro's Cuba," May 20, 1970, Folder 10, Box 1833, DBF Papers.

70. "4th Cuban and American Exposition Fair" flyer, Folder 10, Box 1833, DBF Papers.

71. "COR" to Dante Fascell, "Re: Campaign '70—Cuban-American Exhibition and Fair," June 30, 1970, Folder 10, Box 1833, DBF Papers.

72. In a letter to coauthor Robert C. Mings, Fascell called the study "a noteworthy first step toward filling an obvious void in political intelligence," and found that their findings were "not only sound but also cause for concern." See Dante Fascell to Robert C. Mings, May 10, 1971, Folder 441, Box 1838, DBF Papers.

73. Paul S. Salter and Robert C. Mings, "The Projected Impact of Cuban Settlement on Voting Patterns in Metropolitan Miami, Florida," Folder 441, Box 1838, DBF Papers.

74. Salter and Mings, "The Projected Impact of Cuban Settlement on Voting Patterns in Metropolitan Miami, Florida," Folder 441, Box 1838, DBF Papers.

75. Ibid.

76. Ibid.

77. Bernardo Benes to Dante Fascell, May 8, 1972, Folder 441, Box 1838, DBF Papers.

78. Dante Fascell to Bernardo Benes, May 18, 1972, Folder 441, Box 1838, DBF Papers.

79. Pepper sent form letters to new single or married citizens indicating that as a member of the U.S. House of Representatives he would do whatever he could to further their welfare and that of every other citizen and encouraging him to contact him. Pepper had been requesting and receiving lists of new naturalized citizens in Dade County since at least 1966. See Folder 368, Box 43, Bernardo Benes Papers, CHC.

80. Claude Pepper to John M. Area, September 9, 1968, 369, Box 43, Bernardo Benes Papers, CHC.

81. Dante Fascell to Bernardo Benes, May 18, 1972, Folder 441, Box 1838, DBF Papers.

82. Mayer Finkel to Dante Fascell, July 10, 1972, Folder 441, Box 1838, DBF Papers.

83. Leaflet attached to Finkel to Fascell, July 10, 1972.

Chapter 4

1. María Cristina García, *Havana USA: Cuban Exiles and Cuban Americans in South Florida, 1959–1994* (Berkeley: University of California Press, 1996), 43.

2. Fernando E. C. de Baca to Theodore C. Marrs, March 24, 1975, Folder FG 23 3/20/75–4/8/75, FG 23 Department of Health Education and Welfare, Subject File, White House Central Files, Gerald Ford Presidential Library, Ann Arbor, MI (hereafter Ford Library).

3. Reinaldo Cruz to Gerald Ford, October 21, 1975, Folder—Nuñez Ricardo, Box 2356, Name File, White House Central Files, Ford Library.

4. "Atacan a Ricardo Núñez," *Libertad*, August 15, 1975.

5. Marjorie Lynch to Ted Marrs, July 9, 1976, Folder—Nuñez Ricardo, Box 2356, Name File, White House Central Files, Ford Library.

6. While Cuban refugees no longer had the CRP to support them, they still had an open-door policy and the Cuban Adjustment Act. The demise of the CRP came in the same period as other migrant groups from Latin American increasingly sought out unauthorized immigration as the most viable option to enter the country. Historian Ana Raquel Minian, for example, notes that between the end of the Bracero program in 1965 and 1986, the number of Mexican citizens apprehended in the United States rose 3,000% and that some estimates suggest that 28 million Mexicans entered the United States in the same period without documentation. While the end of the CRP meant less financial support for new Cuban arrivals, the path to legal migration for this population was far simpler than it was for other groups. See Ana Raquel Minian, *Undocumented Lives: The Untold Story of Mexican Migration* (Cambridge, MA: Harvard University Press, 2018), 4–5.

7. Juanita Greene, "Cubans in Dade: 1 in 4 by 1975," *Miami Herald*, June 18, 1971.

8. Roberto Fabricio, "Cubans—at Home, But Homesick," *Miami Herald*, October 29, 1972.

9. Ibid.

10. Ibid.

11. Ibid.

12. Juan M. Clark, "¿Donde viven los Cubanos?," February 15, 1973, Box 50, Series III, Bryan O. Walsh Papers, Barry University, Miami, FL (hereafter Walsh Papers).

13. Clark, "¿Donde viven los Cubanos?," February 15, 1973.

14. Alan Gersten, "Survey Cites Growth of Latin Community," *Miami News*, June 21, 1974.

15. Jorge Mas Canosa, "Deposition of Jorge Mas Canosa," January 10, 1996, Folder 20, Box 1, *New Republic*–Jorge Mas Canosa Collection, 1979–1996, Florida

International University Special Collections, Florida International University, Miami, FL (hereafter FIU Special Collections).

16. Jorge Mas Canosa, "Deposition of Jorge Mas Canosa," February 21, 1996, Folder 22, Box 1, *New Republic*–Jorge Mas Canosa Collection, 1979–1996, FIU Special Collections.

17. See *Bancos y economia*, June 1973, Exile Periodicals Collection, Cuban Heritage Collection, University of Miami, Coral Gables, FL (hereafter CHC).

18. *Bancos y economia*, November 1973, 4–6, Exile Periodicals Collection, CHC.

19. *Bancos y economia*, August 1974, 4, Exile Periodicals Collection, CHC.

20. See *Bancos y economia*, June 1973, and August 1974, Exile Periodicals Collection, CHC.

21. Roberto Fabricio, "Bilingual Status for Dade Sought by Cuban Residents," *Miami Herald*, May 29, 1972.

22. Chuck Gomez, "Spanish Gets You Nowhere in a Crisis," *Miami Herald*, May 29, 1972.

23. Bernardo Benes to Lawrence B. Sheffey, February 23, 1971, Folder 31, Box 4, Bernardo Benes Papers, CHC.

24. José M. Angueiera, "Nuestro derecho a hablar en Español," *Diaro Las Americas*, January 10, 1973.

25. Evaristo R. Savon, "Por unanimidad se aprobó declarar a Dade bilingüe," *Diario Las Americas*, April 18, 1973.

26. Sam Jacobs, "Bilingual Bill Passed by Dade," *Miami Herald*, April 17, 1973.

27. Board of County Commissioners of Dade County, Florida, Resolution Declaring Dade County a Bilingual and Bicultural County, April 16, 1973, Folder 61, Box 7, Bernardo Benes Papers, CHC.

28. Sam Jacobs, "Bilingual Bill Passed by Dade," *Miami Herald*, April 17, 1973.

29. R. Ray Goode to Mayor and Members of Board of County Commissioners, May 29, 1973, Folder 32, Box 4, Bernardo Benes Papers, CHC.

30. "Que pasa?," editorial, *Miami Herald*, April 18, 1973.

31. Bernardo Benes, "County Must Serve Spanish-Speaking," letter to the editor, *Miami Herald*, April 25, 1973.

32. Hilda Inclan, "Cubans Concerned about 'Anti-' Feeling," *Miami News*, November 19, 1974.

33. "Exiled Cubans in Florida Grow More Militant," *Cleveland Plain Dealer*, March 16, 1975.

34. Ibid.

35. Richard McEwen to Phillis Miller, January 18, 1978, Folder 8, Box 1, Bernardo Benes Papers, CHC.

36. Susan Harrigan, "Blemished Bloom," *Wall Street Journal*, November 28, 1979.

37. Anita Casavantes Bradford, *The Revolution Is for the Children: The Politics of Childhood in Havana and Miami, 1959–1962* (Chapel Hill: University of North Carolina Press, 2014), 190.

38. "Exiled Cubans in Florida Grow More Militant," *Cleveland Plain Dealer*, March 16, 1975.

39. Manolo Reboso to Linton Tyler, July 13, 1977, Folder 7, Box 1, Bernardo Benes Papers, CHC.

40. "A Sane Approach to Bi-Lingualism," editorial, *Miami Herald*, January 22, 1975.

41. John McMullan, "Open Letter to My Cuban Friends," *Miami Herald*, August 6, 1978.

42. Ibid.

43. Julio A. Castano to John McMullan, August 8, 1978, Folder 8, Box 1, Bernardo Benes Papers, CHC.

44. Jorge Luis Hernández, "Editorial," August 10, 1978, Folder 8, Box 1, Bernardo Benes Papers, CHC.

45. There are multiple pieces of correspondence between Bernardo Benes, McMullan, and other members of the "Non-Group." See Folder 7, Box 1, Bernardo Benes Papers, CHC.

46. Clark, "¿Donde viven los Cubanos?," February 15, 1973.

47. García, *Havana USA*, 111.

48. "Says 'Cuban Mafia' Label Is 'Irresponsible Reporting,'" *Voice*, July 10, 1970, Folder 199, Box 25, Bernardo Benes Papers, CHC.

49. García, *Havana USA*, 112.

50. Ibid., 113.

51. "¿Qué pasa, USA?," undated with handwritten notes indicating document was written in the early 1980s, Folder 15, Box 3, Series I, Luis Santeiro Papers, CHC.

52. Luis Santeiro, *Fiesta de Quince*, teleplay, undated [presumably 1977], Folder 1, Box 1, Series 1, Luis Santeiro Papers, CHC.

53. Luis Santeiro, *The T.V. Interview*, teleplay, slated for taping June 14, 1977, Folder 8, Box 1, Series 1, Luis Santeiro Papers, CHC.

54. Luis Santeiro, *Citizenship*, originally entitled *Salad Bowl*, teleplay, 1977, Folder 12, Box 1, Series 1, Luis Santeiro Papers, CHC.

55. Translation mine.

56. Santeiro, "Citizenship," 1977.

57. Roberto R. Brauning, "Nuevos ciudadanos sienten alegría y tristeza," *El Miami Herald*, July 5, 1978.

58. José Manuel Casanova to Gerald Ford, December 10, 1975, Folder—Republican National Hispanic Assembly (2), Box 28, Robert T. Hartman Files 1974–1977, Ford Library.

59. Gwen Anderson to Robert T. Hartmann, December 11, 1975, Folder—Republican National Hispanic Assembly (2), Box 28, Robert T. Hartman Files 1974–1977, Ford Library.

60. José Manuel Casanova and Alicia Casanova to Gerald Ford, December 10, 1975, Folder—Republican National Hispanic Assembly (2), Box 28, Robert T. Hartman Files 1974–1977, Ford Library.

61. Jim Cannon to Bob Hartmann, December 16, 1975, Folder—Republican National Hispanic Assembly (2), Box 28, Robert T. Hartman Files 1974–1977, Ford Library.

62. L. F. Chapman Jr., Commissioner Immigration and Naturalization Service, to Robert T. Hartmann, January 13, 1976, Folder—Republican National Hispanic Assembly—Cuban Refugees (2), Box 21, Gwen A. Anderson Files, 1974–1977, Ford Library.

63. Gwen Anderson to Robert T. Hartmann, December 18, 1975, Folder—Republican National Hispanic Assembly (2), Box 28, Robert T. Hartman Files 1974–1977, Ford Library.

64. Bobbie Greene Kilberg to Antonin Scalia, February 12, 1976, Folder—Naturalization of Cuban Refugees, Box 6, Counsel to the President Bobbie Greene Kilberg 1974–1977, Ford Library.

65. Bobbie Greene Kilberg to Jim Connor, Paul O'Neil, and Tom Aranda, September 15, 1976, Folder—Naturalization of Cuban Refugees, Box 6, Counsel to the President Bobbie Greene Kilberg 1974–1977, Ford Library.

66. Antonin Scalia, "Memorandum for the Attorney General," August 30, 1976, Folder—Naturalization of Cuban Refugees, Box 6, Counsel to the President Bobbie Greene Kilberg 1974–1977, Ford Library.

67. Press Release, September 16, 1976, Folder —Naturalization of Cuban Refugees, Box 6, Counsel to the President Bobbie Greene Kilberg 1974–1977, Ford Library.

68. Hector D. Carrio to Evelle J. Younger, October 6, 1976, Folder—Cannon, James, Box 120, Robert T. Hartmann Papers, Ford Library.

69. Stephen Low to Brent Scowcroft, December 16, 1975, Folder—CO 39 Cuba, 6/1/75–12/31/75, Box 15, CO 39 Cuba, Subject File, White House Central Files, Ford Library.

70. Maurice A. Ferré to Gerald Ford, March 3, 1975, Folder—CO 39 Cuba, 4/1/75–5/31/75, Box 15, CO 39 Cuba, Subject File, White House Central Files, Ford Library.

71. Ed DeBolt to Jerry Jones, April 29, 1976, Folder—DeBolt Subject File—Cuban, Box A13, Chairman's Office, President Ford Committee Records, 1975–1976, Ford Library.

72. Robert M. Levine, *Secret Missions to Cuba: Fidel Castro, Bernardo Benes, and Cuban Miami* (New York: Palgrave, 2001), 89.

73. José Manuel Casanova to Gerald Ford, "The Cuban Paper," October 1974, Folder 7, Box 1, Bernardo Benes Papers, CHC.

74. García, *Havana USA*, 47.

75. María de los Angeles Torres, *In the Land of Mirrors: Cuban Exile Politics in the United States* (Ann Arbor: University of Michigan Press, 1999), 89–90.

76. García, *Havana USA*, 47.

77. Cyrus Vance to Jimmy Carter, February 5, 1977, Folder 5, Box 12, Plains File, Jimmy Carter Presidential Library, Atlanta, GA (hereafter Carter Library),

78. Vance to Carter, February 5, 1977.

79. Torres, *In the Land of Mirrors*, 102.

80. Jim Purks to Jack Watson, January 31, 1977, Folder ST 9 1/20/1977–8/31/1978, Executive, Box ST-7, States-Territories, Subject File, White House Central File, Jimmy Carter Presidential Papers, Carter Library.

81. Robert A. Pastor to Zbigniew Brzezinski, October 8, 1977, Folder 4, Box 11, Staff Material: North/South, Carter Library.

82. Levine, *Secret Missions to Cuba*, 4.

83. Ibid., 81.

84. Ibid., 5.

85. Viron Vaky and Robert Pastor to David Aaron and David Newsom, August 4, 1978, Folder 2, Box 60, Zbigniew Brzezinksi Material: Brzezinski Office File, Staff Office Files, Carter Library.

86. Zbigniew Brzezinksi to Hamilton Jordan, September 18, 1978, Folder 7, Box 45, Staff Material: North/South, Carter Library.

87. García, *Havana USA*, 47.

88. National Security Council North–South Evening Report to Zbigniew Brzezinksi, September 8, 1978, Folder 1, Box 15, Zbigniew Brzezinksi Material: Staff Evening Reports File, Staff Office Files, Carter Library.

89. Torres, *In the Land of Mirrors*, 95.

90. Natasha Mella to Conrado Rodríguez and Andrés Nazario Sargen, September 19, 1978, Folder 2, Box 3, Alpha 66 Records, CHC.

91. Torres, *In the Land of Mirrors*, 95.

92. Levine, *Secret Missions to Cuba*, 125.

93. Ibid., 120.

94. Torres, *In the Land of Mirrors*, 95.

95. "Soy el director de 'Látigo,'" editorial, *Látigo*, January 1979.

96. "Con Cuba, contra los traidores," editorial, *Látigo*, February 1979.

97. Ward Sinclair, "The Two Sides of a Negotiator for Castro's Prisoners," *Washington Post*, December 3, 1978.

98. Levine, *Secret Missions to Cuba*, 135.

99. Antonio Venciana, statements to WQBA, transcript, October 5, 1978, Folder 494, Box 57, Bernardo Benes Papers, CHC.

100. Levine, *Secret Missions to Cuba*, 135.

101. Ibid., 196.

102. Torres, *In the Land of Mirrors*, 100.

103. Levine, *Secret Missions to Cuba*, 136–139.

104. Bernardo Benes and Alfredo Durán to Phil Wise, September 21, 1979, Folder 2, Box 9, Donated Historical Material—King, Mary, Carter Library.

105. Mary E. King to Alonzo L. McDonald, October 16, 1979, Folder 2, Box 9, Donated Historical Material—King, Mary, Carter Library.

106. Ibid.

Chapter 5

1. Peter Michelmore, "From Cuba with Hate," *Reader's Digest*, December 1982, 222.

2. Ibid., 223.

3. Ibid., 224.

4. Fabiola Santiago, "Cubans' Image at a Low in U.S., Official Says," *Miami Herald*, August 15, 1982.

5. Guillermo Martinez, "Mariel Myths Feed Venom across Nation," editorial, *Miami Herald*, November 18, 1982.

6. Ana Veciana-Suarez, "Cubans Blast Reader's Digest Story on Mariel Refugees," *Miami Herald*, November 19, 1982.

7. Roberto Fabricio, "Reader's Digest Mariel Article Well Reasoned," *Miami Herald*, November 20, 1982.

8. The *Journal of American Ethnic History* published a forum on disability and immigration policy in 2005, with Douglas C. Baynton writing a central article and several scholars responding. For the centrality of disability exclusion to these laws see Douglas C. Baynton, "Defectives in the Land: Disability and American Immigration Policy, 1882–1924," *Journal of American Ethnic History* 24, no. 3 (Spring 2005): 34.

9. See Silvia Pedraza, *Political Disaffection in Cuba's Revolution and Exodus* (New York: Cambridge University Press, 2007), 152–153.

10. Jo Thomas, "2,000 Who Want to Leave Cuba Crowd Peru's Embassy in Havana," *New York Times*, April 6, 1980.

11. Mirta Ojito, *Finding Mañana: A Memoir of a Cuban Exodus* (New York: Penguin Press, 2005), 68–93.

12. María Cristina García, *Havana USA: Cuban Exiles and Cuban Americans in South Florida, 1959–1994* (Berkeley: University of California Press, 1996), 55.

13. Pedraza, *Political Disaffection in Cuba's Revolution and Exodus*, 152–153.

14. Ojito, *Finding Mañana*, 100–101.

15. María de los Angeles Torres, *In the Land of Mirrors: Cuban Exile Politics in the United States* (Ann Arbor: University of Michigan Press, 1999), 105.

16. Thomas, "2,000 Who Want to Leave Cuba Crowd Peru's Embassy in Havana."

17. García, *Havana USA*, 55.

18. Ojito, *Finding Mañana*, 115–117.

19. García, *Havana USA*, 56.

20. Ojito, *Finding Mañana*, 117.

21. Torres, *In the Land of Mirrors*, 109.

22. García, *Havana USA*, 56.

23. Carl J. Bon Tempo, *Americans at the Gate: The United States and Refugees during the Cold War* (Princeton, NJ: Princeton University Press, 2008), 180.

24. García, *Havana USA*, 56.

25. Associated Press, "Cuba Cancels Staging-Area Exile Flights," *Boston Globe*, April 19, 1980.

26. Jo Thomas, "Costa Rica Offers to Accept All 10,000 from Cuba Embassy," *New York Times*, April 21, 1980.

27. Torres, *In the Land of Mirrors*, 105.

28. Associated Press, "Miami Exiles Go to Cuba to Bring Back Refugees," *Boston Globe*, April 21, 1980.

29. Janet Battaile, "Cuban Exiles' Boats Pick up 40 Refugees," *New York Times*, April 22, 1980.

30. Jo Thomas, "Harbor in Cuba A Floating City of 1,300 Boats," *New York Times*, April 27, 1980.

31. Cuban-Haitian Task Force, "Chronology," Folder Task Force Chronology 5/13/80–9/28/80, Box 28, Subject File, Records of the Cuban-Haitian Task Force, Jimmy Carter Presidential Library, Atlanta, GA (hereafter cited as Carter Library).

32. Juan Carlos Piñera, "Personal Stories," *Mariel: 25 Years Later: The Journey, the Stories* (Miami: *Miami Herald*, April 3, 2005), Digital Repositories at Duke, 28, https://repository.duke.edu/dc/caribbeansea/csmep03026.

33. Lissette Mendez, "Personal Stories," 26.

34. García, *Havana USA*, 63.

35. Niza Motola, "Personal Stories," 27.

36. García, *Havana USA*, 63–64.

37. Central Susquehanna Intermediate Unit Adult School for Cuban Refugees, "Teaching Oral English to Cuban Refugees Report 4: Cuba: As Told by Cuban Refugees," October 24, 1980, Folder Cuba as Told by Cuban Refugees, Box 35, Subject File, Records of the Cuban-Haitian Task Force, Carter Library.

38. Central Susquehanna Intermediate Unit Adult School for Cuban Refugees, "Teaching Oral English to Cuban Refugees Report 4: Cuba: As Told by Cuban Refugees," October 24, 1980.

39. Daniel Benítez, "Personal Stories," 22.

40. Julio Capó Jr., "Queering Mariel: Meditating Cold War Foreign Policy and U.S. Citizenship among Cuba's Homosexual Exile Community, 1978-1994," *Journal of American Ethnic History* 29, no. 4 (Summer 2010): 83.

41. Capó, "Queering Mariel," 86–87.

42. Ibid., 88.

43. García, *Havana USA*, 64.

44. Ojito, *Finding Mañana*, 208.

45. Elizabeth Caballero, "Personal Stories," 23.

46. Tomás Díaz, "Personal Stories," 23.

47. Bon Tempo, *Americans at the Gate*, 173.

48. Ibid., 177.

49. Cuban-Haitian Task Force, "Chronology."

50. Robert Pastor to Zbigniew Brzezinkski, Stu Eizenstat, Frank White, and Jack Watson, May 9, 1980, Folder Cuban Refugees, 5/80, Box 70, Lloyd Cutler Files, Carter Library.

51. Stu Eizenstat, Jack Watson, and Zbigniew Brzezinkski to President Jimmy Carter, May 13, 1980, Folder Cuban Refugees, 5/80, Box 70, Lloyd Cutler Files, Carter Library. (Emphasis in the original.)

52. Stu Eizenstat, Jack Watson, and Zbigniew Brzezinkski to President Jimmy Carter, May 13, 1980.

53. Myles Frechette, "Insider's View," *Mariel: 25 Years Later: The Journey, the Stories* (Miami: *Miami Herald*, April 3, 2005), Digital Repositories at Duke, 28, https://repository.duke.edu/dc/caribbeansea/csmep03026.

54. James Reston, "The Carter Cuban Policy," *New York Times*, May 16, 1980.

55. Historians like Ana Raquel Minian have shown how economic factors like deindustrialization, stagflation, and increased economic inequalities drove many U.S. citizen "to fear that they were becoming economically redundant and responded by positing 'illegal aliens' as the truly superfluous." See Ana Raquel Minian, *Undocumented Lives: The Untold Story of Mexican Migration* (Cambridge, MA: Harvard University Press, 2018), 47–48.

56. James Reston, "The Carter Cuban Policy," *New York Times*, May 16, 1980.

57. "Send Us Your Bums, Fidel," editorial, *Chicago Tribune*, April 20, 1980.

58. García, *Havana USA*, 65.

59. Edward Schumacher, "Retarded People and Criminals Are Included in Cuban Exodus," *New York Times*, May 11, 1980.

60. Ibid.

61. Olga E. Vives to editor, *U.S. News & World Report*, May 6, 1980, Folder Mariel Boatlift—Clippings, Vertical File, CHC.

62. Carl Lindskoog, *Detain and Punish: Haitian Refugees and the Rise of the World's Largest Immigration Detention System* (Gainesville: University of Florida Press, 2018), 40.

63. These efforts are detailed in Chapter 6.

64. Myles Frechette, "Insider's View," *Mariel: 25 Years Later*, April 3, 2005, 19.

65. George Putnam to Roger Winter, Mary Spillane, and Denis Gallagher, May 1, 1980, Folder 61, Box 21, Series II, Cuban Refugee Center Records, CHC.

66. George Putnam to Roger Winter, May 2, 1980, Folder 61, Box 21, Series II, Cuban Refugee Center Records, CHC.

67. George Putnam to Roger Winter, May 2, 1980.

68. George Putnam to Roger Winter, May 5, 1980, Folder 61, Box 21, Series II, Cuban Refugee Center Records, CHC.

69. Manuel A. Varona, Juan Pérez-Franco, and Ricardo Aparicio to Victor Palmieri and Chris Holmes, September 8, 1980, Folder Camp Consolidation [2], Box 1, Subject File, Records of the Cuban-Haitian Task Force, Carter Library.

70. George Putnam to Roger Winter, May 6, 1980, Folder 61, Box 21, Series II, Cuban Refugee Center Records, CHC.

71. See George Putnam to Roger Winter, May 12, 1980, and George Putnam to Roger Winter, May 7, 1980, Folder 62, Box 21, Series II, Cuban Refugee Center Records,

CHC. See also, George Putnam to Roger Winter, May 19, 1980,Folder 62, Box 21, Series II, Cuban Refugee Center Records, CHC.

72. George Putnam to Roger Winter, May 19, 1980.

73. George Putnam to Roger Winter, May 18, 1980, Folder 62, Box 21, Series II, Cuban Refugee Center Records, CHC.

74. George Putnam to Roger Winter, May 17, 1980, Folder 62, Box 21, Series II, Cuban Refugee Center Records, CHC.

75. George Putnam to Roger Winter, May 18, 1980 (8:15 am), Folder 62, Box 21, Series II, Cuban Refugee Center Records, CHC.

76. George Putnam to Roger Winter, May 18, 1980 (1:15 pm), Folder 62, Box 21, Series II, Cuban Refugee Center Records, CHC.

77. George Putnam to Roger Winter, May 20, 1980.

78. Barbara Lawson to Christian R. Holmes, September 26, 1980, Folder Camp Consolidation [2], Box 1, Subject File, Records of the Cuban-Haitian Task Force, Carter Library.

79. George Putnam to Roger Winter, May 20, 1980.

80. George Putnam to Roger Winter, May 21, 1980, Folder 62, Box 21, Series II, Cuban Refugee Center Records, CHC.

81. Ellen Hampton, "Cop Finds Special Passenger," *Miami Herald*, May 17, 1980.

82. Ibid.

83. Anthony Ramirez, "In a Strained Miami, Cubans and Haitians Help the Boat People," *Wall Street Journal*, May 2, 1980.

84. Anthony Ramirez, "Making It: Miami Cubans Prosper by Sticking Together, Aiding Later Refugees," *Wall Street Journal*, May 20, 1980.

85. Bon Tempo, *Americans at the Gate*, 180.

86. Anthony Ramirez, "In a Strained Miami, Cubans and Haitians Help the Boat People," *Wall Street Journal*, May 2, 1980.

87. Bon Tempo, *Americans at the Gate*, 180.

88. Ibid., 182.

89. Lindskoog, *Detain and Punish*, 13.

90. Ibid., 2–3.

91. Anthony Ramirez, "In a Strained Miami, Cubans and Haitians Help the Boat People," *Wall Street Journal*, May 2, 1980.

92. Susan Buchanan and Jay LaRoche to Silvia González, January 11, 1981, Folder 36, Box 20, Series II, Cuban Refugee Center Records, CHC.

93. Daryl B. Harris, *The Logic of Black Urban Rebellions: Challenging the Dynamics of White Domination in Miami* (Westport, CT: Praeger Publishers, 1999), 63.

94. Ibid., 66.

95. Marvin Dunn and Andrea Loring, "Consumer Issues in Riot Areas of Miami: A Preliminary Report to the White House," May 24, 1980, Folder—Miami–Dade Chamber of Commerce [2], Box 373, Subject Files, Jack Watson's O-A, Cabinet Secretary & Intergovernmental Affairs, Staff Office, Carter Presidential Papers, Carter Library.

96. Susan Harrigan and Charles W. Stevens, "Roots of a Riot," *Wall Street Journal*, May 22, 1980.

97. Cheryl F. Wright to Frank Jones, June 4, 1980, Folder—Miami–Dade Chamber of Commerce [2], Box 373, Subject Files, Jack Watson's O-A, Cabinet Secretary & Intergovernmental Affairs, Staff Office, Carter Presidential Papers, Carter Library.

98. Ernest G. Green and Lamond Godwin to Frank N. Jones, June 6, 1980, Folder—Miami–Dade Chamber of Commerce [2], Box 373, Subject Files, Jack Watson's O-A, Cabinet Secretary & Intergovernmental Affairs, Staff Office, Carter Presidential Papers, Carter Library.

99. Marvin Dunn and Andrea Loring, "Consumer Issues in Riot Areas of Miami: A Preliminary Report to the White House," May 24, 1980.

100. Harris, *The Logic of Black Urban Rebellions*, 77.

101. George Putnam to Roger Winter, May 18, 1980 (8:15 am).

102. "Miami: A Time for Healing," editorial, *Miami Herald*, November 3, 1980.

103. Anthony Ramirez, "Making It: Miami Cubans Prosper by Sticking Together, Aiding Later Refugees," *Wall Street Journal*, May 20, 1980.

104. Susan Harrigan and Charles W. Stevens, "Roots of a Riot," *Wall Street Journal*, May 22, 1980.

105. Harris, *The Logic of Black Urban Rebellions*, 98.

106. Susan Harrigan and Charles W. Stevens, "Roots of a Riot," *Wall Street Journal*, May 22, 1980.

107. Gene Eidenberg and Bruce Kirschenbaum to Jimmy Carter, May 25, 1980, Folder—Miami Riots—Dade County Civil Disturbances (2), Box 252, Cabinet Secretary Paula Schneider's Subject Files, Staff Offices, Carter Presidential Papers, Carter Library.

108. Richard Hite to Gene Eidenberg, John White, and Rodger Schlickeisen, August 18, 1980, Folder—Miami Riots—Dade County Civil Disturbances (1), Box 252, Cabinet Secretary Paula Schneider's Subject Files, Staff Offices, Carter Presidential Papers, Carter Library.

109. Cuban-Haitian Task Force, "Chronology."

110. García, *Havana USA*, 68.

111. Ibid, 63.

112. Mario A. Rivera to James Giganti, August 10, 1980, Folder—Tent City, Box 28, Subject File, Records of the Cuban-Haitian Task Force, Carter Library.

113. Christian R. Holmes to Eugene Eidenberg, September 4, 1980, Folder 5, Box 1, Fort Chaffee Collection, CHC.

114. Anthony Ramirez, "In a Strained Miami, Cubans and Haitians Help the Boat People," *Wall Street Journal*, May 2, 1980.

115. Murray Meyerson to Jimmy Carter, July 30, 1980, Folder 99, Box 23, Series II, Cuban Refugee Center Records, CHC.

116. In appendix to Harold T. Toal to Claude D. Pepper, October 2, 1980, Folder—Miami Operations [1], Box 6, Subject File, Records of the Cuban-Haitian Task Force, Carter Library.

117. Commission Pro-Justice Mariel Prisoners, "The Mariel Injustice (In the Year of the 200th Anniversary of the American Constitution," 10, Folder—Various Publications on Mariel Boatlift, Cuban, 1980–2005, Box 3, Caribbean Sea Migration Collection, Duke University Special Collections, Duke University, Durham, NC (hereafter Duke Special Collections).

118. Rafael Peñalver, interview with author, digital recording, Coral Gables, FL, March 14, 2013.

119. Alejandro Portes and Alex Stepick, *City on the Edge: The Transformation of Miami* (Berkeley: University of California Press, 1993), 161.

120. Jo Thomas, "Miami Area Divided Over Ballot Proposal to Drop Spanish as Second Official Language," *New York Times*, November 2, 1980.

121. Ibid.

122. "Miami: A Time for Healing," editorial, *Miami Herald*, November 3, 1980.

123. George Volsky, "Approval of Antibilingual Measure Causes Confusion and Worry in Miami Area," *New York Times*, November 9, 1980.

124. Portes and Stepick, *City on the Edge*, 161.

125. Mary Ellen Higgin, "'Non-Latin White' an Offensive Term,'" letter to the editor, *Miami Herald*, September 23, 1982.

126. Fred Moffett, "The Real Refugees," letter to the editor, *Miami Herald*, August 18, 1982.

127. John McMullan, "Will Last Bigots Please Leave," editor's comment, *Miami Herald*, September 26, 1982.

128. Charles Whited, "Miami Cubans Fight Threat to Hard-Won Pride," *Miami Herald*, September 23, 1982.

129. Jay Ducassi, "Bad Reviews May Drive *Scarface* Filming Elsewhere," *Miami Herald*, August 20, 1982.

130. Demetrio Pérez, Jr., "A Commissioner's Objection to 'Scarface,'" letter to the editor, *Miami Herald*, September 2, 1982.

131. Guillermo Martinez, "Filming of 'Scarface' Harms Cuban Image," *Miami Herald*, August 28, 1982.

132. James Kassir, "Movie will Hurt," letter to the editor, *Miami Herald*, August 9, 1982.

133. F. Mennitto, "Offensive Move," letter to the editor, *Miami Herald*, August 14, 1982.

134. Ana F. Crucet, letter to the editor, *Miami Herald*, August 27, 1982.

135. Edgardo O. Meneses, letter to the editor, *Miami Herald*, September 4, 1982.

136. Stu Schneider, "Can the Film," letter to the editor, *Miami Herald*, September 16, 1982.

137. "Wanted: Scarface," *Miami Herald*, September 1, 1982.

138. Anthony Ramirez, "Making It: Miami Cubans Prosper by Sticking Together, Aiding Later Refugees," *Wall Street Journal*, May 20, 1980.

139. Jo Thomas, "Miami Area Divided over Ballot Proposal to Drop Spanish as Second Official Language," *New York Times*, November 2, 1980.

Chapter 6

1. Mark S. Hamm, *The Abandoned Ones: The Imprisonment and Uprising of the Mariel Boat People* (Boston: Northeast University Press, 1995), 8, 24–25.

2. Rafael Peñalver, interview with author, digital recording, Coral Gables, FL, March 14, 2013.

3. Carlos Harrison, "Cubans Riot in Louisiana," *Miami Herald*, November 22, 1987.

4. Hamm, *The Abandoned Ones*, 5–6.

5. Fred Grimm, "Cuban Inmates Riot in Atlanta," *Miami Herald*, November 24, 1987.

6. United States Department of Justice, Federal Bureau of Prisons, "A Report to the Attorney General on the Disturbances at the Federal Detention Center, Oakdale, Louisiana and the U.S. Penitentiary, Atlanta, Georgia," February 1, 1988, Folder 7, Box 8, Series II, Cuban Detainees' Litigation Paper Records, 1981–1994—MSS 734, James G. Kenan Research Center at the Atlanta History Center, Atlanta, GA (hereafter Cuban Detainee Papers).

7. From the transcript of Agustín Román's message to the rioting detainees, included in Carlos Harrison, Christopher Marquis, and Martin Merzer, "Oakdale Prison Siege Ends," *Miami Herald*, November 30, 1987.

8. Peñalver interview.

9. Peter Slevin, "Washington Gives Cuban Foundation Clout, Legitimacy," *Miami Herald*, October 11, 1992.

10. María Cristina García, *Havana USA: Cuban Exiles and Cuban Americans in South Florida, 1959–1994* (Berkeley: University of California Press, 1996), 147.

11. The Cuban American National Foundation, "Cuban American National Foundation," circa 1988, Folder—[Pocket Folder] The Cuban American National Foundation [1988] (OA-ID 08276-014), Karen Barnes Files, White House Office of National Service, George H. W. Bush Presidential Library, College Station, TX (hereafter George H. W. Bush Library.)

12. Interview with Jorge Mas Canosa, 1993, Item 445, Cuban Living History Project, Florida International University Special Collections, Florida International University, Miami, FL (hereafter FIU Special Collections).

13. Mas Canosa, 1993, Item 445, Cuban Living History Project.

14. María de los Angeles Torres, *In the Land of Mirrors: Cuban Exile Politics in the United States* (Ann Arbor: University of Michigan Press, 1999), 115.

15. Jorge Mas Canosa, "Deposition of Jorge Mas Canosa," April 11, 1996, Folder 2, Box 2, *New Republic*–Jorge Mas Canosa Collection, 1979–1996, FIU Special Collections.

16. Torres, *In the Land of Mirrors*, 115.

17. García, *Havana USA*, 147.

18. Mas Canosa, "Deposition of Jorge Mas Canosa."

19. In 1985, Eduardo Arocena, an anti-Castro activist who was already serving a life sentence for a bombing carried out in New York City, was convicted of seven bombings of businesses and Latin American consulates in Miami from 1979 to 1983.

Arocena was suspected of being the leader of the terrorist group Omega 7, which was responsible for anti-Castro acts in Florida, New Jersey, and New York between the mid-1970s and mid-1980s. See "Anti-Communist Guilty in 7 Miami Bombings," *New York Times*, April 14, 1985.

20. García, *Havana USA*, 147.

21. Interview with Jorge Mas Canosa, 1993, Item 445, Cuban Living History Project.

22. Mas Canosa, "Deposition of Jorge Mas Canosa."

23. García, *Havana USA*, 147.

24. Mas Canosa, "Deposition of Jorge Mas Canosa."

25. Anthony Boadle, "Lieberman a Close Ally of Miami's Cuban Exiles," *Reuters*, August 11, 2000.

26. Torres, *In the Land of Mirrors*, 116.

27. García, *Havana USA*, 149–150.

28. Gaeton Fonzi, "Who Is Jorge Mas Canosa?," *Esquire*, January 1993, 86.

29. Torres, *In the Land of Mirrors*, 115.

30. Ibid., 116–117.

31. Interview with Jorge Mas Canosa, 1993, Item 445, Cuban Living History Project.

32. Alfonso Chardy, "Reagan Rips Castro Rule as 'Fascist,'" *Miami Herald*, May 21, 1983.

33. Fonzi, "Who Is Jorge Mas Canosa?," 86.

34. García, *Havana USA*, 148.

35. Gaeton Fonzi, "Who Is Jorge Mas Canosa?," 86.

36. García, *Havana USA*, 148.

37. Ibid.

38. Andres Viglucci, "Rock, Sports News Lure Cuban Listeners," *Miami Herald*, May 26, 1985.

39. Lourdes Meluza, "Broadcasts' Mild Tone Criticized," *Miami Herald*, May 26, 1985.

40. Sandra Dibble, "Cuban-Americans Reap the Rewards of Diligent Effort," *Miami Herald*, May 26, 1985.

41. See García, *Havana USA*, 148; Georgie Anne Geyer, "Coup at Radio Martí?," editorial, *Washington Times*, March 13, 1990; and "Their Man in Havana," editorial, *Washington Post*, March 18, 1990.

42. García, *Havana USA*, 149.

43. Torres, *In the Land of Mirrors*, 115.

44. Andress Viglucci and Sandra Dibble, "Director Says He Was Forced Out of Radio Martí," *Miami Herald*, March 13, 1990.

45. Sandra Dibble, "Radio Martí Chief Ordered to Clear Office," *Miami Herald*, March 15, 1990.

46. Jorge Mas Canosa, "Betancourt's Power Grab Failed," *Miami Herald*, March 17, 1990.

47. "Unplug the Connection," editorial, *Miami Herald*, March 17, 1990.

48. "Their Man in Havana," editorial, *Washington Post*, March 18, 1990.

49. García, *Havana USA*, 150.

50. Mas Canosa, "Deposition of Jorge Mas Canosa."

51. García, *Havana USA*, 150.

52. Ana Raquel Minian, *Undocumented Lives: The Untold Story of Mexican Migration* (Cambridge, MA: Harvard University Press, 2018), 200.

53. "Cuban American National Foundation Private Sector Program," circa 1992, Folder—[Pocket Folder] The Cuban American National Foundation [1988] (OA-ID 08276-014), Karen Barnes Files, White House Office of National Service, George H. W. Bush Library.

54. "Revised Cuban Refugee Program," April 29, 1961, Folder Cuba, Subject Exiles 1961, Box 48, National Security Files, Presidential Papers, Papers of John F Kennedy, John F. Kennedy Presidential Library, Boston, MA. (hereafter JFK Library).

55. "Cuban American National Foundation Private Sector Program."

56. Bonnie M. Anderson, "Latest Arrival of Cubans Ends Cruel Joke of Destiny," *Miami News*, September 12, 1988.

57. "Cuban American National Foundation Private Sector Program."

58. "Xavier Suarez," *Miami Herald Tropic* magazine, September 28, 1986.

59. Jon Nordheimer, "Man in the News: Xavier Luis Suarez," *New York Times*, November 14, 1985.

60. "Xavier Suarez."

61. Ibid.

62. Ibid.

63. Rick Hirsch, "Suárez arrolla," *El Miami Herald*, November 13, 1985.

64. Xavier Suarez, "I'll Knock Down 'Dividing Walls,' Mayor Says," *Miami Herald*, November14, 1985.

65. Rick Hirsch, "Suarez Vows He Will Unite Miami," *Miami Herald*, November 14, 1985.

66. Sonia L. Nazario, "Freedom of Speech Is a Debatable Issue for Many in Miami," *Wall Street Journal*, June 2, 1986.

67. While the Nicaraguan refugees were not given the same welcome as the Cubans had, their numbers in Miami grew significantly and diversified in terms of class by the late 1980s. See Alejandro Portes and Alex Stepick, *City on the Edge: The Transformation of Miami* (Berkeley: University of California Press, 1993), 152–157.

68. Howard W. French, "Mandela Travels to Miami amid Protests over Castro," *New York Times*, June 29, 1990.

69. Arthur S. Hay, "Black Groups Plan a Miami Boycott to Protest City's Treatment of Mandela," *Wall Street Journal*, August 6, 1990.

70. "Miami Mayor's Apology Still Needed to End Economic Boycott," *Atlanta Daily World*, December 20, 1990.

71. Luis Feldstein Soto, "Los Lehtinen, pareja estelar de la política," *El Nuevo Herald*, September 6, 1989.

72. Luis Feldstein Soto, "It's Ros-Lehtinen, 53–47%," *Miami Herald*, August 30, 1989.

73. Ibid.

74. Liz Balmaseda, "Ileana Ros-Lehtinen Charges the Hill," *Miami Herald*, November 19, 1989.

75. Barrie Tron to K.T., May 8, 1989, Folder—Cuban American National Foundation [OA-ID 01907-129], Barrie Tron Files, White House Office of Public Affairs, George H. W. Bush Library.

76. Luisa Yanez, "Exiles Here Show Support for President," *Miami News*, December 9, 1986.

77. Gladys Nieves, "Salmán: Orgulloso de ser republicano," *El Nuevo Herald*, August 13, 1988.

78. Jorge Mas Canosa, open letter, October 10, 1984, Folder 665, Box 1863, Dante B. Fascell Congressional Papers, 1955–1993, University of Miami Special Collections, University of Miami, Coral Gables, FL (hereafter DBF Papers).

79. L.N. to Dante B. Fascell, May 5, 1992, Folder 845, Box 1879, DBF Papers

80. Charles A. Whitehead to Bob Graham, Lawton Chiles, Claude Pepper, Dante Fascell, et al., July 16, 1985, Folder 6, Box 1867, DBF Papers.

81. It should be noted that, as Carl Lindskoog has shown, while the indefinite detention of thousands of Marielitos had characteristics that differentiated it from other forms of immigration detention, when Ronald Reagan took office the practice of immigrant detention was being applied primarily to Haitians seeking asylum. See Carl Lindskoog, *Detain and Punish: Haitian Refugees and the Rise of the World's Largest Immigration Detention System* (Gainesville: University of Florida Press, 2018), 74.

82. Ibid., 33.

83. Norman A. Carlson to David Hiller, April 9, 1981, Folder—Justice, Dept. of [2], Box 25, Subject File, Records of the Cuban-Haitian Task Force, Jimmy Carter Presidential Library, Atlanta, GA (hereafter cited as Carter Library).

84. Gary Leshaw to Joan Potter, April 15, 1987, Folder 2, Box 8, Series II, Cuban Detainee Papers.

85. United States Department of Justice Federal Bureau of Prisons, "A Report to the Attorney General on the Disturbances at the Federal Detention Center, Oakdale, Louisiana and the U.S. Penitentiary, Atlanta, Georgia," February 1, 1988, Folder 7, Box 8, Series II, Cuban Detainee Papers.

86. Norman A. Carlson to David Hiller, April 9, 1981, Folder—Justice, Dept. of [2], Box 25, Subject File, Records of the Cuban-Haitian Task Force, Jimmy Carter Presidential Library, Atlanta, GA (hereafter cited as Carter Library).

87. Commission Pro-Justice Mariel Prisoners, "The Mariel Injustice (in the Year of the 200th Anniversary of the American Constitution)," 1987, 10, Folder Various Publications on Mariel Boatlift, Cuban, 1980–2005, Box 3, Caribbean Sea Migration Collection, Duke University Special Collections, Duke University, Durham, NC (Hereafter Duke Special Collections).

88. Rafael Peñalver, interview with author, digital recording. Coral Gables, FL, March 14, 2013.

89. Commission Pro-Justice Mariel Prisoners, "The Mariel Injustice," 10.

90. Deborah S. Ebel to Douglas Roberto, July 6, 1983, Folder 1, Box 10, Series II, Cuban Detainee Papers.

91. Rigaberto Méndez Suárez to Atlanta Legal Aid Society, June 2, 1986, Folder 3, Box 14, Series II, Cuban Detainee Papers.

92. Peñalver interview.

93. Hamm, *The Abandoned Ones*, 85–87.

94. United States Department of Justice Federal Bureau of Prisons, "A Report to the Attorney General on the Disturbances at the Federal Detention Center, Oakdale, Louisiana and the U.S. Penitentiary, Atlanta, Georgia," February 1, 1988, Folder 7, Box 8, Series II, Cuban Detainee Papers.

95. Affidavit of Manuel García-Díaz, June 25, 1981, Folder 6, Box 9, Series II, Cuban Detainee Papers.

96. Kenneth A. Hindman to William C. Thompson, May 6, 1985, Folder 5, Box 10, Series II, Cuban Detainee Papers.

97. Gary Leshaw to Joan Potter, April 15, 1987, Folder 2, Box 8, Series II, Cuban Detainee Papers.

98. William C. Thompson to Carla Dudek, October 1, 1986, Folder 4, Box 14, Series II, Cuban Detainee Papers.

99. Transcript reproduced in Commission Pro-Justice Mariel Prisoners, "The Mariel Injustice," 33.

100. Steve Harvey, "Williams, Gregory Released in D.C., Arrested for Picketing at Atlanta Pen," *Atlanta Constitution*, April 23, 1987.

101. John Lewis, "A Mocking Memory," April 27, 1987, in Commission Pro-Justice Mariel Prisoners, "The Mariel Injustice," 52.

102. Edward A. McCarthy, Agustín Román, and Bryan O. Walsh, "Cuban Detainees in Atlanta," August 19, 1981, Folder—Cuban Detainees in Atlanta, August 9, 1981, Box 40, Series III, Bryan O. Walsh Papers, Barry University, Miami, FL (hereafter cited as Walsh Papers).

103. Peñalver interview.

104. Ibid.

105. Jim Hampton, "Caged Logic on Cuban Prisoners," *Miami Herald*, October 19, 1986. Reprinted in Commission Pro-Justice Mariel Prisoners, "The Mariel Injustice," 80.

106. Tracy Thompson, "Congressman Criticizes Plan to Free Cubans," *Atlanta Constitution*, July 2, 1987.

107. Tina Montalvo, "Influx Could Strain Services," *Miami Herald*, November 22, 1987.

108. Peñalver interview.

109. Fred Grimm, "Desperate Wives Pray for Mercy," *Miami Herald*, November 24, 1987.

110. Luis Feldstein Soto and Tina Montalvo, "'I'm Going to Atlanta,' Bishop Says," *Miami Herald*, November 26, 1987.

111. Peñalver interview.

112. Feldstein Soto and Montalvo, "'I'm Going to Atlanta,' Bishop Says."

113. Hamm, *The Abandoned Ones*, 26–27.

114. Peñalver interview.

115. Ibid.

116. Celia W. Dugger and Fred Grimm, "Inmate Talks Make Progress, but Oakdale Pact Draws Scorn," *Miami Herald*, December 2, 1987.

117. Fred Grimm, Mirta Ojito, and Martin Merzer, "Inmates End Siege," *Miami Herald*, December 4, 1987.

118. Peñalver interview.

119. Gary Leshaw to Joan Potter, August 1, 1988, Folder 2, Box 8, Series II, Cuban Detainee Papers.

120. "First 5 Cubans Are Returned by U.S. under Pact with Castro Concerning Criminals," *New York Times*, December 3, 1988.

121. American Civil Liberties Union of Georgia, "Georgia Civil Liberties," Winter 1990, Folder 2, Box 4, Series 1, Cuban Detainee Papers.

122. Sally Sandidge, "Cuban Detainees' Hearings Nowhere Near 'Fair and Equitable,'" letter to the editor, *Atlanta Constitution*, November 14, 1988.

123. In March 1990, Gary Leshaw of the Atlanta Legal Aid Society filed a complaint with INS commissioner Gene McNary over three law student volunteers being denied access to the four detainees they had traveled to Avoyelles Parish Jail in Marksville, LA, to represent. See Leshaw to McNary, March 1, 1990, Folder 2, Box 12, Series II, Cuban Detainee Papers.

124. Stacy V. Sullivan, "Oakdale Repeat Is Possible, Cuban Says, If Delays Go On," *Alexandria Town Talk*, November 20, 1988.

125. "110 reos Cubanos en huelga de hambre, desde hace siete días," *El Mañana*, July 26, 1989.

126. See Valerie Jo Roberts, "Mini-Riot among Cubans at Pen. Leads to Damage," *Lewisburg Daily Journal*, May 23, 1990; and Angela Simoneaux, "INS Prisoners Riot in Avoyelles Jail," *Baton Rouge Morning Advocate*, June 1, 1990.

127. Ronald Smothers, "Talks at Prison Aim at Release of Ill Hostages," *New York Times*, August 29, 1991.

128. Daniel Klaidman, "Crisis Puts Justice Official in Spotlight," *Fulton County Daily Report*, September 13, 1991.

129. Carla Dudeck to Kenneth Schoen, January 15, 1990, Folder 2, Box 8, Series II, Cuban Detainee Papers.

130. Kirsten Haukebo, "Cuban Refugee Steps out of Prison and into New Life," *Louisville Courier-Journal*, September 11, 1991.

131. Gary Leshaw to Laura McQuade, June 4, 1991, Folder 2, Box 8, Series II, Cuban Detainee Papers.

132. Linda Greenhouse, "Supreme Court Rejects Mariel Cubans' Detention," *New York Times*, January 13, 2005.

133. Andres Viglucci, "Ordeal Unites Cuban Community," *Miami Herald*, December 5, 1987.

134. Guillermo Martinez, "Cuban Community Has Come of Age," *Miami Herald*, December 8, 1987.

135. Peñalver interview.

136. Rodrigo Lazo and Justing Gillis, "Miamians Rebuffed in Atlanta," *Miami Herald*, November 28, 1987.

137. Peñalver interview.

138. Mas Canosa, "Deposition of Jorge Mas Canosa."

139. Alex Stepick, Guillermo Grenier, Max Castro, and Marvin Dunn, *This Land Is Our Land: Immigrants and Power in Miami* (Berkeley: University of California Press, 2003), 47.

140. Miguel Gonzalez-Pando, "Herald, Cuban Groups: Necessary Confrontation," *Miami Herald*, November 4, 1987.

141. Mas Canosa, "Deposition of Jorge Mas Canosa."

142. Fonzi, "Who Is Jorge Mas Canosa?," 88.

143. "Bad Strategy on Cuba," editorial, *Miami Herald*, January 18, 1992.

144. Mas Canosa, "Deposition of Jorge Mas Canosa."

145. Alfonso Chardy and Cynthia Corzo, "Cuban Exiles Leader Says Papers Biased," *Miami Herald*, January 21, 1992.

146. Mas Canosa, "Deposition of Jorge Mas Canosa."

147. Stepick et al., *This Land Is Our Land*, 49.

148. David Lawrence Jr., "No, Mr. Mas, Intimidation Won't Work," *Miami Herald*, March 22, 1992.

149. Gaeton Fonzi, "Who Is Jorge Mas Canosa?," *Esquire*, January 1993, 88.

150. Christopher Marquis, "Embargo Bill's Success Testifies to Exiles' Clout," *Miami Herald*, September 28, 1992.

151. Peter Slevin, "Washington Gives Cuban Foundation Clout, Legitimacy," *Miami Herald*, October 11, 1992.

152. Tom Fielder and Ivan Roman, "Clinton-Mas Meeting Shocks Cuban Miami," *Miami Herald*, October 29, 1992.

153. Stepick et al., *This Land Is Our Land*, 7.

154. Ann Louise Bardach, "Our Man in Miami," *New Republic*, October 3, 1994, 20, 25.

155. Silvia Pedraza, *Political Disaffection in Cuba's Revolution and Exodus* (New York: Cambridge University Press, 2007), 178–179.

156. The economic challenges of the special period, combined with instances of government repression, drove a new wave of disaffection with the revolutionary government. Cultural anthropologist Elizabeth Campisi conducted multiple interviews with balseros that showed how the deprivations and restrictions of the special period led individuals to moments of awareness where they realized their values were not aligned with the reality of life in Cuba. This, in turn, drove their desire to leave the island. See

Elizabeth Campisi, *Escape to Miami: An Oral History of the Cuban Rafter Crisis* (New York: Oxford University Press, 2016), 33.

157. Pedraza, *Political Disaffection in Cuba's Revolution and Exodus*, 8.

158. Ibid.

159. William Jefferson Clinton, "Press Conference by the President," August 19, 1994, Folder—[OA-ID 10140] Cuba Press Conference 8/19/94, Box 28, FOIA 2006-0458-F Baer, Don, Communications, Clinton Presidential Records, William Clinton Presidential Library, Little Rock, AR (hereafter Clinton Library).

160. Clinton, "Press Conference by the President."

161. Adam Goodman, *The Deportation Machine: America's Long History of Expelling Immigrants* (Princeton, NJ: Princeton University Press, 2020), 172.

162. "Continua exodo masivo el Mariel II ha comenzado," *La Voz de la Calle*, August 19, 1994.

163. Andres Viglucci, "In Miami, 'Extreme Confusion,'" *Miami Herald*, August 25, 1994.

164. Félix Masud-Piloto, *From Welcomed Exiles to Illegal Immigrants: Cuban Migration to the U.S., 1959–1995* (Oxford: Rowman & Littlefield Publishers, 1996), xxi.

165. "A Painful Policy, but Right," editorial, *Miami Herald*, August 20, 1994.

166. "A Dizzying, Unfair Change," editorial, *Miami Herald*, August 25, 1994.

167. Ann Louise Bardach, "Our Man in Miami," *New Republic*, October 3, 1994, 20.

168. Liz Balmaseda, "Back and Forth, It's U.S. Policy That's Changed," *Miami Herald*, May 3, 1995.

169. "Best of Bad Options," editorial, *Miami Herald*, May 3, 1995. (Italics in the original.)

170. Andres Viglucci, "Cuba Shift May Stoke Prop 187 Campaigns," *Miami Herald*, May 4, 1995.

171. "Best of Bad Options," editorial, *Miami Herald*, May 3, 1995.

172. Christopher Marquis, "A Crisis in Clout for Exiles," *Miami Herald*, May 14, 1995.

Epilogue

1. Miriam Jordan and Mitchell Ferman, "Stranded on Border, This Migrant Became the Camp Doctor," *New York Times*, December 22, 2019.

2. Phrase quoted in Felix Roberto Masud-Piloto, *With Open Arms: Cuban Migration to the United States* (Totowa, NJ: Rowan & Littlefield, 1988), xiv.

3. "Survey: Most Cubans Forgo 'Exile' Moniker," *Miami Herald*, November 24, 1995.

4. Dexter Filkins and Alfonso Chardy, "Exiles: We Won't Quit until Policy Is Reversed," *Miami Herald*, May 13, 1995.

5. Barbara Crossette, "Cuba, Citing Earlier Intrusions, Defend Downing of 2 Cessnas," *New York Times*, March 7, 1996.

6. David Gonzalez, "Cuban Government Enters Fight for Boy," *New York Times*, November 30, 1999.

7. "Future Unclear for Cuban Boy In Doomed Boat," *New York Times*, November 29, 1999.

8. Rick Bragg, "Standoff Over Cuban Boy's Fate Intensifies," *New York Times*, March 29, 2000.

9. Lillian Guerra, "Elián González and the 'Real Cuba' of Miami: Visions of Identity, Exceptionality, and Divinity," *Cuban Studies* 38 (2007): 4.

10. "Lightning Move Took Agents Just 154 Seconds," *Miami Herald*, April 23, 2000.

11. The anxieties raised by the creation of the wet foot, dry foot and the Elián González affair were also drivers in a Cuban American campaign to restore the Freedom Tower from the disrepair it had fallen into after the federal government had ended operations in the building. See Mauricio F. Castro, "Object Lesson: 'All the Help I Needed, I Got Here': Miami's Freedom Tower and the Freedom Tower's Miami," *Buildings & Landscapes* 23, no. 1 (Spring 2016): 16–28.

12. Kevin Sack, "How Florida Got Close Enough to Fight Over," *New York Times*, November 19, 2000.

13. William Finnegan, "The Cuban Strategy," *New Yorker*, March 15, 2004, http://www.newyorker.com/magazine/2004/03/15/the-cuban-strategy.

14. Miguel A. De La Torre, *La Lucha for Cuba: Religion and Politics on the Streets of Miami* (Berkeley: University of California Press, 2003), 35.

15. Rob Wile, "Miami's Biggest New Wave of Immigrants Looks a Lot Like its Previous Ones," *Miami Herald*, August 5, 2019.

16. Ibid.

17. Peter Baker, "U.S. to Restore Full Relations with Cuba, Erasing a Last Trace of Cold War Hostility," *New York Times*, December 17, 2014.

18. Karen DeYoung, "Obama Ending Special Immigration Status for Migrants Fleeing Cuba," *Washington Post*, January 12, 2017.

19. Sabrina Rodríguez, "Why Trump Is Focused On Making Marco Rubio Happy," *Politico*, August 3, 2020, https://www.politico.com/news/2020/08/03/marco-rubio-trump-latin-america-policy-390858.

20. Yvonne H. Valdez, "U.S. Cancels Private Charter Flights to Cuba," *South Florida Sun Sentinel*, August 13, 2020.

21. Stephania Taladrid, "As Trump Gained Latino Support in Florida, Biden's Campaign Ignored Warnings," *New Yorker*, November 10, 2020, https://www.newyorker.com/news/campaign-chronicles/as-trump-gained-latino-support-in-florida-bidens-campaign-ignored-warnings.

22. In an interview with Miami's NPR affiliate, WLRN, for example, television and radio host Lourdes Ubieta mentioned Venezuelan families voting for Trump and then breaking from the GOP on the downballot based on his policies on Venezuela. See "How Florida Democrats Lost Latino Voters and What They Should Learn From It," WLRN, November 11, 2020, https://www.wlrn.org/2020-11-11/how-florida-democrats-lost-latino-voters-and-what-they-should-learn-from-it?

23. Taladrid, "As Trump Gained Latino Support in Florida."

24. Douglas Hanks, "Miami-Dade Commission Rejects Sick Leave for Contractors after Cuba Comparisons," *Miami Herald*, May 7, 2020.

25. Michael Wilner, David Smiley, Alex Daugherty, and Nora Gamez Torres, "White House, Rick Scott Claim Violence at Floyd Protests Linked to Venezuela," *Tampa Bay Times*, June 10, 2020.

26. Monique O. Madan, "Feds Deport 119 Cubans Back to Havana on Miami Flight," *Miami Herald*, March 5, 2020.

27. Noah Lanard, "Cuba Has Refused Deportation Flights, but ICE Isn't Letting Most Cubans Out of Detention," January 28, 2021, https://www.motherjones.com/politics/2021/01/cuba-has-refused-deportation-flights-so-ice-isnt-letting-most-cubans-out-of-detention/.

28. David Ovalle, Joey Flechas, Vera Bergengruen, Carlos Frías, and Patricia Mazzei, "Cuban Exiles Pour Onto Miami Streets to Celebrate Fidel Castro's Death," *Miami Herald*, November 26, 2016.

29. Ibid.

30. Uva de Aragón, *Morir de exilio* (Miami: Ediciones Universal, 2006), 12 (translation mine).

31. Ibid.

INDEX

Christopher, Warren, 144
Church and Tower (telephone company), 110
CIA (Central Intelligence Agency), 48, 56, 57, 87; on disunity of exile groups, 85; JM/WAVE installation, 68
citizenship, 13, 19, 82, 89; cultural and policy battles over naturalization, 120–27; refugees' embrace of, 103, 120–27; refugees' transition into, 109; reluctant to apply for, 98; Republican Party organizing efforts and, 103; as theme in episode of *¿Qué Pasa, U.S.A.?* 121–24
Citizens of Dade United, 160, 162
civil rights movement, U.S., 19, 101, 188; associated with communism by critics, 94, 211; Cold War and, 223n42; Cuban refugees in opposition to, 20–21
Clark, Juan, 109, 120
Clark, Steve, 129
Clinton, Bill, 178, 199, 200–205; Elián González affair and, 208; shift in Cuban immigration policy, 207; "wet foot, dry foot" policy and, 206
Cold War, 3, 24, 32, 207, 213; American cities shaped by, 22; civil rights and, 223n42; defense industries and, 11; electoral politics in South Florida and, 14; end of, 168, 178, 197, 200, 205; federal funds and economy of the Sunbelt during, 91, 238n32; in Latin America, 11; local politics and, 82; Miami as front in, 33–37; parental rights and unaccompanied children, 47–54; political legacy of, 211; Reagan administration and, 15; refugee civilians and, 4; refugees as living reminders of, 47
Collins, Leroy, 37, 97–98
communism, 2, 3, 5, 58, 183; Miami as "bastion" against, 36; political legacy of Cold War and, 211
Concurrent Resolution 492 (1967), 98–99
Connolly, N. D. B., 26
conservatism, 13, 37, 82–83, 101–2, 114, 181; CANF and, 15, 172, 173, 176, 197, 204; in Democratic Party, 180; fear of civil rights movement and, 94; political legacy of Cold War and, 211. *See also* Republican Party (GOP)
Contras, Nicaraguan, 172, 179

Corzo, Cynthia, 198–99
Costa Rica, refugee flights to, 139
COVID-19 pandemic, 211, 212
CRC (Cuban Revolutionary Council), 84–87
CREC (Cuban Refugee Emergency Center), 41, 55, 61, 62
CRP (Cuban Refugee Program), 6, 19, 47, 95–96, 145, 207; Bay of Pigs Invasion and, 58; calls for reinstatement of, 148; CANF compared with, 177; as Cold War welfare program, 54–60; creation of, 10, 55; economic self-sufficiency of refugees as goal, 68, 72; goals of, 4; phase out of, 105, 106, 133, 241n6; plans for post-Castro Cuba, 59, 60; as product of 1960s liberalism, 46; refugees in professional occupations and, 69, 70, 71, 73; resettlement of refugees and, 13, 62–63, 66–68; U.S. national security apparatus and, 79; white Miamians and, 20
Cruz, Celia, 181
Cuba: American business concerns in, 27; commercial air travel to United States halted, 50, 53, 63; detainees deported to, 192, 195, 212; effects of Soviet collapse on, 201; human rights violations of, 170, 171, 180; idealized memory of, 122, 214; *ley de peligrosidad* (law of dangerousness), 140; nostalgia for, 6, 125, 213; Obama's move toward restoration of diplomatic relations, 209; Peruvian embassy crisis and opening of Mariel, 138–43; post-Soviet economy in, 17; racial history of, 20, 21, 93; refusal to repatriate detained Marielitos, 183–84, 186; "special period" of 1990s, 201, 258n156; U.S. embargo against, 197; visas granted for visits by exile youth groups, 128; war of independence, 27
Cuban Adjustment Act (1966), 83, 202, 239n61, 241n6; path to citizenship and, 13, 82, 89, 98; process of exile stabilization and, 125; rate of naturalization and, 120
Cuban American community: Afro Cubans, 92, 238n37; "coming of age" of, 195–96, 205; as decreasing percentage of Miami's Hispanic population, 209; electoral successes of, 178–81; established before Cuban Revolution, 24; federal government and, 5; growing political power of, 98, 168, 181; influence over U.S. foreign

ACKNOWLEDGMENTS

This book would not have been possible without a tremendous network of institutional and personal support. These acknowledgments are not only in recognition of the impact the organizations and individuals had on the writing of my dissertation and the monograph that grew from it, but on the tremendous impact they had on my life.

I received significant and sustained funding from Purdue University in pursuit of this project. The Department of History generously funded my travel to Miami with the Harold Woodman Graduate Student Travel Grant. The year-long Purdue Research Foundation Grant freed me from on-campus obligations and allowed me to pursue multiple research trips between the summer of 2012 and the fall of 2013. Support from Purdue University's Graduate School in the form of the Winifred Beatrice Bilsland Dissertation Writing Fellowship enabled me to spend a year devoted to writing and finishing my dissertation. Without the assistance I received from Purdue, this project would have been impossible to complete.

Another inestimably important source of support was the Cuban Heritage Collection (CHC) Graduate Fellowship, which allowed me to spend three months in residence at the University of Miami. The Cuban Heritage Collection, the Goizueta Foundation, and the Amigos of the Cuban Heritage Collection provided me with the opportunity to mine the depths of the most significant source of material for this dissertation. I am also forever indebted to the CHC's faculty and staff who helped along the way. I would like to thank María Estorino, Esperanza Bravo de Varona. Gladys Gomez-Rossie, Annie Sansone-Martinez, Meiyolet Méndez, and Rosa Monzon-Alvarez, among others. Despite its rich collections, it might be people who welcome and provide the fellows with a home away from home that are the Cuban Heritage Collection's greatest resource.

I must also thank other organizations that helped provide the assistance necessary to travel to multiple states to research this work. The Samuel Flagg

Bemis Dissertation Research Grant from the Society for Historians of American Foreign relations provided significant support for me to conduct an extended, multistate research trip in early 2013. The John F. Kennedy Library Foundation's Abba P. Schwartz Research Fellowship allowed me to travel to Boston and conduct research at the Kennedy Presidential Library. Likewise, without the funds provided by the LBJ Foundation's Moody Research Grant, I would not have been able to travel to the LBJ Presidential Library in Austin. The Research Travel Grant from the Gerald R. Ford Presidential Foundation also allowed me to access collections essential to this project. I must also thank the archivists and staff of these Presidential Libraries and those of the Jimmy Carter Presidential Library, the George H. W. Bush Presidential Library, and the William J. Clinton Presidential Library. I am also indebted to their counterparts at the University of Miami Libraries Special Collections and University Archives, the Barry University Archives and Special Collections, the Florida International University Special Collections & University Archives, the Rutgers University Special Collections and University Archives, the HistoryMiami Archives and Research Center, the Wilson Library Special Collections at the University of North Carolina, Chapel Hill, Duke University Special Collections, and the James G. Kenan Research Center at the Atlanta History Center.

There were other institutions and individuals who provided me with significant support in my career after graduate school. Claudia Milian and Dell Williams of Duke University's Program in Latino/a Studies in the Global South graced me not only with a postdoctoral fellowship and their friendship, but also with the space and time in which to complete my first major revision of this work. When I needed a place to go after Durham, my dear friend Alex Sayf Cummings helped me keep my career going by recommending me to the history department at Georgia State University. I received significant support and friendship there from colleagues and friends, including Rob Baker, Rachel Ernst, Jared Poley, and Jeff Young. This, in turn, gave me time to do further research in Atlanta and to continue revising the work.

Since arriving at Centre College in 2019, I have received a significant amount of institutional support for the completion of this book. I have also been embraced by the most welcoming and supportive program I could have imagined. As I navigated my first years at a tenure track job and a global pandemic I was glad to have the support and friendship of Steve Beaudoin, Jon Earle, Sara Egge, John Harney, Tara Strauch, Sami Sweis, and Amos Tubb. I have also received excellent advice, support, and friendship from others at the college and in the community, including Danielle La Londe, Stacey Peebles, Matthew Pierce, Mark Rasmussen, Shana Sippy, and Helen Willis. I am lucky to be ensconced into such a supportive community.

I must also thank those senior scholars who have been, over the course of my career, so incredibly generous with their time and mentorship. At the Urban History Association Conference in 2012, Mark Rose was kind enough to read my prospectus and to provide extremely helpful feedback that shaped the course of my project. At another conference that same year, the American Historical Association Annual Meeting, I met a friend and mentor who has done nothing but support me and the development of my career. A. K. Sandoval-Strausz has been a strong ally and a true friend to me in the years I have known him, and I am truly grateful to have met him. Lilia Fernández has also provided invaluable support and spaces in which to evolve my work. I am also forever grateful for the friendship, advice, and example set by friends and scholars like Llana Barber, Julio Capó Jr, Ben Francis-Fallon, and Alyssa Ribeiro.

My first mentors, of course, were those faculty members at the institutions at which I received my education. Jeanie Ayub, as both my International Baccalaureate history teacher and my unofficial college counselor, instilled in me a love of the craft and set me on a path that ultimately led to pursuing a career in history. She was also instrumental in my pursuing an undergraduate education at Vassar College. There I was graciously mentored by faculty members David Schalk, James Merrell, and especially Maria Höhn. My Vassar education prepared me well for the rigors of graduate school and solidified my interest in a career in history.

Once at Purdue, I received the full support of the Department of History. Department Head R. Douglas Hurt's door was always open. He always had time to discuss my plans and provide career advice and provided me with significant opportunities after graduation. Director of Graduate Education John Larson was similarly available and eager to provide an encouraging word tempered by a bit of cynical realism regarding the state of the profession. I am forever indebted to two other instructors at Purdue that helped shape my development as a scholar. Alicia Decker, now at Penn State, helped shape my understanding of the developments of nation and sharpened my understanding of gender as a category of analysis. She was also a true friend and a talented and inspiring coauthor for my first major publication. Michael Morrison also graced me with his friendship and his mentorship. In him I found an example to follow as I found my voice as an instructor.

This work would not exist, of course, without the aid I received from the members of my dissertation committee. Nancy Gabin was always supportive of my work, knowledgeable in multiple historiographies, and instrumental in allowing me to conduct oral history interviews as part of my research. David Atkinson provided another excellent example to follow in teaching undergraduates and helped shape my thinking about borderlands and my contributions to the history of American foreign relations. Jon Teaford was kind enough to step in for Darren Dochuk after the latter moved on from Purdue. He always provided good advice regarding the development of the project and helped to keep me on task regarding the writing of the dissertation over the past year. Darren Dochuk was unwavering in his support and in his dedication to directing my dissertation. He gave me the freedom to pursue this project as my own but maintained rigorous academic standards at every step of the process. He was both a friend and advocate over the years. Without his help and guidance, I could not have written this book.

The same goes for the invaluable help of my editors at the University of Pennsylvania Press. Steve Pitti's insightful suggestions helped me distill the vision of this monograph and to place it in conversation with multiple literatures. He was essential to this work. This book, however, would simply not exist in its current form without the help of Bob Lockhart. Bob came highly recommended by many people whom I respect, and when I had my first meeting with him about this project in Providence, RI, at the Organization of American Historians Conference, I came away thinking he lived up to the hype. In the years since that meeting, Bob has exceeded my expectations and has made this book better with every bit of advice he has provided. I could not have asked for a better, more talented, or more patient editor.

This work would also not have bene possible without the support, inspiration, and friendship, of Purdue's graduate student community. Mason Danner came into the program with me and will forever be not just a friend, but the guy who went through academic "boot camp" with me during our first semester here. Brandon Ward was a sounding board for ideas, a friend, and someone whose great scholarship drove me to work harder and improve myself as a scholar.

Some among the graduate student community helped to make Lafayette home and supported me through some of the darkest days of my life. I will never stop making fun of Kara Kvaran for having publicly (and justifiably) mocked me on New Student Orientation Day. She taught me how to be a graduate student and that I could both be a scholar and have fun on my off time. I must confess that I may have stolen an apartment out from under Karen Sonneliter. This was not done out of malice, or even intentionally, but it allows us to share a former address like we share friendship and a love for gritty HBO shows and British period dramas. Erica Morin shared in our love of good television and was also a true friend from the start. Erica's excitement is infectious, and it helped to get me through some tough times.

Kate Pospisek is a fantastic person who is always a pleasure to be around. If she ever made a bad life decision, it was to marry Patrick Pospisek. Despite our combative relationship, Patrick has one of the sharpest minds I have ever encountered, and he is an unending source of good advice and sarcastic wit. I must also thank Patrick's companion in bitterness, Tim Lombardo. Tim helped make me a better scholar from early on and he was instrumental in helping me settle on a topic for this dissertation. He and Beca Venter have also been amazing friends to me in the past few years. I am truly lucky to have Kate, Patrick, Tim, and Beca in my life.

I am also indebted to friends outside of Purdue who aided me in my graduate career and in my research. Mark Gottlieb spent countless hours editing and commenting on my writing when I entered graduate school. Rich Wing provided encouragement as I was beginning my graduate education and provided me housing when I needed to present my work in New York City and to conduct research in New Jersey. I, however, logged the greatest number of hours on Andrés Olarte's futon at his apartment in Coconut Grove. Andrés provided me a place to stay during multiple research trips to Miami and was a friendly face and a good person to have a beer with whenever I was in the area. I must also thank my friends Sven von Saalfeld, Carlos Molina, and Carlos Campos, for helping me in my journey. My friend Pilar Moulaert was an unwavering source of support and a sympathetic ear to me for years before I started graduate school and she never once wavered.

I also made some very good friends who made my life in Lafayette outside of the history department far more interesting. I am unable to count the hours of genre movie and television shows I watched with Paul Shelton over greasy takeout food, giving me a much-needed escape from the rigors of graduate school. Kurk Bright and Magie Read were good friends, extremely flexible landlords, and have continued to support me in the years since I left Indiana.

I met Nick Gaspar while he was a student at Purdue's history department, and I am glad to continue to know this normal, innocent man. Tyler Wood has been as good a friend as I could ask for and I am not sure what my life would look like without him in it. Rebekah Gaspar has been a pillar of strength for me for years. She is the first person to have edited the text that eventually resulted in this monograph, the person to best call me on my nonsense, and my biggest cheerleader.

I must also thank my family for the essential role that they played in helping me pursue this career and this project. It will forever pain me that my brother Adrian did not live to see me finish this book. Before I left Costa Rica for graduate school my brother told me not to worry about my parents as he would care for them. He was unwaveringly supportive of my pursuit of my dream. His murder was the most painful event in my life, but I will forever remember and love him, and I have dedicated this work to his memory. I have also been aided in my journey by my sister Gabriela and my brother-in-law Felipe. They have been far more generous than I could ever have expected. I must also thank my nieces and nephews, Maria Jose, Marcelo, Daniela, Felipe, and Isabella, for their strong support of me over the past decade. I am also indebted to my Uncle Enrique, my Aunt Amanda, and the rest of my extended family for the support they provided to me, my parents, and my sister in the aftermath of my brother's death.

Finally, I owe everything to my parents Adrian and Beatriz. My parents always believed in the value of education, and they sacrificed much to provide me with the best possible opportunities in life. They did not even bat an eyelash when their son returned from his first year of college in the United States saying he wanted to pursue a career in history. My parents always stood behind me even when I was unsure of myself. Without them, none of this would have been possible.

www.ingramcontent.com/pod-product-compliance
Lightning Source LLC
Chambersburg PA
CBHW030259100426
42812CB00002B/497